Defence Planning as Strategic Fact

Defence Planning as Strategic Fact provides and elaborates on an "upstream" focus on the variegated organizational, political and conceptual practices of military, civilian administrative and political leaderships involved in defence planning, offering an important security and strategic studies supplement to the traditional "downstream" focus on the use of force.

The book enables the reader to engage with the role of ideas in defence planning, of organizational processes and biases, path dependencies and administrative dynamics under the pressures of continuously changing domestic and international constraints. The chapters show how defence planning must be seen as a constitutive element of defence and strategic studies – that it is a strategic fact of its own which merits particular practical and scholarly attention.

As defence planning creates the conditions behind every peace upheld or broken and every war won or lost, *Defence Planning as Strategic Fact* will be of great use to scholars of defence studies, strategic studies, and military studies.

This book was originally published as a special issue of *Defence Studies*.

Henrik Breitenbauch heads the Centre for Military Studies in the Department of Political Science at the University of Copenhagen, Denmark. The Centre advises Denmark's parliament and government on strategy, defence and security issues.

André Ken Jakobsson is a Carlsberg Postdoctoral Fellow at the Centre for Military Studies in the Department of Political Science at the University of Copenhagen, Denmark, with a project on grey zone conflicts and great power politics.

Defence Planning as Strategic Fact

Edited by
Henrik Breitenbauch and André Ken Jakobsson

LONDON AND NEW YORK

First published 2020
by Routledge
2 Park Square, Milton Park, Abingdon, Oxon, OX14 4RN

and by Routledge
52 Vanderbilt Avenue, New York, NY 10017

Routledge is an imprint of the Taylor & Francis Group, an informa business

Chapters 1–7, Conclusion © 2020 Taylor & Francis
Introduction © 2018 Henrik Breitenbauch and André Ken Jakobsson. Originally published as Open Access.

With the exception of the Introduction, no part of this book may be reprinted or reproduced or utilised in any form or by any electronic, mechanical, or other means, now known or hereafter invented, including photocopying and recording, or in any information storage or retrieval system, without permission in writing from the publishers. For details on the rights for the Introduction, please see the chapter's Open Access footnote.

Trademark notice: Product or corporate names may be trademarks or registered trademarks, and are used only for identification and explanation without intent to infringe.

British Library Cataloguing-in-Publication Data
A catalogue record for this book is available from the British Library

ISBN13: 978-0-367-41723-9

Typeset in Minion Pro
by codeMantra

Publisher's Note
The publisher accepts responsibility for any inconsistencies that may have arisen during the conversion of this book from journal articles to book chapters, namely the inclusion of journal terminology.

Disclaimer
Every effort has been made to contact copyright holders for their permission to reprint material in this book. The publishers would be grateful to hear from any copyright holder who is not here acknowledged and will undertake to rectify any errors or omissions in future editions of this book.

Contents

	Citation Information	vi
	Notes on Contributors	viii
	Introduction: Defence planning as strategic fact *Henrik Breitenbauch and André Ken Jakobsson*	1
1	Defense planning beyond rationalism: the third offset strategy as a case of metagovernance *Magnus Christiansson*	10
2	Tradeoffs in defense strategic planning: lessons from the U.S. Quadrennial Defense Review *Jordan Tama*	27
3	The role of ideas in defense planning: revisiting the revolution in military affairs *Benjamin M. Jensen*	50
4	The US perspective on future war: why the US relies upon Ares rather than Athena *Jan Angstrom*	66
5	Rediscovering geography in NATO defence planning *Alexander Mattelaer*	87
6	Questioning the "Sanctity" of long-term defense planning as practiced in Central and Eastern Europe *Thomas-Durell Young*	105
7	Defense planning when major changes are needed *Paul K. Davis*	122
	Conclusion: Coda: exploring defence planning in future research *Henrik Breitenbauch and André Ken Jakobsson*	139
	Index	143

Citation Information

The chapters in this book were originally published in *Defence Studies*, volume 18, issue 3 (September 2018). When citing this material, please use the original page numbering for each article, as follows:

Introduction
Defence planning as strategic fact: introduction
Henrik Breitenbauch and André Ken Jakobs
Defence Studies, volume 18, issue 3 (September 2018) pp. 253–261

Chapter 1
Defense planning beyond rationalism: the third offset strategy as a case of metagovernance
Magnus Christiansson
Defence Studies, volume 18, issue 3 (September 2018) pp. 262–278

Chapter 2
Tradeoffs in defense strategic planning: lessons from the U.S. Quadrennial Defense Review
Jordan Tama
Defence Studies, volume 18, issue 3 (September 2018) pp. 279–301

Chapter 3
The role of ideas in defense planning: revisiting the revolution in military affairs
Benjamin M. Jensen
Defence Studies, volume 18, issue 3 (September 2018) pp. 302–317

Chapter 4
The US perspective on future war: why the US relies upon Ares rather than Athena
Jan Angstrom
Defence Studies, volume 18, issue 3 (September 2018) pp. 318–338

Chapter 5
Rediscovering geography in NATO defence planning
Alexander Mattelaer
Defence Studies, volume 18, issue 3 (September 2018) pp. 339–356

Chapter 6
Questioning the "Sanctity" of long-term defense planning as practiced in Central and Eastern Europe
Thomas-Durell Young
Defence Studies, volume 18, issue 3 (September 2018) pp. 357–373

Chapter 7
Defense planning when major changes are needed
Paul K. Davis
Defence Studies, volume 18, issue 3 (September 2018) pp. 374–390

Conclusion
Coda: exploring defence planning in future research
Henrik Breitenbauch and André Ken Jakobsson
Defence Studies, volume 18, issue 3 (September 2018) pp. 391–394

For any permission-related enquiries please visit:
http://www.tandfonline.com/page/help/permissions

Contributors

Jan Angstrom is a Professor of War Studies at the Swedish Defence University, Sweden, and an Associate Professor in the Department of Peace and Conflict Research at Uppsala University, Sweden.

Henrik Breitenbauch heads the Centre for Military Studies in the Department of Political Science at the University of Copenhagen, Denmark. The Centre advises Denmark's parliament and government on strategy, defence and security issues.

Magnus Christiansson is a PhD Candidate at the University of Stockholm, Sweden. As a Lecturer, he teaches strategic studies, Baltic Sea security, deterrence theory and risk theory.

Paul K. Davis is a Retired Adjunct Senior Principal Researcher at RAND, USA, and a Professor of Policy Analysis in the Pardee RAND Graduate School.

André Ken Jakobsson is a Carlsberg Postdoctoral Fellow at the Centre for Military Studies in the Department of Political Science at the University of Copenhagen, Denmark, with a project on grey zone conflicts and great power politics.

Benjamin M. Jensen holds a dual appointment as a Professor of Strategic Studies at Marine Corps University, USA, and as a Scholar-in-Residence in the School of International Service at the American University, Washington, D.C., USA. He is also a Senior Non-Resident Fellow at the Atlantic Council, USA and an officer in the U.S. Army Reserves, 75th Innovation Command.

Alexander Mattelaer is the Academic Director of the Institute for European Studies at the Vrije Universiteit Brussel and a Senior Research Fellow at Egmont – the Royal Institute of International Relations, Belgium.

Jordan Tama is an Associate Professor in the School of International Service, a Research Fellow at the Center for Congressional and Presidential Studies, and the Co-Director of the Bridging the Gap Project at American University, Washington, D.C., USA.

Thomas-Durell Young is a Senior Lecturer and an Academic Associate for the Comparative Defense Planning Curriculum in the Department of National Security Affairs, the Naval Postgraduate School, is associated with the Institute of Defense Governance, Defense Security Cooperation Agency, USA.

INTRODUCTION

🔓 OPEN ACCESS

Defence planning as strategic fact

Henrik Breitenbauch and André Ken Jakobsson

ABSTRACT
With this special issue of Defence Studies, we situate defence planning as a constitutive element of defence and strategic studies. Indeed, in addition to the usual "downstream" focus on the use or non-use of force, on policy decision-making in foreign relations, military operations and global external engagement, we argue for the utility of an increased "upstream" focus on what is a major part of everyday defence and security policy practice for military, civilian administrative and political leadership: the forward-looking preparations for the armed forces and other capabilities of tomorrow. In particular, the special issue contributions explore two general dimensions of defence planning: the long-term, historical relationship between defence planning and the state including national variations in civil-military relations, and a concurrent tension between defence planning as an administrative, analytically neutral activity and the politics of its organisation and outcomes. In both of these, defence planning appears as a particular case of general planning, as a lens that enables particular foci on the external world to come about on behalf of the state while also sometimes creating institutionalised biases along the way. In this manner, paraphrasing Émile Durkheim, defence planning emerges as a "strategic fact" with dynamics of its own.

This special issue of *Defence Studies* identifies defence planning as a particular object of interest for defence and strategic studies as well as for security studies and the wider International Relations discipline. In doing so, the different contributions draw attention to a little analysed but functionally central part of defence and national security policy, namely the more or less formalised planning efforts that are part and parcel of how major policy and organizational reform, investment and acquisition decisions are made in modern defence policy. By opening the black box of the state in terms of identifying, parsing and discussing the effects of various administrative, organisational and political dynamics associated with defence planning, this special issue also offers the potential for a more general focus shift in defence and strategic studies. It does so by taking a cue from Stephan de Spiegeleire (2012) in suggesting that – in addition to the usual "downstream" focus on the use or non-use of force, on policy decision-making in foreign relations, military operations and global external engagement – it is useful to also move "upstream" towards phenomena well-known to most military as well as civilian defence practitioners, namely activities that bear on how states and their constitutive administrative and political authorities conceive of, plan for, and decide upon *future* defence capabilities rather than the immediate use of the *current* ones.

In sociology, Émile Durkheim famously proposed that social science could and should be established around its own objects of study: that there are such things as "social facts" that are different from the objects of natural science (Durkheim 1982). By giving social science its own dimension, Durkheim paved the way for its modern incarnation. We use Durkheim's example metaphorically here and propose that among the "strategic facts" – constituting together the *raison d'être* for defence and strategic studies – we ought to include also those phenomena that are incorporated under the term defence planning. We propose, in other words, that the study of defence planning should be considered a relevant and integral part of the overall sub-disciplinary landscape in defence and strategic studies as a pertinent strategic fact. This special issue is intended to open up avenues for such an agenda and to inspire others to go down those or parallel roads to produce new and useful strategic knowledge.

Process behind the special issue

This special issue originated with a September 2016 conference on "Long-Term Defence Planning in the NORDEFCO countries" organized by the Centre for Military Studies at the University of Copenhagen. This conference initiated a multi-national research agenda by bringing together the expertise of scholars, officers, and civil servants from seven different countries and was followed by a February 2017 author's workshop at the same venue. Taking these questions to a broader audience, the authors of this special issue then convened a roundtable in October 2017 at the ISSS-ISAC Annual Conference hosted by American University in Washington, D.C. The roundtable again saw a mix of scholars, practitioners and officers weighing in on the papers presented as part of an emerging academic field of defence planning. This special issue has itself been subject to the intricacies of planning for the future and the guest editors would like to thank everyone involved in this process for their valuable contributions. This goes especially to the editors of Defence Studies for their strategic acumen in seeing the perspectives in this special issue and for professionally and patiently tending to the editorial process. The numerous anonymous reviewers also deserve praise. Finally, accolade belongs to the contributing authors who willingly ventured into little visited academic territory, providing maps and ideas to further explore for those who will follow.

Defence planning as an object of study

The erratic nature of security threats faced by the modern state demands planning for war and peace under the pressure of deep uncertainty. This condition essentially makes defence planning a persistent quest to tame Machiavelli's *Fortuna*, the wild river of unforeseen political events and involves the highest of stakes as state survival is ultimately conditioned upon successful defence planning: *si vis pacem, para bellum*. The practical activities, dynamics, conditions, effects, pitfalls and general characteristics associated with actual defence planning, however, have hitherto mostly been a technical issue for practical problem-solvers, making it an understudied subject for International Relations and related sub-disciplines. A case in point is delivered by Colin Gray's intent to provide a "proto-theory" for defence planning (Gray 2014, p. 10). While this effort serves as a motivating factor, it is also a testament to the unexplored state of research. One early example of the link between practitioners and knowledge production on the subject is *U.S. Defense Planning: A Critique* (Collins 1982), a monograph written by a researcher with the Congressional Research Service. A recent and central contribution, Stephan Frühling's *Defence Planning and Uncertainty: Preparing for the Next Asia-Pacific War*, fruitfully explores how uncertainty is addressed in different ideal-typical genres of defence planning as a question of fit between analysis of particular kinds of strategic risk and subsequent codification of requirements (Frühling 2014). Even if this special issue testifies to a growing academic interest in defence planning, practitioners' perspectives are likely to be sought after and a dialogue upheld. The historical under-appreciation of defence planning in academia is called attention to as decision makers and defence planning practitioners are hard pressed to find expert academic counter-parts while confronted with an intensified NATO burden sharing debate in addition to threat proliferation by Russia's aggression against Ukraine, Islamist terrorism and spread of advanced weapons technology that has motivated a number of countries to increase defence spending. The practical reactions to these threats is to a high degree contained in the activity of defence planning such as investing in new and more capable fighter jets, participating in new forms of international defence cooperation, developing new doctrines or more radically reforming the armed forces. The sheer scale of the monies involved and the security interests at stake critically warrant a renewed impetus in the academic debate on the substantial and variegated activities formally or informally related to defence planning.

Rather than assuming that adaption to the new security environment happens automatically – like a chemical reaction – practitioners will instead testify to extensive organizational and analytical efforts prior to and clearly shaping the eventual outcomes of political decision-making. Inside the black box of the state, such processes pass over and link the interfaces of not only (in this case) civilian and military realms, but also across the political and the administrative divide (in practice terms: from analysis to policy), all of which have effects on strategic outcomes, and which therefore have strategic relevance. Little research systematically tackles the extensive chronological dimension of long-term planning on top of the complex political, bureaucratic, and operational dimensions, chains of command, policy formulation and implementation. For a research subject of defence planning to emerge it will likely be productive to acknowledge, engage, and assess also these interface dynamics of its analytical, military, political, administrative and organisational dimensions. In the end, we argue, and following the logical sequence of events, studying the *preparation* of the armed forces of tomorrow is arguably as important as studying the *employment* of the existing armed forces of today.

Defence planning has been established and executed as a practice throughout the totality of human history and has at its most fundamental level aimed to limit the condition of uncertainty to ensure survival of the group, community, nation or state. Indeed, as 19th century historian Otto Hintze argued, " [a]ll state organization was originally military organization, organization for war" (Hintze 1975, 181). Within the contemporary modern nation state, this practice has taken on great complexity through a variety of formal national and international processes (Håkenstad and Larsen 2012), which challenge and renegotiate the civil-military relationship as well as the bureaucratic organization of the state as security threats evolve and proliferate. In this way, what matters in particular to a tentative gesture of opening up for new research such as the present one, is to work from the outside in with regard to delimiting the subject. This special issue therefore takes an explicitly big tent approach to the definition of what defence planning is and how it can be studied – with one particular reservation. In the broadest possible sense, defence planning is all planning related phenomena in the world of defence. Following Merriam-Webster's definition of planning, that would be all activity related to the "establishment of goals, policies, and procedures" at the higher echelons of the world of defence. In theory, this could mean studying all kinds of preparatory and prioritisation oriented processes as defence planning. One example could here include all the various organizational terminology that include planning, such as for example "threat-based", "capability-based", "assumption-based" and "effects-based" planning. But while we acknowledge that efforts to control the employment of armed forces crucially also involve organisational planning – for example, the logistics prepared through the (US) Joint Assistant for Development and Execution's instruments such as the Time-Phased Force and Deployment List clearly pertain to planning in a literal way – the planning phenomena we draw new attention to here address not the question of optimal use of the current armed forces, but rather analytical discussions of future alternatives. In this way, "threat-based", "capability-based" and "assumption-based" planning will count as defence planning, while "effects-based" planning, which is concerned with the optimal use of force, does not. As indicated above, we distinguish "downstream" or force-employment related activities (including such things as effects-based planning and the Time-Phased Force and Deployment List), from our main concern, namely "upstream" activities that are about planning for the future force.

Placing defence planning hierarchically within the political-military nexus, Stephan Frühling states that "strategy and the pattern of strategic risk [that is] to be reduced form the strategic guidance that defence planning has to translate into actual programmes, forces and activities" (Frühling 2014, p. 32). Defence planning's activities, output, and outcome function within this composite nexus institutionalized through Weberian bureaucracy and the practice itself is so vital to any state that it stands as an often-undisputed object. The content ascribed to it and what it is an effect of, however, is more opaque. The contribution in this special issue by Paul Davis defines defence planning – along the lines of our distinction above – as the "deliberate process of planning a nation's future forces, force postures, and force capabilities (as distinct from operations planning on how to employ the forces in war). The planning must consider the near-term, mid-term, and long-term" (Davis, 2018). This definition is helpful in distinguishing between force provisioning and force employment – where the latter is not part of defence planning – but as Davis points out, the assumptions, content, scope, and purpose of defence planning has taken on several different expressions over time in the American practitioner context, in which he himself has played an important part. This continuous debate between defence planning practitioners, located inside or organically related to central policy organizations, on what the activity constitutes is the fertile ground from which this special issue wishes to establish defence planning as a strategic fact.

Establishing defence planning as a strategic fact means, beyond the symbolic gesture, to facilitate the renewal of academic debates on theoretical approaches, methodologies, and empirical experiences and in doing so also contributing to the definition of defence planning as a particular object of academic research. In this pursuit, academic research on defence planning has much to gain from interacting with the expert knowledge of practitioners with long empirical experience in connecting platforms, doctrines, and transformation processes with strategy on multiple levels of state bureaucracy and not least a rapidly developing security environment. While these issues have received individual academic attention and even constitute research fields of their own, the contributions in this special issue illustrate how gaps between them can be bridged. Based on these contributions, the special issue aims to open a discussion that allows for a renewed and promising engagement with a rich empirical reality and a variety of academic approaches.

It is therefore worth highlighting the mix of contributions in this special issue. In a welcome addition to the articles penned (as has become the common standard) from the vantage point of a theoretical framework, the issue contains also two commentaries, authored by prominent scholar-practitioners, both with long experience in the US defence planning orbit including central think tanks and professional military education institutions. Paul K. Davis has for several decades produced influential analytical and programmatic writing about defence planning notably at RAND. Along with colleagues, Davis has played a prominent role in shaping the evolution of American defence planning paradigms. Thomas-Durrell Young likewise has a distinguished career at leading institutions including the Naval Postgraduate School, RAND and the U.S. Army War College. He too has made a mark in US defence planning knowledge production with a particular focus on the adaptation and transformation of American defence planning in Central and Eastern Europe since the end of the Cold War. The contributions by Davis and Young contain in their own right a number of valuable and interesting observations and propositions. In this way, they are also a concrete example of the practitioner proximity preached by this introduction.

The state, planning and the politics of planning

While the contributions in this special issue do differ in the particular ways they exemplify the utility of analysing the domain of defence planning, they all share a concern for understanding and bringing to light how defence planning is more than a mere receptacle of a changing threat horizon, more than an automatic transposition of such contextual, external changes into political priorities and, ultimately, decisions. Defence planning, in other words, in these articles appear, as a strategic fact with dynamics of its own that is not reducible to neither automatic reactions to external change, nor to the purely political decision-making surrounding its processes. In particular, the contributions enable a deepened understanding of two general dimensions of defence planning as a strategic fact, namely the long-term, historical relationship between defence planning and the state including national variations in civil-military relations, and a concurrent perspective on the tension between defence planning as an administrative, analytically neutral activity and the politics of its organisation and outcomes. In both of these dimensions we see examples of how defence planning appears as a particular case of general planning; as a lens that enables particular foci on the external world to come about on behalf of the state while also sometimes creating institutionalised biases or path-dependencies along the way to warrant specific attention to the planning phenomenon as a relevant independent or intermediate variable in the greater field of defence and strategic studies.

In the long term, the relationship between the state and defence planning is, as indicated with the reference above to Hintze, deep and constitutive. Approaching defence planning within the overall context of the state's foreign, defence and national security decision-making offers a macro-perspective, which points to its functionalist genesis between the state and war. In the bellocentric historical sociology of state formation, this is most famously captured by Charles Tilly's dictum that "war made the state and the state made war" whereby external competition and risk of war encouraged the emergence of modern internal state institutions, including permanent, dedicated defence administration organisations (Tilly 1975, 42). In the long term, particular, national trajectories of specific organizations of defence planning affected and affect the forms of planning that arise. Long-term divisions of labour at the civil-military level and related institutionalisations of responsibilities for defence planning appear as a central motif in Jan Angstrom's contribution (Angstrom, 2018). Analysing the role and character of United States military long-term defence planning, Angstrom proposes that there is a link between defence planning practices and deep-seated preferences for a particularly military technique focused approach to military operations where the biased preference for kinetic military activity over political solutions is echoed in both defence planning outcomes regarding military platforms as well as the planning stage of the future visions of war. The deep relationship between the state and defence planning is also echoed in Magnus Christiansson's contribution, which offers an analysis of the United States third offset defence planning strategy (Christiansson, 2018). The article identifies the historical origins of the planning as integral to the evolution of the modern state, locates these in a more contemporary context with the evolution of a rational planning paradigm inside the United States defence structure and discusses how the third offset strategy in important ways represent a new form of "meta-governance" that at the same time demonstrates and purports to be an answer to the limits of the modernist rational planning paradigm. Thomas-Durell Young's contribution combines Angstrom and Christiansson's findings by showing how national path dependencies of military and civilian organization set limits to importing and implementing Long Term Defence Planning (LTDP) from the United States to Central and Eastern European (CEE) states (Young, 2018). A legacy of Communist five-year plans lingers in the bureaucracy of CEE states and shape their perception of defence planning as determining for future action even if the original LTDP intention was the direct opposite, namely to facilitate future flexibility by enabling the production of costed priorities as policy priorities and financial execution. Bridging these two positions is thus a key point for Young.

The origins of rational planning, as Magnus Christiansson observes in his contribution, coincide with the advent of Western modernity around the 18th century. This point in time marks the emergence of the Prussian general staff with its adoption and development of Enlightenment rationality into superior force provision and force employment – and it becomes the (defence) planning organization of reference. During the 19th century, evolution of planning practices and theories interact between the civilian and military domains while these become increasingly demarcated throughout the political-military revolutions as civilian political power hierarchically comes to dominate the military as the wielder of state violence while the military itself establishes a professional information and knowledge production monopoly on defence planning and organized violence. However, from the closing decade of the 20th century onwards, the planning practices and theories of the civilian domain can be observed to penetrate the military domain, through organisational practices such as New Public Management (Norheim-Martinsen 2016).

In more contemporary terms, defence planning has a dynamic of its own with political effects that is not reducible to politics or evolving threat horizons. Even so, or because of this, defence planning is not an isolated phenomenon, but rather an administrative tool with political repercussions. Jordan Tama's contribution shows, like Young, how the way defence planning processes are organized impact the effects of the processes and that there are trade-offs associated with these choices. By incorporating many actors and emphasizing transparency, some defence planning processes can help create broader support and buy-in for subsequent political decisions, whereas others, by keeping the organizational design inclusivity limited are more likely to produce more incisive analytical results (Tama, 2018). Benjamin Jensen's contribution, on the other hand, emphasizes how "programmatic actors" can mobilise the power of ideas to shape agendas inside the defence planning systems with subsequent political effects. Drawing on a related public policy theoretical framework, Jensen shows how the study of defence planning can gain from employing insights from other research stemming from other policy domains. Jensen, like Norheim-Martinsen above, in this way in effect deflates at least part of the particular aura surrounding national security studies by subjecting it to approaches found useful elsewhere, thus challenges the uniqueness of Huntingtonian civil-military relations (Jensen, 2018). In Paul Davis' contribution, we also find a reflection on how the evolution of formalised US defence policy and planning systems since the 1960's have fared in the light of major changes in the international environment. The periods of major change, that Davis constructs based on his long experience with the RAND Corporation, shows how the U.S. defence planning structure with the Department of Defence organizationally at the head has been struggling to adequately predict future conflict situations due to limited planning scenarios and failures of imagination, accentuated under a threat-based defence planning paradigm. His analysis indicates how organizational inertia of the planning system calls for civilian and military strategic leadership and the necessity of reaching outside of established planning processes to access non-standardized analyses. In this way, the analysis also illustrates how United States defence planning has evolved between political change agents and administrative procedures (Davis, 2018). This dynamic of defence planning during major changes is elevated past the state level in Alexander Mattelaer's analysis of the evolving organizing principles of NATO defence planning. Mattelaer's contribution shows how the foundational logic of NATO's geography-based division of labour was abandoned after the end of the Cold War and replaced by capability-based defence planning as a consequence of NATO assuming a global mission. However, as Mattelaer posits, the pendulum is swinging back as geography again took centre stage after Russia's annexation of Crimea. Underscoring that defence planning is more than only a receptacle of volatile international politics, Mattelaer connects the domestic politics driven debate on NATO burden sharing with his recommendation of acknowledging geography through a regional division of labour (Mattelaer, 2018).

The evolution of defence planning

Whether one emphasizes the deep historical conceptual contingencies or the contemporary organizational interplay between administration and politics, between process and advocacy of ideas, the forms and roles of defence planning emerge as important and relevant aspects of overall national security and defence policy, not least with regard to its incremental evolution. This should be of no surprise in a common sense way, since the organisations tasked with planning are in fact given responsibility for identifying and proposing change with regard to the future armed forces of a given nation. But from a defence and strategic studies perspective, it matters because the effects of defence planning point to its existence as more than a mere analytical relay station between changes in the character of war and the subsequent political reorientations of the state. As Davis' evolution of defence planning indicates, governments have had a hard time incorporating change into their defence planning systems, and to accommodate the condition of deep uncertainty. Similarly, Young's account of the challenges posed by (legacy) state-society relations in implementing defence planning systems highlights the immanent national security aspects of bureaucratic organization for the upstream. If Jensen's programmatic actors are able to capture a larger slice of top-level political attention and even budgets, they may also in some instances be able to circumvent blind spots – but they could in the process lose their edge by trading inclusion over analytical focus, as argued by Tama. If defence planning continues to be a military dominated activity, such blind spots as identified by Angstrom could be sustained with negative consequences – or it may be that defence planning itself, as proposed by Christiansson, is breaking into mutually incongruous phenomena, serving both the status quo and the need for future technologies. Accommodating these developments will be of critical concern to not only states but also to international defence planning such as in NATO. As Mattelaer points out, the post-Cold War history of alliance defence planning has created unintended dynamics that must now be renegotiated, aligning national and alliance demands and resources.

If defence planning can in these ways be said to be a strategic fact, this special issue will then have served an important purpose not only through the contributions of the articles but also through the example that they set together with regard to the general utility of studying defence planning as a discrete activity in the larger field of defence, strategic and security studies.

Disclosure statement

No potential conflict of interest was reported by the authors.

Funding

This work was supported by the Carlsbergfondet; Gerda Henkel Foundation.

References

Angstrom, J., 2018. The US perspective on future war: why the US relies upon Ares rather than Athena. *Defence studies*, 18 (3), 318–338.
Christiansson, M., 2018. Defense planning beyond rationalism: the third offset strategy as a case of metagovernance. *Defence studies*, 18 (3), 262–278.
Collins, J.M., 1982. *U. S. defense planning: a critique*. Boulder, CO: Westview Press.
Davis, P.K., 2018. Defense planning when major changes are needed. *Defence studies*, 18 (3), 374–390.
Durkheim, É., 1982. *The rules of sociological method*. New York: The Free Press.
Frühling, S., 2014. *Defence planning and uncertainty: preparing for the next Asia-Pacific war*. Abingdon: Routledge.
Gray, C., 2014. *Strategy and defence planning: meeting the challenge*. Oxford: Oxford University Press.
Håkenstad, M. and Larsen, K.K., 2012. *Long-term defence planning. A comparative study of seven countries*, Oslo Files on Defence and Security, 5/2012.
Hintze, O., 1975. Military organization and the organization of the state. *In*: F. Gilbert, ed. *The historical essays of Otto Hintze*. Oxford: Oxford University Press.
Jensen, B., 2018. The role of ideas in defense planning: revisiting the revolution in military affairs. *Defence studies*, 18 (3), 302–317.
Mattelaer, A., 2018. Rediscovering geography in NATO defence planning. *Defence studies*, 18 (3), 339–356.
Norheim-Martinsen, P., 2016. New sources of military change – armed forces as normal organizations. *Defence studies*, 16 (3), 312–326. doi:10.1080/14702436.2016.1195234.
Spiegeleire, S., 2012. *Taking the battle upstream: towards a benchmarking role for NATO*, Report, Center for Technology and National Security Policy, Institute for National Strategic Studies, National Defense University, Washington, DC, September, http://www.dtic.mil/dtic/tr/full text/u2/a582370.pdf
Tama, J., 2018. Tradeoffs in defense strategic planning: lessons from the U.S. quadrennial defense review. *Defence studies*, 18 (3), 279–301.
Tilly, C., 1975. Reflections on the history of European State-making. *In*: C. Tilly, ed. *The formation of national states in western Europe*. Princeton: Princeton University Press, 3–83.
Young, T.-D., 2018. Questioning the "sanctity" of long-term defense planning as practiced in Central and Eastern Europe. *Defence studies*, 18 (3), 357–373.

Defense planning beyond rationalism: the third offset strategy as a case of metagovernance

Magnus Christiansson

ABSTRACT
This article analyzes U.S. defense planning, and more specifically the public administration of the third offset strategy. The U.S. defense bureaucracy is rooted in a tradition of rational planning, which assumes a process of consistent, value-maximizing choices within specified constrains. The cornerstone in this tradition is the program budgeting system, once created to connect plans with budgets according to preferences. The third offset strategy, aimed at dealing with the challenges of geopolitical competition and budget austerity, is influenced by a different public administration philosophy described as metagovernance. Metagovernance is a challenge to rational planning as it entails an indirect approach of organizing arenas for networks, in which start-up companies and civilian corporations get to interact with government officials in order to identify incrementally suitable acquisition projects. Furthermore, the article contextualizes this tendency in reflexive modernity, in which rationality breaks down due to the pace of societal changes and planning processes constantly become subject to feedback.

Military change and public administration

Norwegian scholar Per Norheim-Martinsen recently argued in "Defense Studies" for a new research agenda for the study of defense organizations (Norheim-Martinsen 2016). After revisiting the story of "defense transformation" in Europe as "normal" defense organizations, which like many other public agencies have been subject to public administration reforms, he made the case for a complementary public administration perspective to explain national differences. Importantly, defense organizations (i.e. the whole defense sector of a country) have also been influenced by general trends in public administration, most notably New Public Management (NPM).

Following in these footsteps, this article is a contribution to a research agenda in which organization of government matters as a source of military change. The decentralization of Weberian hierarchical relations in government associated with NPM lead to the question to what extent these relations have been replaced or alleviated by other mechanisms of trust and control (cf. Norheim-Martinsen 2016, p. 323). This is the central puzzle of this article. While it is certainly true that NPM has been an influential trend in replacing traditional hierarchies in government, in the following, I make the case that it is not the only influence that is of importance.

In this article, I demonstrate that as the U.S. Government has identified a key strategic challenge, its planning response for "the third offset strategy" is organized as metagovernance, i.e. higher order governance through which governance is shaped and facilitated with rules and procedures. In key respects, this is an emerging form of trust and control of contemporary defense agencies that challenges the established U.S. planning procedures, which I identify as rational planning.

The third offset strategy, or formally the U.S. Defense Innovation Initiative, was launched in 2014. There are two main drivers for this initiative: that the technological superiority of the U.S. is challenged by emerging powers and that the Department of Defense and defense industry must prepare to cope with innovation under shrinking budgets and austerity. It was explicitly presented as a contemporary version of the "offset strategies" of the 1950s (resulting in tactical nukes) and 1970s (resulting in standoff precision strike, stealth, wide-area surveillance, and networked forces), where the U.S. tried to compensate for various military shortcomings in the cold war power struggle. Hence, it is often referred to as the third offset strategy.

The third offset strategy is based on the processes in four main arenas for interactive networking between government representatives and commercial actors without traditional connections to defense industry (i.e. robotics, advanced computing, miniaturization, and 3D printing). Thus, it is an iterative process of deliberation and consultation, in which the procedures of developing weapon systems become as important as the weapon systems themselves. Not only does the third offset strategy challenge the rational planning in the U.S. defense system, as described in sociology, it could be interpreted as part of reflexive modernity of contemporary societies. The pace of change in society lead to ambiguities, complexities, and uncertainties that undermine the ability for rational planning, and lead to a constant feedback concerning the planning procedures themselves. While the third offset strategy has been covered in research and think tank reports (cf. FitzGerald *et al.* 2016), it has never been grounded in a clearly elaborated theoretical framework of public administration. Thus, this is a contribution to our understanding of how processes and practices of planning in government are a source for change of defense organizations (cf. Tama 2015, p. 736).

This article is structured around three consecutive arguments. In the first section, I argue that the established U.S. procedures of rational planning are conceptually challenged by the processes and practices of metagovernance. Following this, I make the case that U.S. defense planning is influenced by metagovernance, or more specifically that the third offset strategy is a case of metagovernance. Finally, I interpret metagovernance as linked to reflexive modernity, where defense planning becomes a reflexive project about organizing the organization of innovation. In the following, I turn to the argument about the conceptual difference between rational planning and metagovernance.

Rational planning and metagovernance

Planning is an integral feature of public agencies. Planning is a central aspect of how defense establishments organize themselves, and is thus a key process to study in order to understand relations between actors in them. For the purpose of this article, a plan is a prescription for how to cope with the future, and planning are the processes and practices for how to create such prescription. As noted in previous research, planning matters for organizational changes within agencies (Tama 2015). While this might seem trivial, the point is that different forms of public administration make a difference, and that NPM is not the only source of inspiration. In the following, we will focus on two different administrative philosophies (rational planning and metagovernance) and how they challenge each other conceptually. We will start with rational planning.

The introduction of the management techniques of NPM means that the traditional Weberian centralized hierarchy of bureaucracy is decentralized, which means "a weakening of the mutually reinforcing downward flow of directives and upward flow of information upon which hierarchical systems rest" (Norheim-Martinsen 2016, p. 323). One central feature of NPM is the tendency to use market mechanisms and decentralization in the form of horizontal specialization (i.e. agencies are "broken up" in specific functions). This private sector-style management, often accompanied with the use of language from private corporations, emphasizes explicit performance standards and output/outcome control instead of hierarchical command-and-control.

However, it is equally important to note that as much as the advocates of NPM regard it as contrast to the traditional and centralized bureaucracy (Hood 1991), this self-proclaimed novelty, as well as the controversies surrounding the concept, has often reinforced the view of it as a clean break with Weberian bureaucracies. While NPM was critical of the ability of bureaucracy to plan for societies

> it seems as if the high ambitions concerning planning and control did not disappear, but the objects of rational discourse moved from the wider community to the state organizations, or from the macro level to the micro level of reform. (Jacobsson et al. 2015, p. 11)

Public administration scholar Bob Gregory makes the plausible case that the notion of a contradiction between a rational Weberian hierarchy and the market is due to a misunderstanding as "NPM is the latest and most significant manifestation of ... 'rationalization', the quest for greater calculability in and precision in the management of human affairs". (Gregory 2007, p. 222). After all, NPM "is a child of neo-classical economics and particularly of rational/public choice theory" (Osborne 2006, p. 382). The decentralized market-like customers, contractors, and entrepreneurs in NPM are in fact predicated on the assumption that actors in government rationally calculate their interests. This is where NPM meet rational planning: in the assumption that actors in a process make consistent, value-maximizing choices within specified constrains (Allison and Zelikow 1999, p. 18). This assumption is compatible with analysis of "bureaucratic politics", "turf wars", and also "incentive structures" and "cost-benefit" in defense service production. It is important to underline that rational planning is goal-oriented, as it is propelled by aims and objectives, and the plan itself is substantive, i.e. it answers questions of how to deal with a dangerous world. Thus, regardless of its political context, rational planning is basically a service–delivery mechanism where political decision-makers act as system controllers that decide policy objectives "upstream", and staff/contractors implement/manage that policy "downstream", or at least that is how it is designed to operate.

There is a tradition of rational planning in the U.S. Government. The roots stretch as far back as the Civil War, and a modern precursor was the performance budgeting of the 1950s, inspired partly by practices of World War II planning methods. For more about the evolution of the U.S. planning, see Paul K. Davis "Defense planning when major changes are needed", 2018. The rationalist approach was used during World War II in "operations research" and "systems analysis" in order to maximize industrial production and the war effort. Influenced by these experiences, ideas at RAND as well as private business practices, Secretary of Defense Robert McNamara, and the Pentagon Comptroller Charles Hitch introduced a planning-programming-budgeting (PPB) system in the early 1960s (Novick 1966). The defense budget was divided into seven basic programs (strategic retaliatory forces, continental air and missile defense forces, general-purpose forces, airlift and sealift forces, special research and development, reserve and national guard forces, and general support). Each program was composed of a number of program elements (i.e. Polaris submarines and Minuteman missiles). In other words, programs are "combinations of activities that produce distinguishable products or missions" (Hitch and McKean 1960, p. vi). At the time, the virtues of program budgeting were presented as "usefulness in relating ends to means in a comprehensive fashion" (Wildavsky 1964, p. 135), and to quote two public management scholars, it has been "balancing rational decision-processes, neutral expertise from the military and others, and clear political agendas over an extended planning and budgeting horizon" (McCaffrey and Jones 2005, p. 142). Thus, programs have a key comprehensive function of connecting short-term and long-term planning perspectives, or put differently: plans are linked to budgets through programs.

Program budgeting is focused on productivity and efficiency, which mirrors the fear of bureaucratic ineffectiveness (Wildavsky 1966). Agencies are considered to be able to perform as private enterprises and should be subject to private sector-style management with "business models" which require "output/outcome control". Thus, the meaning of government management is to continuously gather and process information concerning the performance of their agencies. The formal protocol for this process is relatively extensive in the U.S. case, and it is also as fluid as the colors of a chameleon.

Though much has changed in this protocol in U.S. defense planning since the 1960s, most notably reformed under Secretaries of Defense Laird and Rumsfeld and the Goldwater-Nichols Act, the conceptual core of the system is still intact. Programs are formally part of a greater acquisition system, and the core is a rational understanding of the process that connects the strategic objectives of the National Security Strategy (NSS) with the distribution of funds for defense programs (based on their individual performance goals). Though there is a constant debate about how these objectives should be calculated (top-down, bottom-up, etc., cf. Owens 2004), they become components in a rational program process. A scholar used the metaphor of programs "as building blocks of diverse shapes and size, out of which defense policy makers need to select in order to build a good house with an anticipated amount of money". (Tagarev 2009, p. 86). In the current incarnation of PPB, there is a special role of the Deputy Secretary of Defense. Based on the NSS, the Deputy Secretary of Defense is responsible for the process of setting goals, priorities, and objectives for defense programs, as well as recommendations for budgetary allocations to the Secretary of Defense and the President.

Conceptually, there is a separation between policy-makers and civil servants. Policy-makers are supposed to set objectives, targets, and detailed indicators for success, whereas agencies report program results that become the point of departure for the next cycle of budgeting. In this cycle, policy-makers cut or re-prioritize short-term budgets for programs that do not fit the objectives of the long-term plan, and thus the program serves as a "filter" for competing strategic demands. As part of this concept, there have been a number of planning tools to make these calculations: balanced scorecard, benchmarking, process reengineering, defense reviews, to name just a few. Public–private dialog was often a part of this process, but most commonly in a relatively insular environment of networks dominated by established interest groups (sometimes lumped together as "the military-industrial complex").

Metagovernance is an alternative philosophy to rational planning. In this thinking, governance is a plurality of processes that connects government with private and voluntary actors in networks and partnerships, and the point of metagovernance is governance of these interactions. This means that strategic guidance is itself a result of complex mechanisms, which do not only originate from public actors (Klijn and Koppenjan 2000). Thus, metagovernance takes place inside and outside of government only partly for the direct benefit of national security objectives. This means that planning can only be realized in a relatively open environment by a plurality of interacting actors with partly diverging interests. In other words, metagovernance is the governance of governance, i.e. higher order governance through which it is shaped, directed, and facilitated with rules and procedures (Kooiman 2003, Sørensen and Torfing 2009, p. 245).

An important aspect of this philosophy is that there is a different role for government compared to rational planning. In metagovernance, policy-makers still have control, but it is not organized with hierarchical command-and-control methods or in a market logic. The role of public agencies is to define problems, mobilize relevant network actors, facilitate arenas for coordination of stakeholders and networks, and create incentive structures (Jacobsson et al. 2015, pp. 13–16). The planning tools are not radically different in themselves, but they are procedural for control of the planning process, rather than substantively dealing with future strategic threats. They are used to probe questions rather than giving answers. Governments try to control the environment of planning, rather than making the plans directly. The function of arenas is that they bring together network actors with different social backgrounds, identities, and interests which is a method for coordination. This means that government is not a central director, but a mediator and stimulator. Consequently, at the center of the planning is dialog, which mirrors the fear of "noise" where network actors do not understand or accept each other. Metagovernance is to:

- shape and frame the strategic issues for planning.
- organize and manage decentered interactive arenas and networks, including public–private partnerships with delegated authority.
- pool resources from mutually interdependent public, private, and voluntary network actors.

To shape and frame is not to set planning objectives, but rather to change the perception of strategic issues and place planning into a coherent reform story, i.e. a rationale for why planning takes place. Thus, the story of the plan becomes a guide for the involved network actors, where planning means to arrive at conclusions trough a goal-seeking process. In other words, the role of government is to maintain a broad policy agenda supported by a reform story and have a narrative of why and how the network actors can find agreements.

Interaction between network actors with interests in the plan is not spontaneous and needs to be organized. Rather than relying on formal authority, public institutions may create arenas where network actors interact. It may introduce new network actors as participation is defined by stakes, interests, knowledge, resources, and networking capability, rather than position in the Pentagon hierarchy (Torfing, Peters, Pierre and Sørensen 2012). In doing this, the government may include traditionally marginalized actors as well as enhancing competing networks as part of planning. Furthermore, government has an important role in setting scope conditions for the interaction process, like timelines, fiscal, and legal limitations. Thus, organizing in metagovernance is not about instrumental realization of substantive planning objectives.

As conflicts often emerge between the involved network actors, there is a need for public "steering strategies" (Klijn and Koppenjan 2000, p. 140). The rules for planning should continuously be monitored and facilitated. Thus, the crucial aspect of making networks relevant and successful is to "facilitate the alignment of goals, values and cultures" (Sørensen and Torfing 2009, p. 243). In doing this, public agencies may address concerns of the involved network actors, i.e. protect autonomy for private companies or the integrity of voluntary groups. The key challenge is to avoid eliminating the capacity for self-regulation, i.e. a situation when public involvement becomes a burden for the network actors.

Planning in metagovernance is to engage in a learning process. The role of the government is to facilitate this interaction process, and networks and partnerships are more flexible forms of organization than hierarchies. This means that civil servants become active participants together with other network actors, while policy-makers institutionalize processes that work well, and learn from those that do not. Though policy-makers may participate directly, such involvement tends to be a proactive problem-solving interaction with the network, rather than direct participation in the negotiations of the network. An important part of this learning process is to listen to the perceived benefits for the involved network actors ("What's in it for me?") and identify positive and negative incentives for continued cooperation. In the beginning, it might be important to have a few "quick victories with joint ownership" (Sørensen and Torfing 2009, p. 251), and also to reduce risks and transaction costs along the process. However, it is important to note that the learning process is not only substantial, it also has a social and cultural side where the usefulness of the network could be strengthened by increased understanding among the involved actors.

Ultimately, this form of planning is based on trust. It is not possible for the Pentagon to command results, as it relies on networks of actors beyond its direct control. When successful, these networks form "obligational contracts" (Hudson 2004), but this is difficult to achieve in a fluid and dynamic network environment. Despite these challenges, in the following, I argue that the U.S. Government engaged in metagovernance in its Defense Innovation Initiative.

The third offset strategy as a case of metagovernance

In fall 2014, U.S. Secretary of Defense Chuck Hagel launched what he called the "Defense Innovation Initiative" (DII) in two key speeches (Hagel 2014a, 2014b, DoD 2014a). The reform story of DII is based on two underpinning arguments: that the technological superiority of the U.S. is challenged by emerging powers and that the Department of Defense (DoD) and defense industry must prepare to operate with shrinking budgets and austerity. The initiative was explicitly presented as a contemporary version of the "offset strategies" of the 1950s (resulting in tactical nukes) and 1970s (resulting in standoff precision strike, stealth, wide-area surveillance, and networked forces), where the U.S. tried to compensate for various military shortcomings in the cold war power struggle. Hence, the DII is often referred to as "the third offset strategy" (cf. Martinage 2014).

In the reform story, the first rationale of DII is the growing concern for the tech-intensive postures of mainly China and Russia, which are generally regarded as a potential threat to global U.S. ambitions. According to the Quadrennial Defense Review of 2014, the U.S. should be able to defeat a regional adversary while maintaining credible deterrence against other possible adversaries in the rest of the world (DoD 2014b). Today, not only is technological competition global, military high-tech has become globalized. China is expected to become the largest economy in the world, and its ca. 10% annual increase of defense expenditures in the last decades, as well focus on intelligence, sensors, autonomous under-water systems, and long-range radars, is of great concern for the U.S. military. Russia's defense expenditures 2016–2020 are expected to increase with some $700bn. It has developed highly qualified military systems like cruise-missile Iskander, coastal defense missile system SSC-5, anti-air system S-400, as well as electronic warfare systems and cyber capabilities. What is perhaps even more concerning in this narrative is that especially China is estimated to have a higher rate of modernization (also known as "new product pipeline") than the U.S. As former Secretary of Defense Ashton Carter concluded during his tenure: "Russia and China are our most pressing competitors". (Carter 2016a).

The second rationale in the reform story concerns the fiscal environment of austerity. Budget pressure makes it impossible to increase size of forces or viably "outspend" any potential adversary. In the 1960s, U.S. Government investments in research and development (R&D) were roughly twice the size of the private sector. In fact, many of these state investments developed into groundbreaking technologies like micro-chips, GPS, and the Internet, which could "spin-off" into civilian products as well. Today, the global private sector investments in R&D are estimated to $1.9Tn, and this accelerating innovation dwarfs any individual initiatives made by U.S. Government within its defense R&D budget of $71.8bn (Industrial Research Institute 2016, p. 3, DoD 2016a, p. 29). Furthermore, many of the most interesting technologies, including robotics, advanced computing, miniaturization, and 3D printing, are developed in start-up industries with few connections to the traditional defense industry. The structure of defense R&D has shifted, and the large companies of the established "military-industrial complex" are no longer dominant (Ellman *et al.* 2017). In the reform story of Hagel: "We all know that DoD no longer has exclusive access to the most cutting-edge technology or the ability to spur or control the development of new technologies the way we once did". (Hagel 2014b), and later Carter: "When I began my career, most technology of consequence originated in America, and much of that was sponsored by the government, especially DoD. Today, not only is much more technology commercial, but the competition is global …" (DoD 2016a, p. 28).

This reform story is sometimes misunderstood. As noted previously, it is not a vehicle for increased defense spending (Korb and Evans 2017). Neither is it in itself a novelty that the Pentagon is interested in developing and conceptualizing new interesting technologies for the benefit of national security. To a large extent, innovation is what DoD's Office of Net Assessment (ONA) and Defense Advanced Research Projects Agency (DARPA) always have been engaged with, and the armed forces are often interested in innovative ways of using current capabilities. Some of the problems addressed by DII were already identified in the "Defense Transformation Act" during George W. Bush's presidency (cf. Rumsfeld 2003). The crucial issue is that DII should be regarded as a particular form of an acquisition transformation. It is transformative, as it is not only focused on cutting red tape, increasing the speed of the process, centralizing decision-making, making planning more effective or, as one scholar noted, "adopt more flexible bureaucratic structures" (Simón 2016, p. 423).

More crucially, DII is a concerted effort to work around the established processes of rational planning. According to Hagel, "we must change the way we innovate, operate, and do business" (Hagel 2014b), and make "important changes to the way DoD diagnoses and plans for challenges to our military's competitive edge" (Hagel 2014b), which means that "we must be innovative not only in developing the technologies we buy, but also *how* we buy them" (Hagel 2014a). His successor Ashton Carter elaborates on the same subject:

> It's no longer just a matter of what we buy; what also matters is how we buy things, how quickly we buy them, whom we buy them from, and how quickly and creatively we're able to upgrade them and repurpose them to be used in different and innovative ways to stay ahead of future threats. (Carter 2016a, p. 28).

Not only does this mean that the planning process of defense acquisition becomes a central aspect of strategy, rather than an outcome and result of strategy. Moreover, the core of reform is to change the process of how weapons are bought and the reform initiatives are about shaping, directing, and facilitating the acquisition process itself, rather than making a rational capability plan to counter Russia and China. The aim is to "position both DoD and industry to more quickly initiate development, without a long-term commitment, outside the traditional budget cycle" (DoD 2016a, p. 47). During the tenures of Chuck Hagel and Ashton Carter, the political responsibility for implementation lay on Deputy Secretary of Defense Robert Work, and other key actors during the Obama administration included Under Secretary of Defense for Acquisition, Technology, and Logistics Frank Kendall and Assistant Secretary of Defense for Research and Engineering Stephen Welby. When implementing DII, these and other officials organized and activated arenas for networks that develop plans for future capabilities.

There are four main arenas in DII: the Advanced Capability and Deterrent Panel (ACDP), the Long-Range Research and Development Plan (LRRDP), the Defense Innovation Unit-Experimental (DIU-x), and the Defense Innovation Board (DIB). They are the concrete expression of the aim to "reach out to hear from everyone – industry, trade groups, think tanks, and Congress – and finding ways to work together" (Hagel 2014a), and especially "seek proposals from the private sector, including those firms, and from those firms [*sic!*] and academic institutions outside DoD's traditional orbit". (Hagel 2014b). In the operation of these arenas, we find the facilitating and coordinating practices of metagovernance.

Robert Work, together with the Vice Chairman of the Joint Chiefs of Staff and the Deputy Director of National Intelligence, chairs the ACDP in a partnership arrangement with quarterly meetings. Already as a think-tanker, Work developed concepts and ideas about the importance of technological innovation (Work and Brimley 2014), and the need to incorporate them into organizational practices: "The technology is never, never the final answer. You have to be able to incorporate those technologies into new operational and organizational constructs" (Work 2015). At first glance, ACDP seems to have a "top-down" priority function guided by the "Strategic Portfolio Review" that considers the long-term development of the future battlefield. However, the identified tech areas of interest are quite loosely defined as, for example, "space", "air- and strike capabilities", and "technology driven challenges" (the latter includes everything in the cyber domain), which means that it is more of an "oversight panel" (Eliason 2017, p. 8).

Frank Kendall chaired the LRRDP that is loosely inspired by a similar body in the 1970s, and its function is to "identify high-payoff enabling technology investments" in a 15-year perspective (Department of Defense 2014c). It has five working groups comprised of members from different parts of the Pentagon, as well as industry and academia, focused on technological breakthroughs that could be turned into development projects within 5–10 years. The aim of LRRDP is to create a network arena as it will:

> invite some of the brightest minds from inside and outside government to start with a clean sheet of paper, and assess what technologies and systems DoD ought to develop over the next three to five years and beyond. (Hagel 2014b)

The modus operandi of the LRRDP is the "request for information approach", which means that the working groups will "support deliberations" (Welby 2014; Welby in conversation 2016) concerning promising technologies. As explained by Stephen Welby:

> We're hoping that by casting this wide net, we'll be able to harness the creativity and innovation going on in the broader ecosystem and help us think about the future department in a new way./ … /The key opportunity out of this whole effort is to start a discussion. (Lyle 2014)

The DIU-x started as a small cooperation office with around 15 employees in Silicon Valley, and it has expanded with offices in Boston and Austin (Garamone 2016). They serve as networking arenas in regions dominated by innovation without traditional connections to defense industry. The offices are run in a partnership model, featuring representatives from among others Google and the National Security Council. Their purpose is twofold: to identify interesting technologies in the private business and connect them with relevant parts of the defense sector, as well as recruiting personnel for mostly short-term projects for the military. Robert Work explains the purpose of DIU-x:

> DIUx is supposed to be a place where DOD could identify the pieces of potential future capabilities that are of interest. Moreover, DIUx can ask industry if there are any commercial products that it might bring to the table for consideration. DIUx is also a means by which a commercial entity could come to DOD and present a new technology it thinks might be useful, but needs the Department to help them think it through. The whole idea of DIUx … is designed to allow that connection to the commercial industry. (Eliason 2017, p. 9)

Finally, the DIB was created in 2015 and is comprised of 12 persons, chaired by former Google CEO Eric Schmidt, and including the founder of Amazon Jeff Bezos, Chairman of LinkedIn Reid Hoffman, and retired Admiral William McRaven. The purpose of the board is to advice the Secretary of Defense on how to develop defense innovation. As Ashton Carter explained in a speech in 2016:

> I want to learn from them things that we haven't thought of that would be good for us. I'm not expecting them to know about defense. I know about defense, our people know about defense, that's not my problem. I would like to know what's going on in the outside world that I might not know about, that has proven successful, that might be applicable to us. (Mausione 2016)

The function of DIB is to provide the decision-making with a consultative forum for innovation policy rather than strategic issues. It offers the political leaders new ideas from the private sector of how to develop innovation. For example, in 2016, as the first federal authority, the Pentagon used the commercial practice of a hacking challenge ("Hack the Pentagon") in order to improve its cyber security. This project is often heralded as a first initial sign of success for DII.

The actors of DII are engaged in a goal-seeking learning process that is one of the hallmarks of metagovernance. It is quite intuitive that an initiative that explicitly starts with a "clean sheet of paper" must be so. However, it is notable that the involved actors are aware that DII may not be used for rational planning, as the third offset strategy has no direct answer to a substantial strategic problem. As Carter put it, "we are making these investments because we aren't yet exactly certain what or where this offset is gonna come from" (Carter 2016b). The third offset strategy, Vice Chairman of the Joint Chiefs of Staff and ACDP-member Paul Selva, explains:

> It's not an answer, it's a question./ … /If it was a fixed point in space, to which we all could navigate, I would drive those requirements into the Joint Requirements Oversight Council, I would mandate them in every acquisition program that exist in the department, and I would impose them through the Chairman on all of the services, except: it's not an answer, it's a question. (Selva 2016)

As it starts with a question, it is a deliberative and iterative process. As Hagel pointed out, "we won't always get it right, especially early on" (Hagel 2014a), and Work cautioned, "this is not about certainty, it is about testing and moving forward" (Work 2015). For his part, Carter used the metaphor of "seeding" and concluded that one of the most valuable aspect was the learning process: "not only what works, but what could make it work better by being agile and throwing out what does not work, and move on" (DoD 2016b). His credo "keep iterating together, and learning from each other" is probably the most revealing slogan of DII.

As discussed in the literature on metagovernance, there are many obstacles and frictions related to the incentives of the actors in this process. This was foreseen by Hagel as one of the priorities in DII was to make sure that small businesses "have the right opportunities and incentives" to develop the technologies the military need in the future (Hagel 2014a). Though many small start-up companies enjoy advantages in defense acquisition (willingness to pay high per unit cost, engage in multi-year contracts, attraction to DoD test ranges, and access to technology in the DoD), there are also barriers for entry (FitzGerald et al. 2016, p. 39). Perhaps the most fundamental problem is related to the fact that the "U.S. acquisition culture and regulatory structures are not optimized for such collaboration" (FitzGerald and Sayler 2014, p. 16). Another central problem is the image impact on the consumer market of working with the military, yet another concerns intellectual property rights, and the problem that start-up companies do not have as developed networks in the Pentagon as the defense establishment. As with all defense contracting, there tends to be a struggle over risk sharing.

Among the methods used to find a way around these problems are various forms of prize challenges and recruitment efforts (especially concerning software and machine learning), in which individuals and firms get to know the DoD and its acquisition environment. It is interesting to note the growing awareness about the relatively young entrepreneurs for the cooperative efforts, and that the vitality of the networks is based on social interaction: "We have to build a relationship, we have to build a familiarity, we have to build trust" (Carter 2016b).

It is important to note that the third offset strategy is often associated with the acquisition reforms initiated by Secretaries of Defense Gates and Carter, but mostly with Frank Kendall and what is labeled "Better Buying Power" (DoD 2015). Better Buying Power is permeated with NPM terms like "scaling", "streamlining", and the recurring idea that the Pentagon should develop a "new business model". It has been "upgraded" (2.0 and 3.0) with obvious reference to computer software updates, as if organizations could be "re-programmed". The core philosophy is based on the "should-cost model" used by private purchasing organizations as a diagnostic tool to calculate profit margins in negotiations. Though often associated with DII, it should be noted that the rationalization ideas underpinning Better Buying Power is not something new. There have been numerous acquisition reforms and attention to cost-effectiveness, especially following the Goldwater-Nichols Act and later during the Clinton administration (Fox *et al.* 2011).

One may note that the DII does not have any budget in itself. This makes it tempting to disregard it as a symbolic gesture rather than a transformative effort. After all, in the enormous organization of DoD, a few panels and working groups are only a minuscule part. For example, the cost for DIU-x is $45mn for fiscal year 2017, which is a drop in the defense budget sea. However, this lack of direct funding is by design, as DII is primarily about funding projects that will get a larger footprint if they eventually become fruitful. It is not about using programs to link plans to budgets, but using the initiative incrementally to alter programs, plans, and the budget. As Hagel put it: "The Defense Innovation Initiative will shape our programs, plans, and budgets. As the initiative matures over time, I expect its impact on budget to scale up in tandem" (Hagel 2014b). Instead of replacing rational planning in a gigantic reform, the DII uses network arenas to find projects that will influence the established program and budgeting process. After resigning, Kendall elaborated on this philosophy:

> What we were able to do in the last couple of budgets was/ … /we funded the most inexpensive part of the life cycle, which is the early risk reduction phase, it's proof of principle basically. It is not a program. All those demonstrations that DIU-x was talking about … and the long-range planning activity that Steve Welby here did, those are all early stage, relatively inexpensive demonstrations. (Kendall 2017a)

Thus, what is crucial is not the size of the budget for DII, but the philosophy of transformation. To use a different metaphor, given the established procedures of rational planning in the Pentagon, one might say that DII represents small islands in a sea of NPM.

What will become of these islands? In late 2016, U.S. Congress decided to split R&D and acquisition, formerly a combined portfolio for Frank Kendall, into two Under Secretary positions in DoD. In Kendall's final public speech as Under Secretary, he argued that this split was counterproductive and that the provisions of U.S. Congress were "totally divorced from the reality of new product management" (Serbu 2017, see also Kendall 2016, 2017b). It is interesting to note that the key argument for uniting R&D and acquisition is directly related to the ability to facilitate networking in the process from technology to products. This suggests that a key risk for further acquisition transformation is to make initiatives "without understanding the culture and requirements of the entrepreneurial community, inadvertently burning bridges" (FitzGerald and DeJonge Schulman 2016, p. 6).

However, it should be noted that while U.S. Congress emphasizes typical NPM ideas (like fixed-price contract structures that tended to be used by the Reagan administration), it seems also to maintain some of the ambitions of DII. According to U.S. Congress, "acquisition programs … would be carried out mostly if not entirely separate from a program of record" and if regarded as fruitful "feed into the existing program structure when [they are] ready" (Ellman *et al.* 2017, p. 34). Though this implies a more radical decentralization than the iterative incrementalism of the current DII, the idea seems to work around the current processes of the budget cycle. This implicates that the enduring impact of the DII may not be its organizational incarnations (i.e. ACDP, LRRDP, DIU-x, DIB) in themselves, but rather a mindset among bureaucrats as well as entrepreneurs regarding the routines and organization of U.S. defense innovation.

In conclusion, the DII exemplifies the contemporary practices and processes of metagovernance in the defense field. Despite occasional contradictions between the logic behind the narrative and function of the administrative bodies (small islands of metagovernance in a sea of NPM), one may conclude that the U.S. Government has, in an experimental way, started to work around the foundations of rational planning. In the final section, we will look closer at the drivers of this inclination.

Metagovernance and reflexive modernity

Previously in this article, we have noted the tendency in U.S. defense to challenge rational planning with processes and practices of metagovernance. If we accept this analysis, we could also conclude that from the viewpoint of the actors in the Pentagon, for some reason rational planning is problematic for making plans. For some reason, the established processes and practices for planning are challenged. The focus of this last section of the article is on how we should interpret this tendency.

From the perspective of the actors in U.S. defense planning, the shortcomings of rational planning are closely related to the reform story: increasing global and geopolitical competition, the increasing importance of commercial start-up innovation, and the limitations of the defense budget. However, this is not the whole story, and more importantly, it does not provide us with any theoretical framework for interpretation. In order to identify this, we need to look closer at defense planning as a phenomenon, or more specifically, what it is in rational planning that makes it problematic for contemporary strategies.

Though strategy theorist Colin Gray may have a point when arguing that "defense planning is functionally eternal; it is trans-historical" (Gray 2014, p. 6), he also concludes, "indeed, modern defense planning is exactly that, modern" (Gray 2014, p. 31). The point is that the practices of rational planning should be situated in a particular sociological context. While the practice of gathering before a battle to draw up plans is probably as old as warfare itself, a long-term defense plan over years and decades is a product of modernity. The roots of rational planning could be traced back to the societal processes during 1750–1850 that generally has been described as the emergence of modernity in the West (cf. Koselleck 2004). In fact, the term "plan" (in the meaning "make a plan of") originates from the eighteenth century. Thus, historian Williamson Murray is right when he points out that "there is no such thing as 'strategic planning', at least as we conceive it, before the eighteenth century" (Murray 2011, p. 8).

Although rational planning was not the only philosophy for dealing with future challenges in modernity, it became integrated with political decision-making and the growing bureaucracies of the modern state. The proliferation of the nineteenth-century German practice of five-year military budgets (*Quinquennat*) or similar arrangements allowed more complex future factors in military planning, like technical and economic developments. As pointed out by Gray: "Military planning staffs inspired by the Prussian model became the norm by the late nineteenth-century" (Gray 2014, p. 32). As exemplified by the planning-programming-budgeting system in the U.S., military agencies developed and perfected increasingly complex methods, which seemed to enable defense planning to reach beyond observation and into the unknown future.

However, sociology also suggests why rational planning has become increasingly problematic. The central term that describes these challenges is reflexive modernity (Giddens 1990, Beck 1992). In strategic studies, it has been highlighted in general terms by security scholar Mikkel Vedby-Rasmussen (Vedby-Rasmussen 2006). Contemporary rational planning is essentially a "colonization of the future" (Beck 1992) in which rationality breaks down due to the pace of societal changes, and planning processes constantly are subject to feedback. As pointed out by sociologists, this tends to reverse the relationship between past, present, and future in long-term planning. Future events that have not yet occurred become the point of departure for reforms. As often noted by Ashton Carter, the key innovators of the third offset strategy are yet to be identified. This inherent tendency in modernity creates a fundamental sense of uncertainty, as the actions can never be fully forecasted and the pace of changes makes planning inherently difficult.

Truly, this is a way to make sense of the constant complaints regarding the U.S. defense planning system. To take but one example, in an evaluation of the U.S. defense planning process, security analyst Anthony Cordesman has emphasized that "what should be a Planning, Programming, and Budgeting System is now little more than a pointless statistical morass" (Cordesman 2010, p. 8). Despite the sophisticated methods of planning, which all originate from the post-World War II period of "big science", Cordesman observes how decoupled the planning system has become from the interests of the involved actors. One interpretation of this observation is that there are simply limitations in modernity to calculate, predict, and control the future. Instead of extending, in the words of a RAND analyst in the late 1960s, "customary planning horizons into a more distant future and … replace haphazard intuitive gambles, as a basis for planning, by sober and craftsmanlike analysis of the opportunities the future has to offer" (Seefried 2014, p. 28), the science of the planning system has "squandered until further notice their historic reputation for rationality" (Beck 1992, p. 70).

The "runaway world" of reflexive modernity is one way of contextualizing this tendency for rationality to break down (Giddens 1990). It emphasizes the pace, scope, and profoundness of change compared with previous historical periods. Not only is society becoming increasingly complex, the speed of increased complexity increases. This creates a growing gap between our experiences of the past and expectations about the future. While the past is used as a point of reference, it becomes increasingly difficult to know exactly what to learn from it. Consequently, what we know of the past is more and more inadequate for the things we expect of the future.

Importantly, the involved actors of DII often make references to these tendencies. As observed by Principal Deputy Director for National Intelligence Stephanie O'Sullivan: "Technology is changing so fast that it is challenging and stressing governments and societies ability to adapt to the changes it's bringing" (O'Sullivan 2016). Secretary of Defense Carter describes the consequences: "There is a faster pace of change which sets up a fierce competition between the present and the future" (Carter 2016b), and "this era of technological competition is uniquely characterized by an additional variable of speed, such that leading the race now depends on who can out-innovate faster than everyone else" (Carter 2017). In other words, actors in DII signal awareness that speed is not only a promise for substantially solving strategic problems, but also a challenge for defense planning procedures. Thus, this is how we can make sense of the fact that decision-makers like Hagel and Carter are equally focused on how to buy weapons as well as what weapons to buy.

It is this tendency for contemporary states to be constantly dealing with future challenges, while at the same time lacking the substantive instruments to directly deal with them on their own, which creates pressure for constant procedural feedback for the planning process. To paraphrase sociologist Anthony Giddens: defense planning is constantly examined and reformed in light of incoming information about defense planning, thus constituitively altering its character (Giddens 1990, p. 38). This is a way of interpreting the obsession with flexibility and iteration in DII. Almost everyone involved in the third offset strategy have referred to this feedback: to be "agile enough to adapt to surprise" (Eliason 2017, p. 7), to be able to "look ourselves in the mirror" (Carter 2016b) or as Selva put it: "Innovation on a micro level tends to threaten institutions" (Selva 2016).

Thus, it is because of the ambiguities, complexities, and uncertainties of reflexive modernity that government seeks to enter into iterative partnerships with multiple actors, and hierarchical coordination becomes less attractive as point of departure in defense planning. Indeed, hierarchical controls have often become illusionary. As pointed out by Norheim-Martinsen, "military organizations are not anymore the strict hierarchies they used to be" (Norheim-Martinsen 2016, p. 320), and Tama notes in the U.S. case "the limited control of senior officials over large, complex and fragmented departments" (Tama 2015, p. 763). Consequently, this is why the processes and practices of metagovernance become essential to master. While networks are not inherently effective, and the focus on organizing networks certainly creates frustration because of the lack of substantive planning (i.e. Quadrennial Defense Review), networks may partly overcome complexities, facilitate coordination, and enhance legitimacy (Sørensen and Torfing 2009, p. 237). For more about QDR, see Jordan Tama "Tradeoffs in defense strategic planning: lessons from the U.S. Quadrennial Defense Review", 2018.

To conclude, the case of the third offset strategy shows that the processes and practices of metagovernance challenge the rational planning philosophy of a substantive, goal-oriented service–delivery mechanism. The U.S. Government shapes and facilitates a process when defining problems, creating networking arenas, mobilizing relevant network actors, and exploring incentive structures. Key U.S. leaders realize that defense innovation is beyond their own control, and they deal with the strategic challenge of emerging competitors with arenas that connect government officials with non-traditional actors in defense industry.

The effect of these processes and practices is a learning process in which essentially the state is "enabling other organizations" (Page and Wright 2007, p. 4). From a sociological perspective, defense planning becomes a reflexive project, as it is about organizing the organization of innovation, and the drivers for this development are related to the pace of change in modernity, and the inherent tendency for rationality to break down under such circumstances.

It is certainly beyond the scope of this article to elaborate on the implications and consequences of such development. One pressing issue concerns the future of any rationalist and "Huntingtonian" bias in U.S. civil–military relations, i.e. the implications for autonomy and professionalism. Two other questions include the ability to identify and define national interests (Edmunds 2014), as well as the specific skills and characteristics of military officers and civilians in the practices and processes of metagovernance. Nonetheless, it points to the continued relevance of public administration theory and sociological theory in the study of military and strategic developments.

Disclosure statement

No potential conflict of interest was reported by the author.

References

Allison, Graham and Zelikow, Philip, 1999. *Essence of Decision: Explaining the Cuban Missile Crisis*. 2nd ed. New York: Addison-Welsley Publishers.
Beck, U., 1992. *Risk society: towards a new modernity*. London: Sage.
Carter, A., 2016a. Remarks by Secretary Carter at the economic club of Washington, DC [online], 2 February. Available from: http://www.defense.gov/News/Transcripts/Transcript-View/Article/648901/remarks-by-secretary-carter-on-the-budget-at-the-economic-club-of-washington-dc.
Carter, A., 2016b. Keynote speech "the path to the innovative future of defense" at CSIS conference *Assessing the Third Offset Strategy* [online], 28 October. Available from: https://csis-prod.s3.amazonaws.com/s3fs-public/event/161028_Secretary_Ashton_Carter_Keynote_Address_The_Path_to_the_Innovative_Future_of_Defense.pdf.
Carter, A., 2017. Exit memo: department of defense. Taking the long view, investing for the future [online], 5 January. Available from: https://obamawhitehouse.archives.gov/administration/cabinet/exit-memos/department-defense.
Cordesman, A.H., 2010. *U.S. defense planning. Creating reality-based strategy, planning, programming and budgeting*. Washington: CSIS.
Department of Defense, 2014a. The defense innovation initiative [online], 15 November. Washington, DC. Available from: http://archive.defense.gov/pubs/OSD013411-14.pdf.
Department of Defense, 2014b. *Quadrennial defense review 2014* [online], Washington, DC. Available from: http://archive.defense.gov/pubs/2014_Quadrennial_Defense_Review.pdf.
Department of Defense, 2014c. Long-range research and development plan (LRRDP) direction and tasking. *Memorandum* [online], 29 October. Available from: http://www.defenseinnovationmarketplace.mil/resources/LRRDP_DirectionandTaskingMemoClean.pdf.
Department of Defense, 2015. Press briefing on better buying power 3.0 [online], 9 April. Available from: http://www.defense.gov/News/Transcripts/Transcript-View/Article/607039/department-of-defense-press-briefing-on-better-buying-power-30-in-the-pentagon.
Department of Defense, 2016a. *2017 force posture statement: taking the long view, investing for the future*. Washington, DC.
Department of Defense, 2016b. Carter speaks at DoD innovation Hub [online], 11 May. Available from: https://www.defense.gov/Video?videoid=463303.
Edmunds, T., 2014. Complexity, strategy and the national interest. *International affairs*, 90 (3), 525–539.
Eliason, W.T., 2017. An interview with Robert O. Work. *Joint force quarterly*, 84, (1st Quarter, January). Available from: http://ndupress.ndu.edu/JFQ/Joint-Force-Quarterly-84/Article/1038783/an-interview-withrobert-o-work/.
Ellman, J., et al., 2017. *Defense acquisition trends, 2016. The end of contracting drawdown*. Lanham: Rowman & Littlefield/CSIS.
FitzGerald, B., Sander, A., and Parziale, J., 2016. *New foundry. A new strategic approach to military-technical advantage*. Washington: Center for a New American Security.

FitzGerald, B. and DeJonge Schulman L., 2016. *12 months in – 8 months left. An update on Sceretary Carter's innovation agenda*. Washington: Center for a New American Security.
FitzGerald, B. and Sayler K., 2014. *Creative disruption: technology, strategy and the future of global defence industry*. Washington: Center for a New American Security.
Fox, J.R., et al., 2011. *Defense acquisition reform 1960–2009: an elusive goal*. Washington, DC: Center for Military History.
Garamone, J., 2016. Carter announces version 2.0 of defense innovation unit experimental [online]. Available from: http://www.defense.gov/News/Article/Article/757147/carter-announces-version-20-of-defense-innovation-unit-experimental.
Giddens, A., 1990. *The consequences of modernity*. Stanford, CA: Stanford University Press.
Gray, C.S., 2014. *Strategy & defence planning. Meeting the challenge of uncertainty*. Oxford: Oxford University Press.
Gregory, R., 2007. New public management and the ghost of Max Weber: exorcized or still haunting? *In*: T. Christiansen and P. Lægreid, eds. *Transcending new public management. The transformation of public sector reforms*. Aldershot: Ashgate, 232–233.
Hagel, C., 2014a. Opening keynote at 'defense innovation days' conference, organized by the Southeastern New England defense industry alliance, Newport, RI, 3 September [online]. Available from: https://www.defense.gov/News/Speeches/Speech-View/Article/605602.
Hagel, C., 2014b. Reagan national defense forum keynote. Ronald Reagan Presidential Library, 15 November [online]. Available from: http://www.defense.gov/News/Speeches/Speech-View/Article/606635.
Hitch, C.J. and McKean, R.N., 1960. *The economics of defense in the nuclear age RAND Corporation research study*. Cambridge, MA: Harvard University Press.
Hood, C., 1991. A public management for all seasons?. *Public administration*, 69, 3–19.
Hudson, B., 2004. Analysing network partnerships. *Public management review*, 6 (1), 75–94.
Industrial Research Institute, 2016. *Global R&D funding forecast*. Arlington: R&D Magazine. Available from: https://www.iriweb.org/sites/default/files/2016GlobalR%26DFundingForecast_2.pdf.
Jacobsson, B., Pierre, J., and Sundström, G., 2015. *Governing the embedded state. The organizational dimension of governance*. Oxford: Oxford University Press.
Kendall, F., 2016. *Getting defense acquisition right*. Fort Belvoir: Defence Acquisition University Press.
Kendall, F., 2017a. Prospects for defense acquisition in the Trump administration. *CSIS conference*, Washington, DC, 5 April [online]. Available from: https://www.csis.org/events/prospects-defense-acquisition-trump-administration/?block2.
Kendall, F., 2017b. Getting defense acquisition right: remarks and book signing with under secretary of defense Frank Kendall. *CSIS conference*, Washington, DC, 17 January [online]. Available from: https://www.csis.org/events/getting-acquisition-right-remarks-and-book-signing-under-secretary-defense-frank-kendall.
Klijn, E.-H. and Koppenjan, J.F.M., 2000. Public management and policy networks. *Public management: an international journal of research and theory*, 2 (2), 135–158.
Kooiman, J., 2003. *Governing as governance*. London: Sage.
Korb, L.J. and Evans, C., 2017. The third offset strategy: a misleading slogan. *Bulletin of the Atomic Scientists*, 73 (2), 92–95.
Koselleck, R., 2004. *Futures past. On the semantics of historical time*. New York, NY: Columbia University Press.
Lyle, A., 2014. DoD seeks future technology via development plan. *DoD news* [online], 3 December. Available from: http://www.defense.gov/News/Article/Article/603745.
Martinage, R., 2014. *Toward a new offset strategy. Exploring long-term advantages to restore U.S. global power projection capability*. Washington, DC: Center for Strategic and Budgetary Assessments.
Mausione, S., 2016. Ash Carter brings on more innovators to upgrade DoD [online]. Available from: http://federalnewsradio.com/defense/2016/06/ash-carter-brings-innovators-upgrade-dod/.
McCaffrey, J.C. and Jones, L.R., 2005. Reform of program budgeting in the department of defense. *International public management review*, 6 (2), 141–145.
Murray, W., 2011. *War, strategy and military effectiveness*. Cambridge: Cambridge University Press.

Norheim-Martinsen, P.M., 2016. New sources of military change – armed forces as normal organizations. *Defence studies*, 16 (3), 312–326.

Novick, D., 1966. *The origins and history of program budgeting*. Santa Monica, CA: The RAND Corporation.

O'Sullivan, S., 2016. Part I: defining the offset strategy at CSIS conference. *Assessing the third offset strategy* [online], 28 December. Available from: https://www.csis.org/events/assessing-third-offset-strategy.

Osborne, S.P., 2006. The new public governance? *Public management review*, 8 (3), 377–387.

Owens, M.T., 2004. "Strategy and the logic of force planning" in Naval War College. *Strategy and force planning*. 4th ed. Newport: Naval War College Press.

Page, E.C. and Wright, V., eds., 2007. *From the active to the enabling state. The changing role of top officials in European Nations*. Houndmills: Palgrave Macmillan.

Rumsfeld, D., 2003. Taking exception: defense for the 21st century. *Washington Post*, 22 May.

Seefried, E., 2014. Steering the future. The emergence of western futures research and its production of expertise, 1950s to the early 1970s. *European journal of futures research*, 29 (2), 1–12.

Selva, P., 2016. Part I: defining the offset strategy at CSIS conference. *Assessing the third offset strategy* [online], 28 December. Available from: https://www.csis.org/events/assessing-third-offset-strategy.

Serbu, J., 2017. In final speech DoD acquisition chief knocks congressional reforms as unhelpful. *Federal News Radio* 18 January. Available from: https://federalnewsradio.com/defense/2017/01/final-speech-dod-acquisition-chief-knockscongressional-reforms-unhelpful/.

Simón, L., 2016. The 'third' US offset strategy and Europe's 'anti-access' challenge. *Journal of strategic studies*, 39 (3), 417–445.

Sørensen, E. and Torfing, J., 2009. Making governance networks effective and democratic through metagovernance *Public administration*, 87 (2), 234–258.

Tagarev, T., 2009. Introduction to programme-based force development. *In*: H. Bacu-Marcu, F. Philipp, and T. Tagarev, eds. *Defence management: an introduction*. Geneva: Geneva Centre for the Democratic Control of the Armed Forces, 75–92.

Tama, J., 2015. Does strategic planning matter? The outcomes of U.S. national security reviews. *Political Science Quarterly*, 130 (4), 735–766.

Torfing, Jacob, Guy Peters, B., Jon Pierre and Eva Sørensen, 2012. *Interactive Governance: Advancing the Paradigm*. Oxford: Oxford University Press.

Vedby-Rasmussen, M., 2006. *The risk society at war. Terror, technology and strategy in the twenty-first century*. Cambridge: Cambridge University Press.

Welby, S.P., 2014. DoD engineering and better buying power 3.0. *Power point presentation*. Available from: http://www.ndia.org/Divisions/Divisions/SystemsEngineering/Documents/2014_12_10-Welby-NDIA-SED-SP-Mtg-vF.pdf.

Welby, Stephen P. 2016. Conversation with the author at the "Outreach" seminar with U.S. Assistant Secretary of Defense Stephen Welby and Rear Admiral Jonas Haggren, organized by the Security and Defense Industry Organization (SOFF), Stockholm 13 October 2016.

Wildavsky, A., 1964. *The politics of the budgetary process*. Boston, MA: Little, Brown and Company.

Wildavsky, A., 1966. The political economy of efficiency: cost-benefit analysis, systems analysis and program budgeting. *Public administration review*, 26 (4), 292–310.

William, T. Eliason, 2017. An Interview with Robert O. Work. *Joint Forces Quarterly*, 84, 26 January 2017 (http://ndupress.ndu.edu/JFQ/Joint-Force-Quarterly-84/Article/1038783/an-interview-withrobert-o-work/)

Work, R.O., 2015. Remarks by deputy defence secretary robert work at the CNAS defense forum [online]. 14 December. Available from: http://www.defense.gov/News/Speeches/Speech-View/Article/634214/cnas-defense-forum.

Work, R.O. and Brimley S., 2014, January. *20YY. Preparing for war in the robotic age*. Washington: Center for New American Security.

Tradeoffs in defense strategic planning: lessons from the U.S. Quadrennial Defense Review

Jordan Tama

ABSTRACT
Defense ministries conduct strategic planning in various ways. In this article I outline tradeoffs in the design of strategic planning processes, and consider the implications of these tradeoffs for choices about the conduct of defense planning in different circumstances. Whereas an inclusive and transparent planning process is well-suited to building internal and external buy-in for a defense strategy, a more exclusive and opaque process is more likely to generate a defense strategy that departs from the status quo and speaks candidly about key challenges. The design of a defense planning process should therefore be informed by certain features of its context, such as whether the international security environment is stable or in flux and whether the defense ministry enjoys or lacks strong political support. I base the article's findings on an in-depth analysis of the U.S. Quadrennial Defense Review, which served for nearly two decades as the major strategy process of the U.S. Department of Defense. This analysis draws on interviews I conducted of 23 defense officials and experts, as well as primary and secondary sources. More generally, my findings highlight for scholars and practitioners the importance of understanding how planning processes can shape defense and national security policies.

Introduction

While few scholars or practitioners question the importance of strategic planning for defense institutions, assessments of the value of particular defense strategy processes can be remarkably varied. Consider the U.S. Quadrennial Defense Review (QDR), which represented from 1997 to 2014 the principal effort by the U.S. Department of Defense (DoD) to formulate an overarching defense strategy. (A 2016 U.S. law changed the QDR's name to the National Defense Strategy and altered some of the review's requirements.) Many defense experts and practitioners have seen major shortcomings in the QDR, but many have also considered it to have been quite valuable in certain ways.

On the one hand, much of the U.S. defense community has considered the QDR to have been ineffective as a mechanism for formulating defense strategy or driving defense innovation. Michèle Flournoy, who served as under secretary of defense for policy, conveyed this view when she testified to the U.S. Congress in 2015 that "DoD's strategy development process is broken" (U.S. Senate 2015). Flournoy added: "Although the need for a robust, rigorous and regular strategic planning process within the [Defense] Department remains valid, the QDR routinely falls short of this aspiration" (U.S. Senate 2015). Kathleen Hicks, who directed the 2010 QDR, commented along similar lines in an interview conducted for this research: "QDRs are often much more work than what you get out of them" (15 October 2013). More pointedly, Jim Thomas, who served as one of the leaders of the 2006 QDR, has said, "I can't think of a worse way of making good strategy" (Center for Strategic and International Studies 2013). Long-time defense analyst Anthony Cordesman has even quipped, "If God really hates you, you may end up working on a Quadrennial Defense Review" (Cordesman 2009). These and other critics of the QDR observe, in particular, that the review tended to result in lowest-common-denominator restatements of existing U.S. defense policy, rather than driving important changes to U.S. force planning or the allocation of defense resources (Quadrennial Defense Review Independent Panel 2010, Center for Strategic and International Studies 2013, Gunzinger 2013, Cohen 2018).

On the other hand, many defense experts and practitioners have argued that the QDR served a useful role by fostering strategic thinking among DoD leaders, helping the secretary of defense lead the department, aiding the formation of consensus within DoD, socializing ideas among department personnel, explaining U.S. defense policy to foreign militaries, providing a clear rationale for defense budget proposals, or aiding legislative oversight of defense matters. For instance, in interviews conducted for this research, individuals knowledgeable about the QDR made the following statements:

- "By putting strategic planning in the inbox of decision-makers, the QDR forces them to think about strategic questions" (DoD official, April 2013).
- "Every secretary [of defense] wants to get his arms around the department. [The QDR] is the best way to do it" (David Ochmanek, 7 September 2013).
- "[The QDR is] a vehicle to get everyone's big picture thinking on the same page" (DoD official, June 2013).
- "The [QDR] report has an impact on discourse in DOD. People take cues from it" (former DoD official, June 2013).
- "People [in Congress] and in the Pentagon treat the QDR as an opportunity to validate their preferences on force structure and the budget" (congressional official, May 2013).
- "[The QDR] is a tool for extracting data from the Pentagon" (former DoD official, February 2013).

It is puzzling that the same strategic review process could generate such a range of perceptions. One of my goals in this article is to explain why defense officials and experts can have widely varying views of the same defense strategy process, and, in particular, why the same process can be viewed very favorably in some respects and very unfavorably in others. The answer, I argue, is rooted in the multiple functions that strategy processes can serve, the impossibility of a single process serving all of these functions well, and differences among officials and experts in the emphasis they place on these different functions.

Put another way, the design of a strategy process involves choices that can enable the process to be valuable in some respects and less useful in other respects. The heart of this article outlines three key design choices – regarding the inclusivity, transparency, and schedule of a review – and explains their typical effects. First, making a strategic review more inclusive boosts the likelihood that the review will be accepted and implemented by the bureaucracy, but decreases the likelihood that it will depart sharply from the status quo. Second, making a review more transparent increases the likelihood that it will generate buy-in among external actors – such as lawmakers and foreign partners – but reduces the likelihood that it will discuss security threats, institutional weaknesses, or other sensitive matters frankly. Third, mandating that a review be conducted periodically according to a fixed calendar ensures that senior officials will devote some time to strategic questions, but prevents officials from scheduling strategic planning based on their decision making needs.

Given these tradeoffs, policymakers or analysts may form quite different judgments about the value of a strategy process depending on what potential outcome they focus on or value most. Neither enthusiastic supporters nor harsh critics of a given strategy process are necessarily off-base; they are just seeing the process from different perspectives.

Greater recognition of these trade-offs can also help to inform sound choices by policy makers about how to develop defense strategy in particular contexts. For example, major strategic innovation may be paramount during times of sudden and dramatic change in the international environment, necessitating a nimble and relatively closed strategy process. On the other hand, buy-in – facilitated by inclusiveness and transparency – may be more important during times when the context for defense strategy is rather stable.

These trade-offs, moreover, are not limited to U.S. defense policy making. Indeed, they are inherent in efforts by any sizable institution to establish policies or plans for its future behavior. Outside the United States, some countries regularly conduct major defense reviews akin to the QDR, while others employ markedly different defense planning processes (Cornish and Dorman 2010, Gray 2010, De Spiegeleire 2011, Håkenstad and Knus 2012). These processes also involve design choices regarding their inclusivity, transparency, and schedule. My goal in this article is to use an in-depth analysis of the QDR to generate conclusions about the tradeoffs associated with these choices that apply to all countries that conduct defense planning.

In what follows, I explain how I conceive of defense planning, review existing knowledge about the benefits and limitations of different strategic planning approaches, present a detailed analysis of the QDR, and identify lessons based on this analysis for the development and study of defense policy. The core of my analysis explains how the perceived strengths and weaknesses of the QDR reflect certain choices about how the QDR is carried out. I show that the QDR has failed to satisfy everyone in part because it has been expected to do many things at the same time, from developing new strategic doctrine to explaining U.S. defense goals to external constituencies. Through choices regarding the QDR's inclusivity, transparency, and schedule, policy makers have enabled QDRs to be better-suited to some of these functions than others.

More generally, these findings add to knowledge by enhancing understanding of the links between planning processes and planning outcomes, which have been under-examined not only in defense and strategic studies, but also in public administration and management literature (Poister *et al.* 2010, Breitenbauch and Jakobsson 2018).

What we know from prior research

For the purpose of this article, I follow the lead of some other scholars in conceiving of defense planning broadly, rather than associating it only with the development of military plans. For instance, Colin Gray defines defense planning as "preparations for the defense of a polity in the future (near-, medium-, and far-term)" (Gray 2014, 4). In another broad definition, Magnus Håkenstad and Kristian Knus-Larsen define long-range defense planning as "a process by which a given state arrives at political decisions regarding the future development of the structure, organization and capabilities of their armed forces" (Håkenstad and Knus 2012, 12).

Seen this way, defense planning is narrower than a government's effort to develop grand strategy – which encompasses military and non-military tools of national power – but broader than operational military planning. In other words, it involves the development and review of options concerning defense strategy, military force structure, and other defense policies and programs that extend beyond operational and near-term considerations. The QDR served as the principal tool with which DoD sought to conduct this type of high-level strategic planning for a period of nearly two decades, and the process that produces the National Defense Strategy now plays this role in DoD.

This conception of defense planning is consistent with some definitions of strategic planning in other contexts. For instance, leading public administration scholars define strategic planning as a "deliberative, disciplined effort to produce fundamental decisions and actions that shape and guide what an organization (or other entity) is, what it does, and why" (Bryson *et al.* 2018). Based on this definition, the development of a grand strategy or an overall defense strategy represents a form of strategic planning, but operational military planning does not.

Public administration and management scholars have also assessed the value of strategic planning for public and private sector organizations, and considered the merits of different approaches to the conduct of strategic planning. On the whole, studies have found that government agencies and private firms benefit from both structured and unstructured strategic planning activities (Brews and Purohit 2007, Poister *et al.* 2010, Bryson 2011, Elbanna *et al.* 2016). At the same time, previous research suggests that there should not be a "one size fits all" approach to strategy development, as strategy development needs vary considerably across different types of organizations and different circumstances. For many businesses that operate in rapidly changing market conditions and have relatively nimble workforces, effective strategy development can center mainly on informal and flexible processes. Indeed, highly structured strategic planning has been out of fashion in much of the business world for the past few decades based in large part on a belief that formal planning activities are not conducive to innovation and adaptability (Mintzberg 1994, Mintzberg *et al.* 2009, Popescu 2017).

Consistent with these broader patterns, strategic and security studies scholars have also shown that national security and defense strategies need not be centered on formal plans. While some official planning documents have certainly been important in guiding government and military decision makers, security and defense strategies have often emerged rather organically or become manifest only through the statements or behavioral patterns of policymakers and other officials (Goldgeier 1998, Dueck 2008, 2015, Drezner

2009, Mahnken 2012, Brands 2014, 2018, Edelstein and Krebs 2015, Krebs 2015, Goldgeier and Suri 2016, Jensen 2016, Silove 2016, 2018, Becker and Malesky 2017, Cohen 2017; Christiansson 2018, Popescu 2018).

Nevertheless, structured strategic planning processes can clearly benefit many public sector organizations. These benefits can be particularly substantial for government institutions that are large or complex, have numerous stakeholders, rely heavily on collaboration with external partners, or rely heavily on long-term capital investments (Wilson 1989, Berry 1994, Brews and Purohit 2007, Mintzberg *et al.* 2009, Bryson 2011, Moynihan and Hawes 2012, Tama 2015, 2018). Several of these characteristics – large size, complexity, many stakeholders, heavy reliance on collaboration, and heavy reliance on capital investments – clearly characterize most defense ministries, suggesting that structured strategy development processes should be particularly valuable for them. Indeed, structured strategic planning largely originated in military institutions (Freedman 2013, 2017).

Yet defense ministries do not all conduct defense planning in the same way. Just within North America and Western Europe, there exists an array of approaches to the development of defense strategy. For instance, in recent years Sweden, Finland, and the Netherlands employed well-established, formal structures to prepare long-term defense strategy documents, whereas Denmark and the United Kingdom employed more ad hoc approaches (Håkenstad and Knus 2012). Countries also vary in terms of whether their development of defense strategic guidance occurs according to a preset calendar – i.e. every four years – or whenever the political leadership sees a need for it (Håkenstad and Knus 2012). Such differences suggest the need for analyses of the tradeoffs involved in different defense planning processes. In what follows, I take a step toward greater understanding of such tradeoffs by examining how the QDR's design influenced the review's perceived strengths and weaknesses.

The U.S. Quadrennial Defense Review

The QDR dates back to 1996, when the U.S. Congress enacted a law requiring the secretary of defense to conduct every four years a comprehensive examination of defense strategy, force structure, modernization plans, and other defense programs and policies (U.S. Congress 1996, Tama 2017). The law also required the secretary of defense to submit an unclassified report on the results of the review to Congress, among other specific requirements.

Since the 2014 QDR, Congress has twice enacted new legislation that changed some of the review's requirements (U.S. Congress 2014, 2016). The most recent such law, enacted in December 2016, renamed the report resulting from the review the National Defense Strategy. This new law also requires the report to be classified, requires the separate issuance of an unclassified summary of the strategy, and requires DoD to assess the strategy's implementation and whether the strategy requires revision during each year in which a new strategy is not being issued (U.S. Congress 2016).

DoD completed five QDRs under the old legislative requirements – in 1997, 2001, 2006, 2010, and 2014 – and issued the first National Defense Strategy under the new requirements in January 2018. My analysis is based on the QDRs that were completed under the old requirements, but I also consider the significance of the recent legislative changes below.

My analysis builds on an ample preexisting set of publications on the QDR by scholars and scholar-practitioners (Snodgrass 2000, Davis 2002, Donnelly 2005, Gordon, John 2005, Henry 2005, Fitzsimmons 2006, Flournoy 2006, O'Hanlon 2007, Cordesman 2009, Spring and Eaglen 2009, Ucko 2009, Daggett 2010, Hicks and Brannen 2010, Sharp 2010, Center for Strategic and International Studies 2013, Gunzinger 2013, Chiu 2014, Brimley and Schulman 2016, Karlin 2017, Cohen 2018, Larson et al. 2018, Wormuth 2018). I add to this literature by examining the tradeoffs involved in key design choices concerning how the QDR was carried out.

My analysis is based on a review of QDR documents, other primary and secondary sources related to the QDR, and interviews I conducted of 23 U.S. defense officials and experts. I selected people to interview who had possessed governmental responsibilities closely connected to the QDR or had demonstrated substantial expertise about the QDR through publications. I started by requesting interviews with officials who had been heavily involved in the 2010 QDR – the most recent review when I began this research in 2011 – including Office of the Secretary of Defense (OSD) officials who had played central roles in overseeing or coordinating the review. Since many of these officials had served in OSD during prior QDRs too, I asked them questions about previous QDRs as well as about the 2010 QDR. I also asked these officials for the names of other individuals who had played important roles in previous QDRs, and then sought interviews with those former officials. In addition, I sought interviews with individuals who had coordinated defense policy in the White House during one or more of the QDRs, served in key defense policy oversight roles as congressional staff during one or more QDRs, authored reports by the Congressional Research Service or U.S. Government Accountability Office about one or more QDRs, or published articles or think tank reports that demonstrated substantial expertise about the QDR. Most of the people in the last of these categories also possessed first-hand experience with one or more of the QDRs as a result of prior service in DoD. Out of 34 people that I contacted, 23 agreed to be interviewed.

I sought interviews with this cross-section of officials and experts in order to ensure that the interview subjects represented a range of professional responsibilities and that any biases they might possess would likely vary. The interview subjects spanned individuals with stronger and weaker stakes in the perceived outcomes of the QDR (for instance, OSD officials who coordinated a QDR might be more likely than others to want observers to see the review as innovative or impactful). In addition, most of the people I interviewed had been deeply involved in defense policy or defense policy debates for well over a decade, giving them insights that were based on several iterations of the review, rather than on just one iteration of it. Moreover, in my interviews, I asked individuals to provide their assessments based on all QDRs about which they had direct experience or substantial knowledge. To encourage candid responses, I gave each interview subject the option of conducting the interview on the record or on a not-for-attribution basis.

Nevertheless, I recognize that interview subjects may sometimes provide – wittingly or unwittingly – incomplete or inaccurate information. To guard against the possibility of such information leading me to reach faulty conclusions, none of this article's conclusions are based solely on the comments of a single individual. Instead, they are based on the totality of the interviews and on the various written documents I examined, including

QDR reports, other government documents, and secondary sources. These written sources provided useful triangulation on the information from interview responses that should increase confidence in the validity of my conclusions.

The review's inclusiveness

While the process used to conduct the QDR varied somewhat from one iteration to the next, DoD typically carried it out in a structured and inclusive manner (Snodgrass 2000, Gordon, John 2005, Center for Strategic and International Studies 2013, Tama 2016, Cohen 2018, Larson *et al.* 2018). Each QDR was led by civilian strategy and policy officials in OSD. These officials coordinated QDR working groups composed of representatives from various components of DoD, including the military services and the military's joint (or inter-service) staff. The final product of each QDR was a report issued by the secretary of defense that described U.S. defense strategy and force structure plans in broad terms.

Perceptions of the QDR's outcome were heavily influenced by the review's inclusive design, particularly the participation in the review of key stakeholders from different parts of DoD. Review participants and defense experts maintain that this inclusiveness facilitated the reaching of consensus among department stakeholders about important issues, enabled DoD leaders to gain bureaucratic buy-in for some of their priorities, and aided the socialization of review ideas among DoD personnel. At the same time, the review's inclusiveness led the review typically to result only in incremental changes to defense strategy and marginal changes to the allocation of resources among defense programs. While inclusiveness can be beneficial in bringing into consideration the ideas of a greater number of people, during the QDR it was usually embodied in bureaucratized processes that made it less likely that the resulting report would deviate substantially from the status quo.

In 1961 – more than three decades before DoD began conducting the QDR – Samuel Huntington noted:

> "Strategic programs, like other major policies, are not the product of expert planners, who rationally determine the actions necessary to achieve desired goals. They are the result of controversy, negotiation, and bargaining among officials and groups with different interests and perspectives.... Some measure of departmental consensus... is essential to any policy" (Huntington 1961, 146, 168).

Although small groups of defense strategists could surely have formulated more innovative strategies than the strategies that were expressed in the QDR reports, less inclusive processes would probably have diminished the extent to which the military services and other parts of the defense bureaucracy became invested in the strategies. Indeed, when DoD leaders have attempted to formulate strategy in a more ad hoc manner, they have encountered a backlash from the bureaucracy that has rendered their efforts ineffective. For instance, in 2001, Donald Rumsfeld sought to circumvent the QDR process by tapping an informal set of advisors with the development of strategic ideas that would advance his defense transformation agenda. This approach backfired, as it led uniformed military officers and civilian career officials to resist his agenda strongly (Came and Campbell 2010). More generally, Barry Watts, former director of program analysis and evaluation at DoD, has written: "To paraphrase Clausewitz, military institutions, like their corporate counterparts, are capable of mounting resistance to unwelcome strategic decisions that is inconceivable unless one has experienced it" (Watts 2012, 61). Put another way, former DoD strategist Jim Thomas observed that DoD officials are habituated to the institution operating as "a consensual organization" (interview, 21 May 2013).

Given these characteristics of DoD – which are shared by most bureaucratic organizations – the QDR served importantly as a means of bringing the department's different stakeholders under the same tent. One DoD official noted that the QDR "forces people to hash out issues and look at issues the same way" (interview, April 2013). Another DoD official commented: "If the process is open, people in the department may feel like they had their chance to weigh in, even if they don't like the changes" (interview, June 2013).

For secretaries of defense, the QDR's inclusiveness also helped them put their imprint on DoD. Barry Pavel, who has led or participated in the development of numerous defense strategy statements at DoD and the White House, observed that "secretaries [of defense] understand the QDR is their best chance to change the organization" (interview, 21 June 2013). Even though the QDR did not result in major transformation, some secretaries were able to use it to embed some of their priorities more strongly into the institution.

Consider the following example. Robert Gates became secretary of defense in December 2006. With the next QDR not due until 2010, Gates decided to release a broad strategic document that outlined his vision for DoD in 2008 (interview of Thomas Mahnken, 22 May 2013). This document – called the National Defense Strategy (the document should not be confused with the new, post-2016 name for the QDR) – emphasized the importance of balancing the need to prepare for future security challenges with the need to prevail in the irregular conflicts in which the United States was engaged at the time (U.S. Department of Defense 2008, 1). Thomas Mahnken, who served as a principal author of the document as deputy assistant secretary of defense for policy planning, noted that this idea was designed to prod DoD to prioritize winning current wars more highly than it had been doing (interview, 22 May 2013).

Gates then sought to use the 2010 QDR process as a tool for institutionalizing this shift toward greater emphasis on ongoing conflicts (Hicks and Brannen 2010). For instance, the 2010 QDR called for increasing investments in intelligence, surveillance, and reconnaissance in the form of manned and unmanned aircraft. Kathleen Hicks, who served at the time as deputy under secretary of defense for strategy, plans, and forces, noted that some parts of the department resisted this proposal because they wanted the money to be spent on other items, but Gates used the QDR process to ensure that that his priority would be captured not only by the strategy statement, but also by the associated fiscal year 2011 DoD budget proposal (interview, 13 October 2013). In the absence of a participatory process, it may have been more difficult for Gates to move forward with this initiative because a decision by him to do so without the QDR's imprimatur may have seemed less legitimate to some stakeholders and therefore generated even stronger resistance.

In addition, the QDR's inclusiveness contributed to its ability to socialize new ideas throughout the department. Although the QDR did not generate major changes in U.S. force structure, it served as the forum through which some important new strategic ideas were developed and propagated. For instance, DoD strategists first developed the notion of "building partnership capacity" as a key means of addressing security challenges as part of the 2006 QDR (Barry Pavel, interview, 21 June 2013). This idea subsequently became a major theme of the 2010 QDR and a central principle of defense strategy during the Obama administration (U.S. Department of Defense 2010, McInnis and Lucas 2015). To take another example, DoD strategists developed ideas that turned into what became known as the "pivot" or "rebalance" to Asia during the 2010 QDR. More specifically, much of the strategizing related to the repositioning of U.S. Marines to Darwin, Australia and the deployment of U.S. littoral combat ships to Singapore was done during this QDR (Shawn Brimley, interview, 15 May 2013, Kathleen Hicks, interview, 15 October 2013).

While defense strategists are certainly capable of developing new ideas in the absence of a formal review process, the QDR helped to diffuse the ideas throughout the bureaucracy (Matthew Kroenig, interview, 20 June 2013; Barry Pavel, interview, 21 June 2013). Even in instances when a strategic idea was not generated by the QDR itself, the idea's endorsement by the QDR often gave it "additional heft" (Shawn Brimley, interview, 15 May 2013).

While some of this socialization would likely have occurred even if the review process was not highly participatory, the involvement of the military services and other DoD elements in the QDR gave them an ownership stake in the report. This stake, in turn, gave them greater incentive to propagate the report's ideas within their own institutions.

On the other hand, the QDR's inclusiveness contributed heavily to the pattern of each review largely preserving the status quo in U.S. defense strategy and force planning, rather than changing them substantially to match shifts in the international environment. Defense analyst Mark Gunzinger observes that none of the QDRs "created a new vision for how the U.S. military should prepare to meet the nation's security challenges" (Gunzinger 2013). Similarly, Jim Thomas commented, "All the QDRs have tried to move us away from the 1993 Bottom-up Review, and have only done so a little bit" (interview, 21 May 2013).

For instance, the 1993 Bottom-up Review called for being "able to win two major regional conflicts that occur nearly simultaneously" (Aspin 1993, 7), and the first QDR stated similarly that DoD must be "able to deter and defeat large-scale, cross-border aggression in two distant theaters in overlapping time frames" (U.S. Department of Defense 1997, 12). By 2010, the QDR placed increasing emphasis on preparing for a range of other security challenges, but reiterated the importance of maintaining the "ability to prevail against two nation-state aggressors" (U.S. Department of Defense 2010, vi). Even the 2014 QDR – issued during a period of fiscal austerity that had already resulted in a scaling down of U.S. defense goals (see the discussion below of the 2012 Defense Strategic Guidance) – included a modified version of the two regional war construct. It stated: "If deterrence fails at any given time, U.S. forces could defeat a regional adversary in a large-scale multi-phased campaign, and deny the objectives of – or impose unacceptable costs on – another aggressor in another region" (U.S. Department of Defense 2014, 22).

The QDR's repeated failure to generate substantial strategic change was influenced by the inclusive process used to conduct the review. David Ochmanek, who served from 2009–14 as deputy assistant secretary of defense for force development, observed, "The larger the formal entity in a strategy process, the more likely you are to get the least common denominator, the conventional wisdom" (interview, 7 September 2016). Along similar lines, another former DoD official noted, "The best strategies are developed by small groups, not in large formal reviews" (interview, February 2013).

Moreover, different components of DoD – particularly the military services – were able to use their involvement in the QDR to fight to protect their turf. As a result, it was much easier for defense officials to issue a QDR report that added some new initiatives to the status quo than to issue a report that shifted resources from one part of the military to another – as would have been necessary to carry out major changes to force planning (DoD official, interview, May 2013). The most common type of strategic or policy change resulting from the QDR was therefore a new or increased investment in an area considered to be of growing importance, without a matching cut someplace else.

For instance, in the midst of the George W. Bush administration's war on terrorism, the 2006 QDR generated decisions to increase the size of U.S. special operations forces and boost U.S. spending on medical countermeasures against biological threats (Ucko 2009, Jim Thomas, interview, 21 May 2013, former DoD officials, interviews, May-October 2013). But those changes were not accompanied by reductions in spending on systems that were of little utility for irregular warfare and nontraditional threats. As one participant in that review recalled, "We did a hard scrub on the F-35 [a stealth combat aircraft], but the building didn't have the guts to make any changes on that" (former DoD official, May 2013).

These limitations of the QDR are further underscored by a comparison of the QDR with a major U.S. defense review that was carried out in a more top-down manner than the QDR. This review was ordered by President Barack Obama in 2011, after the U.S. Congress had enacted legislation that cut U.S. government spending sharply and set strict caps, through a mechanism known as sequestration, on government spending in future years (Williams 2017). Notably, these budget caps applied to both defense and non-defense spending. In this context, then-Under Secretary of Defense for Policy Michèle Flournoy recalled:

> "The president had a stroke of genius to say, 'Rather than do this is a big staff exercise – bottom-up – I want to use this as an opportunity to bring my leadership team together.' He called the secretary [of defense], the chiefs [of the military services], and all of the [combatant commanders] together at the White House for two or three different meetings of multiple hours each and said, 'This is a challenge we share. How are we going to do this with half a trillion less over the next ten years?'".... The process was much less formal and much less bureaucratic than the QDR process (Michèle Flournoy, interview, 24 July 2013).

The Obama-led process resulted several months later in the public issuance of a new strategic document called the Defense Strategic Guidance, or DSG (U.S. Department of Defense 2012b). This eight-page report was more than ten times shorter than most QDR reports, but broke from preexisting strategy more heavily than any QDR report did. The DSG report stated that the U.S. military would "no longer be sized to conduct large-scale, prolonged stability operations" – a major change following a decade in which the Pentagon had increasingly shifted its focus toward conducting and preparing for such missions (U.S. Department of Defense 2012b, 6). This shift was accompanied by a large cut in the size of the U.S. Army and Marine Corps (U.S. Department of Defense 2012a).

While these changes were clearly driven by the tighter fiscal environment that faced DoD starting in 2011, they were greatly facilitated by the top-down leadership provided by Obama in driving the process. Indeed, under Obama's direction, the DSG report was drafted by some of the most senior uniformed and civilian defense leaders, including the deputy secretary of defense and vice chairman of the joint chiefs of staff (Kathleen Hicks, interview, 15 October 2013). With the president pushing his most senior defense advisors to come up with a plan for adapting U.S. defense strategy to the new budgetary realities, the bureaucratic inertia that often made it difficult to change strategy dramatically in the QDR was greatly mitigated. Nor is it coincidental that this streamlined and top-down process was associated with a review that had not been mandated by Congress. Whereas the various requirements of the legislation mandating the QDR incentivized DoD to employ highly bureaucratized processes in carrying out the QDR, the absence of legislative requirements for the DSG freed senior officials to conduct that review with a high degree of flexibility. The result was a process that many defense officials considered to be more consequential than the QDR (Shawn Brimley, interview, 15 May 2013, Michèle Flournoy, interview, 24 July 2013, Kathleen Hicks, interview, 15 October 2013).

The results of a set of major independent U.S. defense reviews further underscore how review outcomes can be shaped by the nature of participation in them. In conjunction with mandating the QDR, Congress established a non-governmental panel charged with providing an independent assessment of the QDR and offering its own recommendations for U.S. defense strategy. Some iterations of this panel were named the National Defense Panel (NDP), while another was named the Quadrennial Defense Review Independent Panel. (Congress similarly established an independent panel to assess the new National Defense Strategy, named the Commission on the National Defense Strategy of the United States.) Each of these panels consisted of a relatively lean operation composed of former defense officials and defense experts. For instance, the 2014 NDP, which was led by former Secretary of Defense William Perry and former CENTCOM Commander John Abizaid, included a total of just ten panel members and eleven staff – all from outside government (National Defense Panel 2014, 73–81).

This type of structure enabled the independent panels to question military service priorities and call for far-reaching strategic innovation. For instance, the 1997 NDP urged that DoD advance an ambitious agenda of defense transformation, while criticizing the services for focusing on procuring systems that would soon become outdated (National Defense Panel 1997, iii; Mahnken 2001, Kagan 2006). This recommendation departed markedly from the 1997 QDR, which did not significantly alter the status quo in overall defense strategy (Snodgrass 2000, Gordon, John 2005). More recently, the 2014 NDP moved away from the two regional war construct more clearly than any QDR did. It argued that the United States should be prepared to defeat large-scale aggression in one theater and simultaneously thwart aggression in *multiple* other theaters (emphasis mine), while defending the homeland and carrying out counterterrorism operations (National Defense Panel 2014, 26). This recommendation was based on an assessment by panel members that the United States was facing "perhaps the most complex and volatile security environment since World War II" (Flournoy and Edelman 2014).

The repeated creation of these independent panels also reflected congressional dissatisfaction with the QDR's output. Legislators initially created the NDP as part of the QDR legislation based on a concern that the QDR would become a status quo-oriented process captured by the defense bureaucracy (Tama 2017). Some legislators responsible for defense policy concluded that this is exactly what happened with the review. For instance, House Armed Services Committee Chairman Buck McKeon commented in 2014 that the QDR had served only as "validation of a force structure that the services admit is driven by budget constraints," rather than as "an opportunity to bring together key national security stakeholders and strategic thinkers to discuss and debate how we can shape the longer-term direction of our forces, their missions, and their capabilities" (U.S. House of Representatives 2014a, 1–2). For McKeon and other key legislators, the NDP served as a mechanism to enable more forward-leaning and innovative strategizing (U.S. House of Representatives 2014b).

The review's transparency

Defense officials and experts also report that the QDR's outcomes were shaped by the requirement in the original QDR legislation that the review result in an unclassified report to Congress. Since unclassified reports to Congress can also be shared by legislators with journalists or other individuals outside of Congress, this requirement was equivalent to requiring that the QDR report be issued publicly. Given that reality, DoD opted to make each QDR report directly available to the public. Put another way, the unclassified report requirement ensured that there would be some measure of transparency with respect to the QDR.

On the positive side, this requirement enabled the five QDR reports to serve as useful devices for DoD leaders to explain the department's goals and initiatives to a variety of external audiences, including not only congressional officials, but also journalists, defense contractors, and foreign governments and militaries. This was particularly important with respect to congressional officials, since DoD needed regularly to persuade legislators to support its budgetary and legislative requests. As one indication of the extent to which the review was useful in this regard, then-Secretary of State Hillary Clinton once noted the following in explaining why she intended to establish a quadrennial State Department review:

> "I served for six years on the Armed Services Committee in the Senate. And it became very clear to me that the QDR process… provided a framework that was a very convincing one to those in the Congress, that there was a plan, people knew where they were headed, and they have the priorities requested aligned with the budget, and therefore, people were often very convinced that it made good sense to do whatever the Defense Department requested" (U.S. Department of State 2009).

Moreover, Clinton is not alone in having this perception. Quantitative data from my interviews show that the QDR's public relations function represented one of its main perceived effects. As part of my interviews of defense experts and practitioners, I asked the interview subjects to assess the impact of the QDR in a number of areas. More specifically, I asked them to assess how much impact the QDR has had on a scale of 1–7, with 1 representing no impact and 7 representing very large impact, in each of the following areas: defense policy and programming, defense management and organization, defense budgeting, DoD's public relations, and preparing DoD leaders to make future strategic decisions. As Table 1 shows, the average rating of the interview subjects that answered these questions was 4.3 for impact on DoD's public relations, second only to the average rating of 4.46 for impact on preparing DoD leaders to make future strategic decisions. (I discuss the latter type of perceived impact later in the article.)

Conversely, the original legislative mandate that the QDR report be provided to Congress and published in an unclassified manner helped Congress perform its critical functions of overseeing DoD and legislating defense policies. In particular, the report enhanced congressional understanding of DoD and gave legislators ammunition for trying to hold department officials accountable for their success or failure in meeting the goals expressed in the report (congressional officials, interviews, May-June 2013). In addition, legislators used the report to inform and rationalize their design of defense legislation. A congressional staff member noted: "The QDR helps our own internal process on the NDAA [the major annual defense bill]. We look at whether the DoD budget request aligns with the QDR" (interview, May 2013). Congressional officials added that it was common in hearings and meetings for legislators to ask service chiefs if something they were asking for was in the QDR (interviews, May-June 2013). In this way, the report made it easier for legislators to avoid advancing legislation that served parochial military interests and was inconsistent with overall defense strategy.

While a classified report to Congress could also serve these functions to some extent, the unclassified character of the QDR reports enabled legislators to refer to the reports in legislative proposals and to discuss them at any congressional hearing or on the floor of the House or Senate, rather than being restricted to referring to them only in classified settings. Moreover, since one of the common motivations of legislators in conducting oversight of the executive branch is to demonstrate to voters that they are influencing public policy, the ability to refer to the reports in public fora gave legislators greater incentive to use them as oversight tools.

Yet the unclassified character of the QDR reports also contributed to a tendency in these reports to gloss over many important security risks and challenges, rather than discussing and prioritizing them frankly and explicitly. Since the reports were going to be accessible to the public, DoD officials had an incentive to produce reports that concealed the department's weaknesses, downplayed potential concerns about the stability of friendly countries, refrained from indicating how the department planned

Table 1. Assessments of the U.S. Quadrennial Defense Review's impact.

Area of impact	Average interview response
Preparing DoD leaders to make future strategic decisions	4.46
DoD's public relations	4.30
Defense policy and programming	3.78
Defense budget	3.25
Defense management and organization	2.21

Note: These interview data are based on 21 interviews conducted between 2011 and 2016. (In two other interviews I conducted for this research, time constraints prevented me from asking the interview subject this set of questions or the interview subject declined to answer them.) For each question, I asked interview subjects to assess the QDR's impact on a scale of 1–7, with 1 representing no impact and 7 representing very large impact. Before asking the questions, I informed the subjects that I would not attribute to them their answers in any resulting publication. In some cases, interview subjects opted to give distinct answers for individual QDRs. In those cases, I treat their average rating across the reviews they rated as their answer for the purpose of these tabulations.

to counter or defeat potential adversaries, and avoided statements that might raise hackles or increase tensions with other countries (Jim Thomas, interview, 21 May 2013, former DoD official, interview, February 2013). As Shawn Brimley, who served as the principal drafter of the 2010 QDR, commented in an interview conducted before Congress changed the QDR's requirements to make its report classified, "You can't talk about China or Iran or talk about taking risks in the QDR because we've decided the report is unclassified" (interview, 15 May 2013).

Moreover, it is much harder to prioritize among security threats and challenges in an unclassified report since a ranking of security dangers can antagonize governments or other actors that appear high on the list and expose defense officials to charges that they are neglecting dangers that appear lower on the list. In addition, when a defense report is unclassified, defense officials may focus as much during the review process on how the report will be received by external audiences as on the substance of the defense strategy, thereby reducing the report's value as a strategic document (Center for Strategic and International Studies 2013, Brimley and Schulman 2016).

Furthermore, by incentivizing DoD to stick to rather general and anodyne policy statements in the QDR reports, the unclassified requirement made it harder to move forward with implementation once the reports were completed. In particular, since the QDR reports were written mainly in broad language, time-consuming follow-on efforts were needed to translate those big ideas into actionable guidance. Yet when such efforts were initiated, the lack of specificity in many QDR statements made the implementation processes themselves contentious. Brimley noted, "After the QDR, the under secretary for [acquisition, technology, and logistics] and the under secretary for policy use the QDR in internal processes, but because [the QDR report is] vague you're back to arguing first principles" (interview, 15 May 2013).

This implementation problem was magnified by the original QDR legislation's lack of any requirement that the report's implementation be subsequently assessed. In the absence of such a requirement, QDR implementation was quite uneven. Following the 2006 QDR, DoD Deputy Secretary of Defense Gordon England ordered the creation of implementation roadmaps and the establishment of about a dozen groups charged with ensuring that these roadmaps were being followed. Participants in this process recalled that it facilitated progress on some issues, but was only partially effective (Jim Thomas, interview, 21 May 2013, former DoD officials, interviews, May-October 2013). After the 2010 QDR, OSD also issued implementation guidance, but the implementation effort was not sustained (Shawn Brimley, interview, 15 May 2013, DoD official, interview, 24 May 2013).

Recognition of these shortcomings contributed to the decision by Congress in 2016 to make the QDR report classified and to require DoD to assess the report's implementation during each year in which a new quadrennial report is not being issued (Brimley and Schulman 2016). This should make it easier for defense officials to write openly about and prioritize security risks and challenges, while incentivizing defense officials to give sustained attention to the report's implementation (Brimley 2017). However, it is important to recognize that the change to a classified report will not be costless, as it will make it harder for DoD to use the report as a communications device and limit the extent to which the report serves as a reference point for congressional discussions about defense matters.

The review's fixed schedule

A final important design feature of the QDR was the legislative requirement that DoD conduct the review once every four years. The original legislation also mandated that the report be completed within the first four months of a presidential term. Following complaints from executive branch officials that this did not give a new administration sufficient time to complete a thorough review, Congress subsequently moved back the review's deadline (Henry 2005). The third, fourth, and fifth QDRs were each due early in the second year of a presidential term.

There was a clear logic to this schedule, as it gave an incoming or reelected administration a substantial period of time to determine its national security and defense strategy before it had to issue the QDR report. In principle, the report could then serve as the foundation for the administration's defense policies for the remaining three years of the presidential term.

The requirement that a review be conducted every four years was also beneficial because, in the absence of such a requirement, senior defense officials might have gone through a full presidential term without giving as much consideration to important strategic questions. Matthew Kroenig, a DoD strategist during the George W. Bush and Obama administrations, commented: "If you don't formally mandate a strategic review, big picture strategic thinking might never happen because policymakers are consumed with the day-to-day" (interview, 20 June 2013). Interestingly, congressional officials who oversee DoD saw the review's value in part in the same way. U.S. Representative Mac Thornberry, a congressional leader on defense issues, observed: "If Congress does not require a look at the bigger picture, nobody else is going to" (interview, 1 August 2013). A congressional defense aide commented similarly: "The [QDR] legislation is a forcing function for the secretary of defense to conduct a review" (interview, May 2013).

Relatedly, the QDR helped some senior defense officials become better prepared for making future decisions during the remainder of their tenure in office. A former DoD official commented, "The greatest value of the QDR is probably the process of having strategy discussions, more than the product" (interview, February 2013). This insight is consistent with other research on strategic planning, which has found that the greatest contribution of formal planning often lies in helping leaders understand their organizations and strategic matters more thoroughly (Kaplan and Beinhocker 2003, Erdmann 2009). Dwight Eisenhower famously captured this insight when commenting that "plans are useless... planning is indispensable" (Nixon 1962, 235). As Table 1 shows, my interview subjects rated the impact of the QDR on preparing DoD leaders to make future strategic decisions more highly than its impact on any other dimension about which I asked the interview subjects, suggesting that the review's value in this respect was indeed substantial. Given this benefit of the QDR, the review's value would have been diminished if it was conducted less frequently than every four years or was conducted later in a presidential term, when many senior officials would have less time remaining in their positions.

However, a fixed quadrennial schedule also had a couple of downsides. Most importantly, senior leaders may have the greatest need for a strategic review at a time that does not correspond to the quadrennial schedule, such as a moment when the strategic or political environment suddenly changes. The 2012 Defense Strategic

Guidance, which was issued shortly after a dramatic shift in the fiscal environment, illustrates this possibility. Although the Obama administration's ability to conduct the DSG despite the legislative requirements for a QDR shows that a quadrennial review requirement does not preclude the conduct of reviews at other times, review fatigue following a large quadrennial review may make leaders reluctant to order additional reviews even if a real need to update defense strategy exists. The U.S. Congress tried to address this problem in 2016 by requiring DoD to assess whether U.S. defense strategy needs updating during each year in which the new National Defense Strategy is not being completed. This requirement should make it more likely that U.S. defense strategy will be adjusted when circumstances warrant doing so in the future.

A remaining deficiency of the U.S. defense planning calendar is that it is often poorly synchronized with the production of broader U.S. national security strategy reports. While recent U.S. presidents issued an NSS once per term, they frequently produced these reports after the QDR had already been completed (Larson *et al.* 2018, 253–254). For instance, Barack Obama released his second term NSS nearly a year after the 2014 QDR had been released (U.S. Department of Defense 2014, Obama 2015). Logically, the NSS should precede and inform a defense planning document, with the latter document serving as an application of the president's overall national security strategy to the area of defense. But the fixed calendar for the QDR made it more difficult for administrations consistently to issue the strategic documents in their logical order.

This problem of sequencing was mitigated somewhat by the broad character of these documents, which allowed officials to nest them within each other regardless of the order in which they were issued. But no matter how such documents are sequenced, it is clearly important for defense strategies to be formulated in close coordination with plans to employ other tools of national power, such as diplomacy, intelligence, trade, and foreign assistance (Breitenbauch 2015).

Lessons and implications

In this concluding section, I consider what general lessons and implications can be derived from the U.S. experience with the QDR. I begin by discussing some lessons for defense practitioners and conclude by identifying some implications for defense scholars.

For defense practitioners, the main takeaway from this research is that recognizing the trade-offs associated with different ways of conducting strategic planning can help to inform sound choices about the design of strategic planning processes in various circumstances. Defense officials can craft such processes in ways that place them in different locations on several spectrums. In the preceding analysis, I focused in particular on choices concerning the extent of a review's inclusiveness or exclusivity, transparency or opacity, and fixed or flexible schedule. The QDR generally fell closer to the inclusive and transparent ends of these spectrums, while being conducted according to a preset schedule. As shown above, such design features entailed both benefits and costs. The QDR's inclusivity helped the review's ideas spread through the bureaucracy and facilitated their implementation, but resulted in reports that few people considered to be visionary or transformative. The QDR's transparency allowed DoD leaders to use the review as an effective public relations device, but prevented them from openly discussing security risks and vulnerabilities in the reports. The QDR's fixed schedule ensured that DoD leaders devoted some time to high-level strategic questions each presidential term, but meant that the review did not always occur when leaders most needed it.

A choice to make a strategic planning process more or less inclusive, more or less transparent, and more or less flexible in terms of its calendar therefore should depend on the needs of decision-makers in particular contexts. For instance, at times when the strategic or political environment is undergoing a major and rapid shift, it will tend to be important for defense policy makers to be able to conduct a review quickly and to privilege top-down direction over broad participation, since such design features will enhance the prospects that the review will produce ideas in a timely manner that break from the status quo. By contrast, in times of greater strategic or political stability, it will often make more sense to privilege deliberation and consensus-building over quick decision-making or innovation.[1] To take another example, when a defense ministry lacks strong external support, it may be advisable for the ministry to seek greater backing by conducting a highly transparent review, but when a ministry enjoys strong preexisting support, the benefits of transparency are more likely to be outweighed by the downsides associated with being unable to speak candidly about key security matters. Moreover, the same principles should apply to government-wide national security strategic planning processes too. Table 2 summarizes the advantages and disadvantages associated with designing a strategy process in the different ways discussed in this article, as well as the circumstances in which certain design choices are the most sensible.

This research also has broader implications for defense and strategic planning scholars. For defense scholars, the principal implication is that it is important to devote attention to the policy making process when studying the defense policies of countries. While a rich literature on bureaucratic politics exists (Allison 1969, Halperin and Clapp 2006), the study of governmental decision making processes – which tend to be hard to quantify – fell out of vogue in political science and international relations scholarship over the past several decades. At the same time, the field of strategic studies has focused more on the "downstream" relationships between defense policies and war or peace than on the "upstream" governmental processes that shape those policies (Breitenbauch and Jakobsson 2018).

Table 2. Key tradeoffs in the design of defense strategy processes.

Design feature	Strength	Weakness	Suitable condition for design feature
Inclusive	Conducive to internal buy-in	Not conducive to departure from status quo	Strategic stability
Exclusive	Conducive to departure from status quo	Not conducive to internal buy-in	Strategic shock
Transparent	Conducive to external buy-in	Not conducive to candor about threats and vulnerabilities	Agency lacks sufficient external support
Opaque	Conducive to candor about threats and vulnerabilities	Not conducive to external buy-in	Agency possesses adequate external support
Fixed schedule	Ensures high-level planning is conducted	Timing of planning not based on decision maker needs	Strategic stability
No fixed schedule	Ensures timing of planning is based on decision maker needs	High-level planning might not be conducted	Strategic shock

However, the evidence presented in this article, and elsewhere in this special issue, suggests that the design of a strategic planning process can affect the content of a country's defense policies (Ångström 2018). Further research on the relationship between policy processes and defense policy outcomes would therefore be worthwhile. In developing such research conceptually, defense scholars might find it useful to draw, as I have done, on the work of public administration scholars who have conceptualized key aspects of the policy process, particularly with respect to public sector strategic planning.[2]

In addition, scholars could build on this research empirically by documenting more systematically the features and outcomes of various defense planning processes. Such work could include charting the number of their participants, the structure of their operations, the proportion of their ideas that departed from the status quo, the extent to which they shared information with external audiences, and the rate at which their recommendations were implemented. These and other data could facilitate rigorous testing of hypotheses about the links between planning processes and outcomes across a range of strategy processes – for instance, by enabling scholars to classify each planning process with a high degree of confidence as involving high, medium, or low levels of inclusiveness, transparency, and other characteristics.

One potential extension of this research would be to theorize how strategic planning by defense officials can be shaped by a variety of principals. An extensive literature has examined the dynamics between principals and agents, particularly the extent to which an agent behaves independently when a principal delegates authority to it. For instance, scholars have theorized the extent to which international institutions act independently of the countries that grant them authority, as well as the extent to which government agencies act independently of the legislatures that authorize their programs (Weingast 1984, Waterman and Meier 1998, Hawkins et al. 2006). Along similar lines, strategic review processes are sometimes mandated by a principal outside the institution conducting the review, such as a legislature.

Moreover, the participants in strategic reviews are sometimes accountable not only to a single principal, but to multiple principals. For instance, depending on their institutional position, DoD officials involved in a strategic review might be accountable to more senior officials within OSD, superiors in one of the military services, and/or members of Congress. But such principal-agent relationships will tend to vary in their importance for different review participants – e.g. most military officers participating in a strategic review will tend to place greater weight on the preferences of their service's leadership than on the preferences of other principals.

Analogous dynamics involving multiple principal-agent relationships characterize defense planning processes in many countries, and offer fertile ground for further theorizing and empirical analysis. In addition to elucidating planning by individual defense ministries, such research could be particularly valuable in enhancing understanding of defense planning by multinational organizations, such as NATO, that are accountable to numerous countries. Within such organizations, the behavior of strategic planners may be influenced both by the preferences of their superiors within the organization and by the preferences of their national government or military. While scholars have examined ways in which the behavior of agents is shaped by multiple principals in other contexts (Spiller 1990, Whitford 2005, Hawkins et al. 2006), greater attention to the importance of these types of dynamics in defense planning could further enhance our understanding of how and why defense institutions develop certain strategies and policies.

Notes

1. See Davis and Wilson (2011) and Davis (2018) for a related argument that it is important to prioritize experimentation and imagination over standardization and consensus when the security context is changing dramatically. See Cohen (2018), 60–63 for a different related argument: that the difficulty of predicting future strategic needs means that it may be best for defense reviews to make only incremental changes to defense strategy.
2. See Jensen (2018) for an application of other policy process theory that sheds light on links between defense planning and policy.

Acknowledgments

I am grateful to the participants at a February 2017 workshop at the Centre for Military Studies at the University of Copenhagen and to the anonymous reviewers for very helpful feedback on earlier versions of this paper. I thank IBM Center for the Business of Government, American University, and the School of International Service at American University for their support of this research. I am also grateful to Edward Lucas, Kate Tennis, and Balazs Martonffy for excellent research assistance.

Disclosure statement

No potential conflict of interest was reported by the author.

Funding

This research was supported by the IBM Center for the Business of Government, American University, and the School of International Service at American University.

References

Allison, G.T., 1969. Conceptual models and the Cuban missile crisis. *American political science review*, 63 (3), 689–718. doi:10.2307/1954423.
Ångström, J., 2018. The US perspective on future war: why the US relies upon Ares rather than Athena. *Defence studies*, 18 (3), 318–338.
Aspin, L., 1993. *Report of the bottom-up review*. Arlington, VA: U.S. Department of Defense.
Becker, J. and Malesky, E., 2017. The continent or the 'grand large'? Strategic culture and operational burden-sharing in NATO. *International studies quarterly*, 61 (1), 163–180. doi:10.1093/isq/sqw039.
Berry, F.S., 1994. Innovation in public management: the adoption of strategic planning. *Public administration review*, 54 (4), 322–330. doi:10.2307/977379.
Brands, H., 2014. *What good is grand strategy? Power and purpose in American statecraft from Harry S. Truman to George W. Bush*. Ithaca: Cornell University Press.

Brands, H., 2018. Choosing primacy: U.S. strategy and global order at the dawn of the post-cold war era. *Texas national security review*, 1 (2), 8–33.
Breitenbauch, H.Ø., 2015. Defence planning. *Academic foresights*, 13. Available from: http://www.academic-foresights.com/Defence_Planning.html.
Breitenbauch, H. and Jakobsson, A.K., 2018. Defence planning as strategic fact: introduction. *Defence studies*, 18 (3), 253–261.
Brews, P. and Purohit, D., 2007. Strategic planning in unstable environments. *Long range planning*, 40 (1), 64–83. doi:10.1016/j.lrp.2006.12.001.
Brimley, S., 2017. Getting the pentagon's next national defense strategy right. *War on the rocks*, 24 May. Available from: https://warontherocks.com/2017/05/getting-the-pentagons-next-national-defense-strategy-right/
Brimley, S. and Schulman, L.D., 2016. Au Revoir QDR. *War on the rocks*. 14 June. Available from: https://warontherocks.com/2016/06/au-revoir-qdr/
Bryson, J.M., 2011. *Strategic planning for public and nonprofit organizations: a guide to strengthening and sustaining organizational achievement*. 4th. San Francisco: Jossey-Bass.
Bryson, J.M., Edwards, L.H., and Van Slyke, D.M., 2018. Getting strategic about strategic planning research. *Public management review*, 20 (3), 317–339. doi:10.1080/14719037.2017.1285111.
Came, T. and Campbell, C., 2010. The dynamics of top-down organizational change: Donald Rumsfeld's campaign to transform the U.S. defense department. *Governance: an international journal of policy, administration, and institutions*, 23 (3), 411–435. doi:10.1111/(ISSN)1468-0491.
Center for Strategic and International Studies, 2013. *Preparing for the 2014 quadrennial defense review: conference proceedings, presentations, and key takeaways*. Washington, DC: Center for Strategic and International Studies.
Chiu, D., 2014. Dr. Daniel Chiu on the pentagon's newest challenges. Great decisions podcast series. Foreign Policy Association. Available from: https://foreignpolicyblogs.com/2014/05/06/dr-daniel-chiu-pentagons-newest-challenges/
Christiansson, M., 2018. Defense planning beyond rationalism: the third offset strategy as a case of metagovernance. *Defence studies*, 18 (3), 262–278.
Cohen, R.S., 2017. *Air force strategic planning: past, present, and future*. Santa Monica, CA: RAND Corporation.
Cohen, R.S., 2018. *The history and politics of defense reviews*. Santa Monica, CA: RAND Corporation.
Cordesman, A.H., 2009. *Reforming defense decisionmaking: taking responsibility and making meaningful plans*. Washington, DC: Center for Strategic and International Studies.
Cornish, P. and Dorman, A.M., 2010. Breaking the mould: the United Kingdom strategic defence review 2010. *International Affairs*, 86 (2), 395–410. doi:10.1111/j.1468-2346.2010.00888.x.
Daggett, S., 2010. *Quadrennial defense review 2010: overview and implications for national security planning*. Washington, DC: Congressional Research Service.
Davis, P.K., 2002. *Analytical architecture for capabilities-based planning, mission-system analysis, and transformation*. Santa Monica, CA: RAND Corporation.
Davis, P.K., 2018. Defense planning when major changes are needed. *Defense studies*, 18 (3), 374–390.
Davis, P.K. and Wilson, P.A., 2011. *Looming discontinuities in U.S. military strategy and defense planning*. Santa Monica, CA: RAND Corporation.
De Spiegeleire, S., 2011. Ten trends in capability planning for defence and security. *RUSI journal*, 156 (5), 20–28. doi:10.1080/03071847.2011.626270.
Donnelly, T., 2005. *Quadrennial defense review time*. Washington, DC: American Enterprise Institute. Available at: https://www.aei.org/publication/quadrennial-defense-review-time/
Drezner, D.W., ed., 2009. *Avoiding trivia: the role of strategic planning in American foreign policy*. Washington, DC: Brookings Institution Press.
Dueck, C., 2008. *Reluctant crusaders: power, culture, and change in American grand strategy*. Princeton: Princeton University Press.
Dueck, C., 2015. *The Obama doctrine: American grand strategy today*. Oxford: Oxford University Press.

Edelstein, D.M. and Krebs, R.R., 2015. Delusions of grand strategy: the problem with Washington's planning obsession. *Foreign affairs*, 94 (6), 109–116.

Elbanna, S., Andrews, R., and Pollanen, R., 2016. Strategic planning and implementation success in public sector organizations: evidence from Canada. *Public management review*, 18 (7), 1017–1042. doi:10.1080/14719037.2015.1051576.

Erdmann, A.P.N., 2009. Foreign policy planning through a private sector lens. *In*: D.W. Drezner, edited by. *Avoiding trivia: the role of strategic planning in American foreign policy*. Washington, DC: Brookings Institution Press, 137–158.

Fitzsimmons, M., 2006. The problem of uncertainty in strategic planning. *Survival*, 48 (4), 131–146. doi:10.1080/00396330601062808.

Flournoy, M., 2006. Did the pentagon get the quadrennial review right? *Washington quarterly*, 29 (2), 67–84. doi:10.1162/wash.2006.29.2.67.

Flournoy, M. and Edelman, E., 2014. *Cuts to defense spending are hurting our national security*. Washington Post. 19 September. Available from: https://www.washingtonpost.com/opinions/cuts-to-us-military-spending-are-hurting-our-national-security/2014/09/18/6db9600c-3abf-11e4-9c9f-ebb47272e40e_story.html?utm_term=.1884bdf88b46.

Freedman, L., 2013. *Strategy: A history*. Oxford: Oxford University Press.

Freedman, L., 2017. The meaning of strategy, Part 1: the origins. *Texas national security review*, 1 (1), 90–105.

Goldgeier, J. and Suri, J., 2016. Revitalizing the U.S. national security strategy. *Washington quarterly*, 38 (4), 35–55. doi:10.1080/0163660X.2015.1125828.

Goldgeier, J.M., 1998. NATO expansion: the anatomy of a decision. *Washington quarterly*, 21 (1), 83–102. doi:10.1080/01636609809550295.

Gordon, John, I.V. 2005. *The quadrennial defense review: analyzing the major defense review process*. Doctoral Dissertation. George Mason University.

Gray, C., 2010. Strategic thoughts for defence planners. *Survival*, 52 (3), 159–178. doi:10.1080/00396338.2010.494883.

Gray, C., 2014. *Strategy and defence planning: meeting the challenge of uncertainty*. Oxford: Oxford University Press.

Gunzinger, M., 2013. *Shaping America's future military: toward a new force planning construct*. Washington, DC: Center for Strategic and Budgetary Assessments.

Håkenstad, M. and Knus, K.L., 2012. *Long-term defence planning: a comparative study of seven countries*. Oslo: Norwegian Institute for Defence Studies.

Halperin, M.H. and Clapp, P.A., 2006. *Bureaucratic politics and foreign policy*. 2nd edition. Washington, DC: Brookings Institution Press.

Hawkins, D.G., et al., eds, 2006. *Delegation and agency in international organizations*. Cambridge: Cambridge University Press.

Henry, R., 2005. Defense transformation and the 2005 quadrennial defense review. *Parameters*, 35 (4), 5–15.

Hicks, K.H. and Brannen, S.J., 2010. Force planning in the 2010 QDR. *Joint force quarterly*, 59, 137–142.

Huntington, S.P., 1961. *The common defense: strategic programs in national politics*. New York: Columbia University Press.

Jensen, B.M., 2016. *Forging the sword: doctrinal change in the U.S. Army*. Stanford, CA: Stanford University Press.

Jensen, B.M., 2018. The role of ideas in defense planning: revisiting the revolution in military affairs. *Defence studies*, 18 (3), 302–317.

Kagan, F., 2006. *Finding the target: the transformation of American military policy*. New York: Encounter Books.

Kaplan, S. and Beinhocker, E.D., 2003. The real value of strategic planning. *MIT sloan management review*, 44 (2), 71–76.

Karlin, M., 2017. *Recommendations for future national defense strategy*. Washington, DC: Brookings Institution Policy Brief.

Krebs, R.R., 2015. *Narrative and the making of national security*. Cambridge: Cambridge University Press.
Larson, E.V., et al., 2018. *Defense planning in a time of conflict: a comparative analysis of the 2001-2014 quadrennial defense reviews, and implications for the Army*. Santa Monica, CA: RAND Corporation.
Mahnken, T.G., 2001. Transforming the U.S. Armed Forces: rhetoric or reality? *Naval college war review*, 54 (3), 85–99.
Mahnken, T.G., ed, 2012. *Competitive strategies for the 21st century: theory, history, and practice*. Stanford: Stanford University Press.
McInnis, K.J. and Lucas, N.J., 2015. *What is 'building partner capacity'? Issues for Congress*. Washington, DC: Congressional Research Service.
Mintzberg, H., 1994. *The rise and fall of strategic planning*. New York: The Free Press.
Mintzberg, H., Ahlstrand, B., and Lampel, J., 2009. *Strategy safari: your complete guide through the wilds of strategic management*. 2nd edition. Harlow, UK: Pearson.
Moynihan, D.P. and Hawes, D.P., 2012. Responsiveness to reform values: the influence of the environment on performance information use. *Public administration review*, 72 (S1), S95–S105. doi:10.1111/j.1540-6210.2012.02653.x.
National Defense Panel, 1997. *Transforming defense: national defense in the 21st Century*. Arlington, VA: National Defense Panel.
National Defense Panel, 2014. *Ensuring a strong U.S. defense for the future*. Washington, DC: U.S. Institute of Peace.
Nixon, R., 1962. *Six crises*. Garden City, NJ: Doubleday.
O'Hanlon, M., 2007. *The politics of defense planning*. New York: NYU Wagner Graduate School of Public Service and John Brademas Center for the Study of Congress.
Obama, B., 2015. *National security strategy*. Washington, DC: The White House.
Poister, T.H., Pitts, D.W., and Edwards, L.H., 2010. Strategic management research in the public sector: a review, synthesis, and future directions. *American review of public administration*, 40 (5), 522–545. doi:10.1177/0275074010370617.
Popescu, I., 2017. *Emergent strategy and grand strategy: how American presidents succeed in foreign policy*. Baltimore: Johns Hopkins University Press.
Popescu, I.C., 2018. Grand strategy vs. emergent strategy in the conduct of foreign policy. *Journal of strategic studies*, 41 (3), 438–460. doi:10.1080/01402390.2017.1288109.
Quadrennial Defense Review Independent Panel, 2010. *The QDR in perspective: meeting America's national security needs in the 21st century*. Washington, DC: U.S. Institute of Peace.
Sharp, T., 2010. *Vision meets reality: 2010 QDR and the 2011 defense budget*. Washington, DC: Center for a New American Security.
Silove, N., 2016. The pivot before the pivot: U.S. strategy to preserve the power balance in Asia. *International Security*, 40 (4), 45–88. doi:10.1162/ISEC_a_00238.
Silove, N., 2018. Beyond the buzzword: the three meanings of 'grand strategy'. *Security studies*, 27 (1), 27–57. doi:10.1080/09636412.2017.1360073.
Snodgrass, D.E., 2000. The QDR: improve the process to improve the product. *Parameters*, 30 (1), 57–68.
Spiller, P.T., 1990. Politicians, interest groups, and regulators: a multiple-principals agency theory of regulation, or 'let them be bribed'. *Journal of law and economics*, 33 (1), 65–101. doi:10.1086/467200.
Spring, B. and Eaglen, M., 2009. *Quadrennial defense review: building blocks for national defense*. Washington, DC: Heritage Foundation.
Tama, J., 2015. Does strategic planning matter? the outcomes of U.S. national security reviews. *Political science quarterly*, 130, 4. doi:10.1002/polq.12395.
Tama, J., 2016. *Maximizing the value of quadrennial strategic planning*. Washington, DC: IBM Center for the Business of Government.
Tama, J., 2017. The politics of strategy: why government agencies conduct major strategic reviews. *Journal of public policy*, 37 (1), 27–54. doi:10.1017/S0143814X15000148.

Tama, J., 2018. How an agency's responsibilities and political context shape government strategic planning: evidence from US federal agency quadrennial reviews. *Public management review*, 20 (3), 377–396. doi:10.1080/14719037.2017.1285114.

U.S. Congress, 1996. National defense authorization act for fiscal year 1997. *Public law*, 104–201. 110 STAT. 2422

U.S. Congress, 2014. National defense authorization act for fiscal year 2015. *Public law*, 113–291.128 STAT. 3294.

U.S. Congress, 2016. National defense authorization act for fiscal year 2017. *Public law*, 114–328.130 STAT. 2000.

U.S. Department of Defense, 1997. *Report of the quadrennial defense review*. Arlington, VA: U.S. Department of Defense.

U.S. Department of Defense, 2008. *National defense strategy*. Arlington, VA: U.S. Department of Defense.

U.S. Department of Defense, 2010. *Quadrennial defense review report*. Arlington, VA: U.S. Department of Defense.

U.S. Department of Defense, 2012a. *Defense budget priorities and choices*. Arlington, VA: U.S. Department of Defense.

U.S. Department of Defense, 2012b. *Sustaining U.S. global leadership: priorities for 21st century defense*. Arlington, VA: U.S. Department of Defense.

U.S. Department of Defense, 2014. *Quadrennial defense review 2014*. Arlington, VA: U.S. Department of Defense.

U.S. Department of State, 2009. *Town hall on the quadrennial diplomacy and development review*. Available from: https://2009-2017.state.gov/secretary/20092013clinton/rm/2009a/july/125949.htm

U.S. House of Representatives, 2014a. Committee on armed services. Hearing on the 2014 quadrennial defense review. H.A.S.C. 113-102. 3 April.

U.S. House of Representatives, 2014b. Committee on armed services. Hearing on national defense panel assessment of the 2014 quadrennial defense review. H.A.S.C. 113-130. 2 December.

U.S. Senate, 2015. Committee on armed services. Hearing to receive testimony on improving the pentagon's development of policy, strategy, and plans. S. Hrg. 114-395. 8 December.

Ucko, D.H., 2009. *The new counterinsurgency era: transforming the U.S. military for modern wars*. Washington, DC: Georgetown University Press.

Waterman, R.W. and Meier, K.J., 1998. Principal-agent models: an expansion? *Journal of public administration research and theory*, 8 (2), 173–202. doi:10.1093/oxfordjournals.jpart.a024377.

Watts, B., 2012. Barriers to acting strategically: why strategy is so difficult. *In*: T.G. Mahnken, edited by. *Competitive strategies for the 21st century: theory, history, and practice*. Stanford: Stanford University Press, 47–67.

Weingast, B.R., 1984. The congressional-bureaucratic system: a principal agent perspective (with Applications to the SEC). *Public choice*, 44 (1), 147–191. doi:10.1007/BF00124821.

Whitford, A.B., 2005. The pursuit of political control by multiple principals. *Journal of politics*, 67 (1), 29–49. doi:10.1111/j.1468-2508.2005.00306.x.

Williams, L. M. 2017. *The budget control act and the defense budget: frequently asked questions*. Washington, DC: Congressional Research Service.

Wilson, J.Q., 1989. *Bureaucracy: what government agencies do and why they do it*. United States: Basic Books.

Wormuth, C., 2018. Can Mattis succeed where his predecessors have failed? *Foreign policy*. 23 January. Available from: https://foreignpolicy.com/2018/01/23/matiss-defense-strategy-offers-old-wine-in-a-new-bottle/.

The role of ideas in defense planning: revisiting the revolution in military affairs

Benjamin M. Jensen

ABSTRACT
Which ideas shape defense planning and why? The following paper builds on over 80 interviews with senior defense officials to dissect the origin, evolution, and fall of the Revolution in Military Affairs (RMA), a major post-Cold War US defense innovation paradigm. In studying the emergence and diffusion of the RMA concept, my research suggests a central role for collective actors sharing constitutive ideas about practice and competing for legitimate authority and influence in the defense establishment. The rise of the RMA as an organizing idea in U.S. defense planning is thus not reducible to bureaucratic competition, technological determinism, or strategic culture as an external set of norms. Rather, it can be portrayed as a social process involving boundary activation by bureaucrats and soldiers (re)interpreting their key tasks and core missions for future war.

Ideas & revolutions

Much of defense discourse in the 1990s, an era of shrinking budgets and strategic realignment, dealt with defining a Revolution in Military Affairs (RMA), how the combination of information-technology and precision strike called for new systems, organizations, and doctrine fundamentally altering warfare. In 1994, Andrew Krepenvich, then Director of the Defense Budget Project, published an article in the *National Interest* entitled "Cavalry to computer; the pattern of military revolutions" discussing ten military revolutions that changed the world. The work reflected a public presentation of what was a growing research program in the Office of Net Assessment (ONA), a small unit in the Office of the Secretary of Defense headed by Andrew Marshall, a Presidential Appointee since the Nixon administration and former RAND Corporation analyst.[1]

Marshall was involved with a series of debates about the potential of precision weapons dating back to his days at RAND and questions about long-range accuracy, laser-guided munitions, and cruise missiles with a network of defense officials and strategic thinkers that included Albert Wohlsetter, Paul Wolfowitz, Donald Rumsfeld, and Richard Perle among others. The question was not just the extent to which war would change, but what it implied in terms of U.S. strategy and defense planning. This sentiment was best captured in 1996 by Zalmay Khalilzad, then Director of the Strategy, Doctrine and Force Structure program for RAND's Project Air Force and one of the co-authors of the 1992 Defense Planning Guidance that called for a two-major theater war strategy, who argued that the central challenge for U.S. grand strategy was sustaining a position of global preeminence through maintaining technological superiority in the defense sphere (7).

Yet, how do scholars make sense of the rise of an idea and its advocates in defense bureaucracies and their relative ability to influence policy and planning? Which ideas matter and why? In exploring these questions, this article contributes to the larger research agenda on the politics and practice of defense planning (Breitenbauch and Jakobsson 2018).

With respect to RMA and defense transformation, at one level it would be easy to dismiss the fanfare as nothing more than rhetorical acumen, a sales pitch designed to capture resources amidst declining budgets or an extension of party ideology. In another reading, exogenous factors, the weight of large-scale historical change between a loosely defined modern industrial and information based post-industrial society alters the confirmation of war (Toffler 1984a, 1984b, 1991, Van Creveld 1989, 1991).[2] In this reading, RMA is a structural condition, not a strategic choice based on the intellectual musings of bureaucrats.

Whether a lie, a deep structure, or something more, RMA remains a central idea in modern defense organizations. Students in Professional Military Education systems study the idea. Emerging defense ideas carry the DNA of the RMA. From AirSea Battle and its vision of blinding precision strikes against mainland China as a means of countering anti-access/area denial to the Third Offset and its emphasis on game changing technologies that sustain defense dominance, the RMA is part of the genetic code in the U.S. defense bureaucracy.[3]

In studying the emergence and diffusion of the RMA concept, my research suggests a central role for collective actors sharing ideas and competing for legitimate authority and influence over sectoral policy making (Genieys and Smyrl 2008a, 2008b, Genieys 2010, Hassenteufel *et al.* 2010). This insight about the role of small groups waging a war of ideas inside defense organizations is a new perspective in security studies (Jensen 2016a, 2016b). Agents, not enduring structures, seek to solve problems and, in the process, shape the practice of defense planning. Programmatic actors are the positive counterpart to veto players, seeking to advance an agenda as opposed to stop an alternative (Tsbelis 2002, Hassenteufel *et al.* 2010).

In the following paper, I will establish an analytical basis for examining the intersection of ideas and agents in defense planning using the RMA debate as an exploratory case. This case shows the intersection of multiple networks around a single program outlining a new theory of victory for future warfare. Triangulating the space occupied by networks organized around ideas requires situating the programmatic actor framework with respect to concepts from relational sociology, institutionalism, and organizational theory. In this respect, my work extends William Genieys and Marc Smyrl's work on programmatic actors in French social policy (Genieys and Smyrl 2008a, 2008b, Genieys 2010). Specifically, the programmatic actor model I derive from their work is about tracing how ideas diffuse in policy communities.

Programmatic actors

Programmatic actors are relatively small groups of policy specialists predominately located inside government connected by their advocacy of a shared bundle of ideas and problem-solving prescriptions not reducible to material self-interests and preferences along institutional lines.[4] Rather, the interests associated with programs are defined in terms of the relative influence of individual actors inside government defined as *Herrschraft*, or legitimate authority (Genieys and Smyrl 2008a, 2008b). This authority may allow individual actors to capture additional resources inside government, but the capture of resources may not always produce increased legitimacy. As a collective actor, programmatic actors are held together by the extent to which they are connected by a given set of ideas, defined in terms of boundary activation, and predisposed towards advancing policy options that increase the resonance of these ideas and hence their individual authority.[5] The struggle at the heart of government is best viewed as contentious bureaucrats advancing divergent programs.

In the Goffman sense of the term, a program is a "frame," acting as a schema of interpretation that organizes how events and interactions are understood (Goffman 1974, 27). Inherent in any defense program are bundles of assumptions about what constitutes a threat, cause-effect relationships related to strategy development, and logics of appropriateness that define procurement and weapons design. They form a constitutive as opposed to regulative logic. Programs are the cosmology of bureaucrats, how they understand the rules, norms, and organizing principals of their particular domain of practice.[6] As such, they tend to be focused on technical issues nominally associated with policy specialists and not reducible to a particular party ideology and only loosely linked to broader social discourses.

By its very definition, a program is relational, connecting social sites and actors, and in the process, activating boundaries (Emirbayer 1997, Jackson and Nexon 1999, Tilly 2005). While linking ideas, norms, culture, and other approximations of ideational factors to the policy formation process is neither novel nor new, what standouts in a programmatic actor orientation is the conceptualization of identity as relational site of competition inside government. Programs are vehicles of socialization and boundary activation for contentious bureaucrats.

The programmatic actor framework begins from the assumption of organizational anarchy common in much of the policy process literature (Kingdon 1984; Sabatier Sabatier and Jenkins-Smith 2007). Competition is rampant among different bureaucratic actors, individual policy specialists, and broader advocacy networks. As used here, competition is not singularly defined by material interests, the turf and money bureaucrats are hypothesized to horde in strict rationalist renderings. Rather, competition is just as prevalent around the articulation of discrete policy logics, or programs, that frame options. This contestation over interpretation is as central as the search for resources and allies inside government. A war of idols defines the search for legitimate authority inside government. *If where you sit determines where you stand, seating is often shaped by who you know and the beliefs that bind you together.*

If the actors are small groups at the commanding heights of a bureaucracy, their objective is prestige and authority. In a Weberian turn, reform is thus at least partially a function Herrschaft, efforts to legitimate authority within a formal organization that produces viable career paths of its associated members and thus (re)produces the program that holds them together. Within any bureaucracy there is a process of creative destruction as actors seek to innovate as a means of legitimating and sustaining their respective program absent external shocks. In defense, these actors cut across multiple categories including senior officers, elected officials, civil servants, and industrial interest-groups. That said, they are relatively small groups, bound together by the program and thus differentiated from advocacy coalitions. They are not reducible to party lines or competing sub-organizations (i.e. service rivalry). Rather, they are generalized groups of policy professionals that are not unitary, but prone to competition, contestation, and intrigue

To date, case studies pioneering the programmatic actor model have focused on European healthcare policy (Genieys 2010). This grows from earlier studies by Genieys and Hassenteufel on social policy (Hassenteufel *et al.* 1999). Since 2010, the emphasis has been on seeking a more generalizable set of propositions that derive from the model through cross-national comparison of health care sector reform (Hassenteufel *et al.* 2010) and the defense sector (Joana and Smith 2006). Furthermore, an edited volume in 2010 looked at expanding the scope beyond healthcare to other public policy sectors (Genieys 2010).

The programmatic actor model begins with the assumption that small groups compete for legitimacy authority and influence inside government. Note that the actual content of policy and policy implementation is assumed to be more contingent and subject to standard arguments about interest formation.[7] The emphasis in a programmatic actor model is policy formulation, the articulation of possible paths given the underlying program and actors associated with it. By formulating, translating, and mobilizing their programs, as discrete policy logics, these agents play a constitutive role within the policy formation process. This constitutive role should be observable along two dimensions: 1) the context of policy; and 2) the number of policy proposals.

The extent to which new policy frames and their circulation as the formation of new policy options are present should correspond with the configuration of a program actor network. First, the following attributes need to be observed to hold that a programmatic actor network was present and sufficient to influence the articulation of policy options: 1) *organization*, a coherent network organized around a set of ideas that both define a particular problem set and mobilize solutions; 2) *capacity*, evidence that this programmatic network had either direct or indirect access to the policy process; and 3) *resonance*, indications that the programmatic actor network sought to expand its influence through perpetuating the program and increasing its corresponding legitimate authority.

Furthermore, each category has variation depending on the degree to which it is present and latent attributes. Organizations can be either heterogeneous or homogenous depending on the degree to which they allow participants and ephemeral or enduring depending on the longevity of the programmatic network and its member's participation. One would expect to find organizations that are more homogenous and enduring to be associated with increased policy options. Capacity can be thought of on a spectrum running from low, no direct access to the policy process, to high, access to both formulation and implementation. One would expect to find high capacity associated with increased generation of policy options linked to the program. Last, resonance relates to the degree to which bureaucratic actors use the language of the program and its associated with policy heuristic. If a program is resonant there should be a limited number of frames, or a coherent program, and agent career trajectories should be related to its circulation.

Assuming one is able to identify the presence of a programmatic actor network and prove that they shaped the policy formation process, the next step is to draw out the causal mechanisms associated with the process. The programmatic actor model outlines two ideal-typical processes connecting actors, programs, and policy change that account for the production of legitimate authority and hence the content and character of sectoral debates endogenous to a bureaucracy. These are each associated with a process that explains how policy heuristics intersect the desire for Herrschaft and produce the possibility of policy change even in stable institutional settings prone to isomorphism. This does not seek to replace the possibility of external shocks, bureaucratic interests, or path dependencies. Rather the objective is to locate a particular modality of institutional change that is self-reinforcing and local.

Analyzing these processes requires focusing on causal mechanisms as opposed to co-variation. Mechanisms can be defined as "a delimited class of events that change relations among specified sets of elements in identical or closely similar ways over a variety of situations" (Tilly 2001, 25–26).[8] In analyzing defense policy, I draw on mechanisms associated with social boundary activation.[9] A boundary represents any zone of contrast between internally connected groups (Tilly 2005, 134). These groups share a common representation that is enacted when they come into contact with other groups. In defense, it can be organizational cultures, military branches, even more diffuse ideas and strategies about how to realign sector policy examined here as programs.

Inside a program, as a type of policy boundary, actors exert autonomy and influence through interpretation and reference to the program. It can be further inferred that a program will interact with the communities sense of core mission and tasks (Wilson 1966, 90–110). The programs resonance will be defined in terms of how it links a subunits core mission and tasks to the overarching concept of change. If a common interpretative framework can be established, the program should have a higher degree of bureaucratic buy in.

In analyzing programmatic actor networks that bridge different organizational actors in defense policy, I draw on two boundary activating mechanisms from relational sociology to analyze how programs interact with existing communities and diffuse: *encounter* and *activation/deactivation* (Tilly 2005, 138). Encounter describes the process whereby actors are introduced to new programs. It is a necessary condition as the "encounter" produces the possibility of change. It can be analyzed in terms of mapping the sites of socialization bureaucratic actors used to facilitate the spread of ideas. Encounter implies that two members of previously distinct groups enter the same social space and interact. As they interact, their encounter either "activates" new or existing boundaries or "deactivates" old boundaries. This is the sufficient condition. It can be analyzed in terms of the ways in which programs interact with core missions and tasks (Wilson 1966).

Together these mechanisms concatenate into two processes. The first process, *mobilization*, emerges from the encounter mechanism specified above and identifies how new actors enter a given program thus expanding its influence and prestige. It deals with socialization and the (re)production of programmatic content. The programmatic actor model does not seek to reproduce structural or functional accounts of policy change and contention. This emphasis on agents is similar to rational choice perspectives that predicate their analysis of social action on collective action problems and relatively autonomous, instrumental agents seeking to maximize their interests.

As used here, the emphasis on agents does not reduce social action to the search for instrumental gains measured by material payoffs. Rather, actors search for authority as *the capacity to generate prestige and future gains*. To this end, they align with programs. Alternatively, there might be social sites through which actors are exposed to the underlying ideas that constitute a program. These could include commissions, wargames, and workshops or studies. Last, there might be a distinct cohort effect whereby a critical mass of new entrants to the bureaucracy admires a particular set of ideas.

The second process, *articulation*, emerges from the activation/de-activation social boundary mechanism and concerns how programs are maintained and translated into policy ideas that constitute the basis for change. Programs are expressed as actual policy options via framing. Framing is how actors situate their identities, opponents, and coalitions (McAdams *et al.* 2001, 16). Programs can be conceptualized as similar to the process of category formation. Category formation refers to the process whereby actors are constituted, here a programmatic actor, through common articulation of a distinct set of ideas that bounds them from other actor networks (McAdams *et al.* 2001, 116). As categories form, they drive incessant competition and brokerage as actors align based on boundary activation, seizing opportunities to advance their agenda in opposition to alternatives (McAdams, Tilly, and Tarrow 322). Programs are used to frame options in policy forums. This produces boundary activation that reinforces the program. As policies emerge that carry the programmatic frame, they reify the program and produce legitimate authority and thus increased prestige for associated officials.

To evaluate these claims, the paper will now turn to exploring the emergence of the RMA debate and the extent to which it parallels a programmatic actor hypothesis. The empirical data is derived from multiple sources including secondary historical treatments, archival documents, and over 80 interviews with high level retired officials associated with an individual service, the Department of Defense, or Congress. First to ensure an adequate analysis of capacity, individuals were selected only if they met the following criteria: field grade or higher officer (note: flag officer preferred), GS14 or presidential appointee, and with respect to Congress either staffer or senior aid. Multiple services and political parties were selected in order to ensure that party politics or individual service perceptions did not cloud observation. In analyzing the empirical data, the research examines if without a programmatic actor, the policy environment, the type of options generated and their range would have been different.[10] This implies analyzing the attributes defined above (organization, capacity, and resonance) and the proposed causal mechanisms, mobilization and articulation across four decades: 1970s, 1980s, 1990s, and 2000. The assumption is that program, growing out of the thinking of Andrew Marshall and Albert Wohlstetter as near zero miss, evolves over this period and should see alterations in the configuration of the associated programmatic actors in terms of their organization, capacity, and resonance. These observations allow one to further define the approach and consider the causal mechanisms: mobilization and articulation.

Revisiting the RMA: the role of programmatic actors

The intersection of multiple, defense policy networks around a central set of propositions about future warfare, as a program, is apparent in the emergence of the RMA in the United States. The larger genealogy of the term "revolution in military affairs" can be linked back to two historically linked trajectories. The first trajectory involved a series of Russian doctrinal publications in the 1970s analyzing U.S. experiments with laser-guided weapons and precision weapons and space systems in general. These publications, including the *Scientific-Technical Progress and the Revolution in Military Affairs* (Lomov and Gen 1973) and the writings of Marshal N.V. Ogarkov, which were translated by the United States Air Force and disseminated throughout the defense department by the Military Publishing House. Much of the research emphasized a growing "automated reconnaissance-and-strike complex" that would make it possible to achieve effects similar to those requiring nuclear weapons (Watts 2007, 12). Soviet theorists were carefully studying U.S. operations ranging from Linebacker in Vietnam to Assault Breaker, a program established by future defense secretary William Perry as the Deputy Undersecretary for Defense, Director of Research and Engineering.

The second related trajectory involved a broader discussion of the role of precision in warfare. According to former defense department officials associated with the defense policy board and undersecretary of defense, the deep origins of the RMA are associated with the ideas of Albert Wohlstetter and his push for both precision nuclear and non-nuclear weapons (Interview c 2010). Wohlstetter focused on the prospect of "near zero miss" weapons and how they would alter warfare. The logic was captured in a series of panels organized by the Defense Advanced Research and Projects Agency (DARPA) and Defense Nuclear Agency (DNA) in the early 1970s, the Long Range Research and Development Planning Program. The study had three panels attended by OSD and service representatives organized around advanced technology, munitions, and strategic alternatives, which was chaired by Albert Wohlstetter. Collectively, the panels put forward the idea that near-zero miss or precision weapons would generate "coercive response" options short of full-scale war that would maintain the delicate balance of terror (Paolucci 1975, 23). This logic put a premium on systems designed to "conduct military attacks with associated low collateral damage" including remotely piloted vehicles, or what became UAVs capable of persistent surveillance and cruise missiles, and precision missiles with a range of payloads and objective missions (i.e., deep earth penetrating, guided projectile, rapid mine laying, etc.) (Paolucci 1975, 29). Non-nuclear systems with low circular error probability (50–100 feet) were seen as satisfying "current United States and Allied damage requirements [that required] the use of nuclear weapons" (Paolucci 1975, 45).

In the 1980s, the idea was further articulated as "discriminate deterrence." In 1987 the Reagan White House formed a panel of defense experts to study requirements to meet the security environment likely in 20 years. The resulting Commission on Integrated Long-Term Strategy published its findings January 1988 in a document entitled *Discriminate Deterrence* (Ikle and Wohlstetter 1988). Much of the logic and spirit, from precision weapons and integrating new technology, was directly drawn from the earlier LRRDP report. The Commission, like the earlier project revolved around working groups dedicated towards specific research areas such as sources of change in the future security environment, role of advanced conventional standoff weapons, and technology and national security. Andrew Marshall, head of the Office of Net Assessment led the working group on future security environments, a group that included James G. Roche, future Secretary of the

Air Force and author of their force transformation plan in 2001, Dov Zakheim, future Comptroller of the Defense Department under Rumsfeld, and two academics associated with the Office of Net Assessment, Eliot A. Cohen and Stephen P. Rosen (Watts 2007, 82). On note, the report called for "fast tracking" key weapon systems like stealth and cruise missiles to avoid the "horse cavalry syndrome," essentially a re-aligning of defense priorities that favored DOD over the services (Ikle and Wohlstetter 1988, 48).

Both commissions though were clear that radical change did not limit itself to introducing new weapon systems alone. A former Undersecretary of Defense and Assistant Secretary for Policy and Plans summarized an anecdote attributed to Wohlstetter: if a medieval knight discovered an M-16, what would he do with it? Bludgeon his opponent or begin to engage targets over 300 meters away with precision fire (Interview c 2010).[11] In this reading, the precision revolution was not just about fielding new weapon systems that would tip the balance in the U.S. favor without significantly altering the "balance of terror" but about optimizing the organization in terms of doctrine, planning, and bureaucratic configuration to ensure the full capabilities were harnessed.

In the 1990s, the idea was used to propose concepts about realigning defense priorities. While the major planning documents and strategic concepts that emerged following the end of the Cold War such as the Base Force and Two Major Theater War planning strategy called for largely continuing U.S. military posture albeit at lower, conventional levels, the concept of a "military technical revolution," first proposed in response Soviet readings of U.S. technology advances and related to the genealogy of precision and "near-zero-miss," became a centrifuge for military officers and defense bureaucrats (Interview c 2010).

In 1993, the Office of Net Assessment (ONA) contracted an alumnus, Jeff McKitterick, and his team at the Strategic Analysis Center (SAC) within SAIC to organized a series of workshops and war-games related to explore the Soviet concepts of a military-technical revolution. McKitterick went on to change the name MTR to RMA and organized a series of war-games around key concepts: dominant maneuver and precision engagement. The goal of the workshops was to "infect a young generation of officers with the RMA virus" (Interview h 2010).

In May 1995, the first meeting of the Dominant Maneuver Working Group was convened to analyze a decisive movement to contact involving concepts like a swarm and digital command net (Interview g 2010). This was followed by a September 27 Army Round Table on RMA that included an analysis of small warfighting organizations, using precision to strike an enemies center for gravity, and projecting power from the U.S. chaired by Andrew Marshall, Stephen Rosen, and General Sullivan (Interview g 2010).

The mid 1990s OSD and JCS were also RMA hothouses, with key individuals like Secretary Perry, Chairman Shalikashvili, and Vice Chairman Admiral Owens backing RMA related concepts emerging from its associated concept of "offsetting." Secretary Perry made the case that the weapon systems displayed in the Gulf War were a byproduct of a larger strategy he helped shape as a defense official from 1977 to 1981 called "offsetting" in which technology was used to offset mass (Interview b 2010). That is, disruptive technologies researched by DARPA during his tenure including stealth fighters, more unmanned systems, and JSTARs would enable the U.S. to use less forces when confronting an adversary with superior numbers. He further hypothesized that in the future a "system of systems" could be built that integrated multiple sub-systems to achieve even further offsetting.

As a variant of the transformation thesis complementing the near-zero-miss and reconnaissance-strike-complex, the "system of systems" concept became a central aspect of efforts to usher in the RMA program in the Joint Chiefs of Staff and DOD during the 1990s. On his return to the Pentagon from 1993 to 1997, Perry's career overlapped the movement of Admiral Bill Owens, a career submariner, to the position of Vice Chief of the Joint Staff in 1994. Perry drew on this concept to develop a model of systems integration, or RMA as a system of systems, around three areas: intelligence, surveillance, and reconnaissance (ISR); command, control computer systems, and intelligence processing (C4I), and precision strike (Interview f 2010, Blaker and Manning 1997, 7). Through integrating these subsystems U.S. forces would penetrate the competitors' decision-making cycle, or OODA loop, and be able to rapidly find targets, process the information, select the appropriate weapon system, and engage it with a high level of accuracy before the enemy even knew they were being tracked (Interview a 2010). The concept became the basis for Owens (2001) later book, *Lifting the Fog of War* in which he argued for pursuing an RMA for three reasons: 1) take advantage of the strategic pause brought on by the fall of the Soviet untion; 2) prepare for the rise of China to a status of "near-peer" competitor by 2010–2015; and 3) take advantage of a larger inventory turnover given the need to replace Reagan era legacy systems.

After the 2000 election, the RMA concept underwent further rebranding as "transformation." Part of this change rose from the fact that many felt that the term RMA was being reduced to a foil for increased spending and technology change without getting at the true nature of large-scale innovation. For Marshall, the best analogy of the RMA was the interwar period, an era he commissioned multiple studies on. It was going to be a long, slow process that hinged on changing the way organizations were configured so that they could better realize change. As a mantra of change, this perspective called for changes in leadership dynamics, business practices, and the way the defense bureaucracy as organized to include its underlying culture (Interview d 2010).

The spirit of Rumsfeld's effort to adapt the rhetoric of transformation to apply to organizational change as much as it did weapons procurement is clear in a 10 September 2001 Pentagon speech, one which he felt strongly enough to forward directly to President Bush and Vice President Cheney as a memo entitled "Waste to Warfighting." In the speech he referred to the Pentagon bureaucracy as the "adversary" that is stifling innovation through institutional inertia calling in the process for a "war on bureaucracy." Much of the speech emphasized that a technological revolution had transformed the private sector but failed to impact the bureaucratic processes in the DOD and individual services.

The idea of a transformation that would shape organizational practices in order to accelerate the RMA was reinforced by a series of special studies Rumsfeld initiated after returning to the DOD in 2000 (Interview d 2010). Similar to the discriminate deterrence project, Rumsfeld called for a Defense Strategy Review that framed the future security environment. The strategy review was accompanied by a series of panels designed to jump start transformational thinking (Interview f 2010). The studies were conducted separate from the congressionally mandated QDR process leading to a degree of confusion. Overall, the intent was to use the review and panels as a way of kicking off the QDR and PPBS process.

This confusion also proved a key point of resistance for the individual services. According to a study of the process by SAIC, the J8 used the QDR to work the JCS agenda and protect the individual services. Because it still contained a push for transformation, it produced a large turf battle: to realize transformation would require significant cuts in force structure and pet projects like the Army Crusader (Interview c 2010). The debate was further complicated by the slow pace of confirming civilian officials. Only 3 senior civilian personnel were in place by May 2000 and Rumsfeld tended to view the remaining officials and senior members of the JCS as Clinton loyalists who were not genuinely interested in change. In fact, much of the process of pushing transformation became constructed as an attempt by Rumsfeld to reassert civilian control over a military apparatus, both in the JCS and individual services, who had become accustomed to getting their way with civilian officials (Interview b 2010). Furthermore, while transformation was a "Congress-free zone" individual services would use hearings to lobby Congress and the budgeting process as seen in the Crusader episode where the Army used members to unsuccessfully defend the program (Interview c 2010).

To further push the cause of transformation, Rumsfeld opened the Office of Force Transformation, headed by Admiral Art Cebrowski, a naval aviator close to Admiral Owens and former Secretary Perry. Within the Office they pushed Cebrowski's view of network centric warfare, essentially a operational concept employing Perry and Owens RMA as a systems of systems. Work from the office was quickly picked up and altered by the Navy to produce a series of innovated designs like the Littoral Combat Ship (LCS) and a number of wide ranging organizational initiatives dealing with personnel issues, logistics, and business processes (Interview i 2010).

Revisiting the underlying propositions of a programmatic actor orientation, one should find major defense debates like RMA are not reducible to exogenous shocks or bureaucratic politics. They should be partially explained by small groups that form around particular ideas and advocate for them, movements within governments whose search for legitimate authority influences the policy formation process. In terms of organization, while there was a small group that cut across standard bureaucratic lines it was much more fluid and heterogeneous than previous studies of healthcare policy. The RMA program tended to draw on external academics, small groups in the defense department, and members of individual services.

In terms of organization, in the 1970s Wohlstetter connected with a small cohort of defense intellectuals and bureaucrats through DARPA laying the ground work for the near-zero miss and later RMA program. The group was relative small, but more heterogeneous than the expected value. Beyond defense bureaucrats, academics and think tanks, not explored here, like RAND were actively brought into the policy framing process. Thus a heterogeneous group was associated with the framing a range of policy options derived from the program including increased interest in cruise missiles and experiments with precision weapons like operation Assault Breaker (Interview a 2011).

In fact, organizational heterogeneity continued to be a defining feature in the 1980s and 1990s. In the 1980s, the organization of the program remained more homogenous than one would anticipate with external actors still playing a predominant role as seen in the "Discriminate Deterrence" project. Of interest is the emergence of two nodes within the program: the Wohlstetter network compromising his students and their affiliates in government and the ONA network, or "St. Andrew's Prep" as it is still called by its alumni (Interview f 2010). In the 1990s, the programmatic network involved senior service members like General Sullivan as well as members of the Joint Chiefs of Staff and external contractors like SAIC where ONA alumni worked. Here the results again seem to challenge the homogeneity premise that small coherent groups should be better able to push their agenda. Broader programmatic networks were associated with increased policy formation in the 1990s and 1970s.

After 2000, the group is less heterogonous owing to the way in which RMA shifted from a planning tool to a real debate that involved significant program cuts and cancelations. Battle lines were drawn thus increasing the extent to which the RMA crowd was predominantly located inside OSD and, not explored here, the Navy. The homogenous group, led by now seasoned RMA acolytes who were presidential appointees and long-time ONA veterans, pushed for the widest ranging changes to date including challenging the PPBS process and individual service POMs. Yet the increased volume and severity of the policy options led to other organizations consolidating along service lines with the CJCS and Congress providing further top cover.

Organization, the degree to which a group is homogenous or heterogonous in terms of its membership was not related to the number of policy options generated. In fact, to the contrary in two of the episodes that saw significant policy options generated, the groups were diverse and included a wide range of members.

In terms of capacity, all episodes demonstrated a group of like-minded actors who had access to the policy process. In the 1970s, defense officials had direct access but it was confined to DARPA type experiments and not associated in any meaningful way with service POMs or the larger PPBS process. Here the initial assumption is challenged. Low capacity programmatic actors can generate not only a large array of policy options, but policy outcomes if they target small, disruptive reforms that can later be drawn on by services or the OSD. In the 1990s, the RMA program reached its zenith producing a number of new requirements and procurement concepts. Of note, is the way actors leveraged existing bureaucratic mechanisms, specifically the joint mandated JROC and joint doctrine to push for greater systems integration. After 2000, capacity was highest and the resulting degree of policy formulation increased. That said, it resulted in failure given the stark opposition it generated.

Last, in terms of resonance, the degree to which the program was referenced and actors' career trajectories were impacted, there was corresponding evidence in each episode. In the 1970s, the emergence of near-zero miss generated increased interest in precision that was linked to DARPA programs and working groups. Individuals associated with the programmatic frames early on like the students of Wohlstetter, ONA, and William Perry continued to resurface in each subsequent decade. In the 1990s, the peak of the RMA, the frame took at interesting turn. After 1996, individual services began to claim they were modernizing under the label RMA, as a means of justifying existing procurement timelines and plans. One participant lamented being turned away from every flag officer of the services with the claim, "yeah we are doing the RMA thing" (Interview a 2010). This dynamic indicates an interesting tipping point. Once a programmatic frame becomes omnipresent, it is used as a justification for diverging strategies, and all encompassing but empty mantras of change. In the case of the Army, an early champion of the RMA, it even began to define a separate reform trajectory, transformation, that focused on building an interim, deployable force under General Shinseki. That same term, transformation, was adopted by Rumsfeld as they sought to realign not just procurement but organizational practices to bring about the original programmatic frame, an RMA that dictated trading force structure for technological improvements, disruptive planning processes for established bureaucratic practices like the PPBS and POM systems. This observation relates to the articulation mechanism: it is not only boundary activation that occurs, but definitional slippage and yoking as actors re-appropriate terms and concepts to justify their standing bureaucratic practices.

In terms of the two proposed mechanisms, a wide range of socialization forums and conflicting articulation practices define the programmatic actors. From documents that discuss "infecting officers with the RMA virus" to the wide range of bureaucratic forum that were sought out, mobilization is a key practice in advancing programmatic content. Of interest was the importance of commissions, workshops, panels, and war-games. The ONA proved masterful in punching above its weight. An extremely small office, its careful selection of war-game topics, attendees, and contractors to facilitate the process provided critical sites of socialization in which OSD could connect with individual services like the Army during the dominant maneuver experiments without significantly altering budgets or challenging turf. As seen in the paragraph above, articulation indeed reinforces programmatic resonance but only to a point; eventually either the boundaries are deep enough to cause existing bureaucratic cleavages to be drawn or the term is fashionable enough that everyone uses it thus stripping it of meaning.

Considered with respect to counterfactual analysis, a means of drawing out the logic of the pathway case, the RMA required programmatic actors. Put another way, *no Wohlstetter network or ONA, no revolution.* Individual agents, organized around the idea of precisions, offsetting, and organizational change and generated policy options that cannot be reduced to bureaucratic interest alone. In fact, what stands out is the fact that the major periods of success, the 1970s and 1990s were periods of declining budgets. On the surface this could signal that the RMA was nothing but a tool for DOD or the individual services to justify turf and resource allocation. Yet, such a claim misses a central aspect of the RMA: it was continually used as a justification for altering budget structure and reducing the size of the defense department, especially in Secretary Perry's vision.

Conclusion

This paper explored the extent to which a programmatic actor model, a policy analysis heuristic developed to account for policy change in stable institutional settings, can be applied to the U.S. defense sector. RMA, as a pathway, crucial case was selected to examine the analytical utility of the framework. The initial evidence points to a promising research agenda that requires further study of both the U.S. case and the defense sector in general.

First, the results need to be subject to further clarification, with additional interviews and declassified documents used to scrutinize how and if policy options formulated can be linked to a hypothetical programmatic actor network. Second, other defense bureaucracies need to be analyzed to see how and if the model can explain policy formulation in other military institutions. For example, what policy networks came together as the idea diffused in different cultural and institutional settings in other major military powers like Russia, China, and Israel?

What the exploration does highlight is the central role of ideas in defense planning. Core assumptions actors invoke about future warfare and prevailing theories of victory have a unique causal logic not reducible to standard models of bureaucratic competition or most constructivist accounts. There are, in fact, epistemic defense communities, that cut across organizational stovepipes as the military professional and bureaucrat articulate new programs. These programs are not reducible to structural definitions of culture as a variable. Rather, they are relational and enacted as actors negotiate the meaning of future war and new theories of victory. This suggests an important new research area focusing on the politics of defense planning, the subject of this special issue, as it relates to the military profession and competing discourses inside defense organizations.

Notes

1. For the definitive look at Andrew Marshall and the Office of Net Assessment he founded, from both an organizational and intellectual historical perspective, see Krepenvich and Watts (2015).
2. This line of inquiry can be seen as embodying a policy window type approach in which exogenous shocks produce the possibility of change in otherwise rigid, hierarchical institutions. On the concept of institutional evolution and punctuated equilibrium, see True et al. (1999), Thelen (2003, 2004), and Thelen and Steinmo (1992).
3. In academic circles the publication of a special issue in the *Journal of Strategic Studies* and the release of Dima Adamsky's book on the RMA and strategic culture illustrates there has been renewed interest in the RMA that tends to focus on the subject as a function of cultural antecedents (Adamsky and Bjerga 2010).
4. For an account of the policy process based on institutional rational choice, see Ostrom (1990), Ostrom et al. (1994), Eggertsson (1990), and Moe (1984), (Moe 1990). With respect to incentives inside bureaucracies, see Tullock (1965) and Niskanen (1971).
5. The emphasis on agents advancing ideas finds parallels in Stephen Rosen's earlier work on military innovation and the central role played by career progression in determining whether or not reformists produced lasting institutional change (Rosen 1988, 1991).
6. On the practice turn, see Bueger and Gadinger (2014, 5) and Pouliot (2008).
7. This criteria is drawn from earlier studies by Hassenteufel et al. (2010).
8. For similar definitions of mechanisms, see McAdam, Tarrow and Tilly (2001). There is a wide range of definitions as to what causal mechanisms are and in turn what they can explain. James Mahoney has identified over twenty different definitions. This work draws on Charles Tilly's characterization. For competing definitions, see Schelling (1978), Elster (1989), Coleman (1990), Stinchcombe (1991), Hedström and Swedberg (1998), and George and Bennett (2005). Most definitions deal with the bridging effect of mechanisms, the linking of cause to effect. Where they often depart is the extent to which some accounts preface a cognitive and hence rational choice based account of mechanisms (Schelling 1978, Elster 1989, Bates et al. 1998, Hedström and Swedberg 1998). Tilly also discusses this move in outlining cognitive mechanisms (Tilly 2001, 24).

9. On the concept of social boundaries in sociology, see McAdams *et al.* (2001), Tilly (2001), Tilly (2002), Tilly (2003), and Tilly (2005).
10. This implies a use of counterfactual analysis derived from Weber and the concept of ideal-types. On counterfactuals, see Fearon (1991). Note that in his assessment, counterfactuals are an applicable check on validity as long as they analyze conditions vs. strict causation and that the counterfactual claim is "contenable" with initial facts and conditions (Fearon 1991, 190–191).
11. Accessed from the archive at www.rumsfeld.com.

Disclosure statement

No potential conflict of interest was reported by the author.

Funding

This work was supported by the Centre national de la recherche scientifique [ANR-08-BLAN-0032].

References

Adamsky, D. and Bjerga, K.I., 2010. Introduction to the information-technology revolution in military affairs. *Journal of strategic studies*, 33 (4), 463–468. doi:10.1080/01402390.2010.489700

Bates, R., et al., 1998. *Analytical narratives*. Princeton: Princeton University Press.

Blaker, J.R. and Manning, R.A., 1997. *Understanding the revolution in military affairs: A guide to America's 21st century defense*. Washington, DC: Progressive Policy Institute, defense working paper no. 3.

Breitenbauch, H., and Jakobsson, A. K., 2018. Defence planning as strategic fact: introduction. *Defence studies*, 18 (3), 253–261.

Bueger, C. and Gadinger, F., 2014. *International practice theory: new perspectives*. New York: Palgrave Macmillan.

Coleman, J., 1990. *Foundations of social theory*. Cambridge: Harvard University Press.

Eggertsson, T., 1990. *Economic behavior and institutions*. New York: Cambridge University Press.

Elster, J., 1989. *Nuts and bolts for the social sciences*. Cambridge: Cambridge University Press.

Emirbayer, M., 1997. Manifesto of relational sociology. *American journal of sociology*, 103, 281–317. doi:10.1086/231209

Fearon, J.D., 1991. Counterfactuals and hypothesis testing in political science. *World politics*, 43, 169–196. doi:10.2307/2010470

Genieys, W., 2010. *The new custodians of the state: programmatic elite in French society*. New York, New Brunswick: Transactions Publishers.

Genieys, W. and Smyrl, M., 2008a. Inside the autonomous state: programmatic elites in the reform of french health policy. *Governance*, 21 (1), 75–93. doi:10.1111/gove.2008.21.issue-1

Genieys, W. and Smyrl, M., 2008b. *Elites, ideas, and the evolution of public policy*. New York: Palgrave MacMillan.

George, A.L. and Bennett, A., 2005. *Case studies and theory development in the social sciences*. Cambridge: MIT Press.

Goffman, E., 1974. *Frame analysis: an essay on the organization of experience*. Boston: Northeastern University Press.
Hassenteufel, P., et al., 1999. *L'emergence d'une "elite du Welfare"? Sociologie des sommets de l'Etat en interaction. Le cas des politiques de protection maladie et en matiere de prestations familias*. Paris: M.I.R.E.
Hassenteufel, P., et al., 2010. Programmatic actors and the transformation of European health care states. *Journal of health politics, policy, and law*, 35 (4), 1–19. doi:10.1215/03616878-2010-015
Hedström, P. and Swedberg, R., eds., 1998. *Social mechanisms: an analytical approach to social theory*. Cambridge: Cambridge University Press.
Ikle, F. and Wohlstetter, A., 1988. *Discriminate deterrence*. Washington, DC: Commission on Integrated Long-Term Strategy.
Interview a. 2010. Appointed OSD Official, 5 May.
Interview a. 2011. Appointed OSD Official, 17 January.
Interview b. 2010. OSD Official, 5 May.
Interview b. 2010. Former General Officer, 18 February.
Interview c. 2010. Appointed OSD Official, 13 May.
Interview c. 2010. Former Appointed Department of the Air Force, 24 February.
Interview d. 2010. Appoint OSD Official, 15 May.
Interview f. 2010. Former Senior Officer Serving in OSD, 29 May.
Interview g. 2010. Former General Officer, 22 June.
Interview h. 2010. Former OSD Official, 7 October.
Interview i. 2010. Appointed OSD Official, 2 December.
Jackson, P.T. and Nexon, D.H., 1999. Relations before states: substance, process and the study of world politics. *European journal of international relations*, 5 (3), 291–332. doi:10.1177/1354066199005003002
Jensen, B., 2016a. Escaping the iron cage: the institutional foundations of FM 3-24, counter-insurgency doctrine. *Journal of strategic studies*, 39 (2), 213–230. doi:10.1080/01402390.2015.1115038
Jensen, B., 2016b. *Forging the sword: doctrinal change in the U.S. army*. Pal Alto: Stanford University Press.
Joana, J. and Smith, A., 2006. Changing French military procurement policy: the State, industry, and 'Europe' in the Case of the A400M. *West European politics*, 29 (1), 70–89. doi:10.1080/01402380500389257
Khalilzad, Z., ed., 1996. *Strategic Appraisal 1996*. Washington, DC: RAND Corporation, Project Air Force.
Kingdon, J., 1984. *Agendas, alternatives, and public policy*. New York: Harper Collins Publisher.
Krepenvich, A. and Watts, B., 2015. *The last warrior: Andrew Marshall and the shaping of modern American defense strategy*. New York: Basic Books.
Lomov, C. and Gen, N.A., ed., 1973. *Scientific-technical progress and the revolution in military affairs*. Moscow: Translated by the USAF.
McAdams, D., Tarrow, S., and Tilly, C., 2001. *Dynamics of contention*. New York: Cambridge University Press.
Moe, T., 1984. The new economics of organization. *American journal of political science*, 28, 4. doi:10.2307/2110997
Moe, T., 1990. Political institutions: the neglected side of the story. *Journal of law, economics, and organization*, 6, 213–253. doi:10.1093/jleo/6.special_issue.213
Niskanen, W., 1971. *Bureaucracy and representative government*. Cambridge: Harvard University Press.
Ostrom, E., 1990. *Governing the commons*. New York: Cambridge University Press.
Ostrom, E., Walker, J., and Gardner, R., 1994. *Rules, games, and common-pool resources*. Ann Arbor: University of Michigan Press.
Owens, W.A., 2001. *Lifting the fog of war*. Baltimore: John Hopkins University Press.
Paolucci, P.A. 1975. *Summary report of the Long Range Research and Development Planning Program (LRRDP)*. Falls Church: Lulejian & Associates, Declassified 1983.

Pouliot, V., 2008. The logic of practicality: a theory of practice of security communities. *International organization*, 62 (2), 257–288. doi:10.1017/S0020818308080090

Rosen, S.P., 1988. New ways of war. *International security*, 13 (1), 134–168. doi:10.2307/2538898

Rosen, S.P., 1991. *Winning the next war: innovation and the modern military*. Ithaca: Cornell University Press.

Sabatier, P. and Jenkins-Smith, H., 2007. The advocacy coalition framework: an assessment. *In*: P. Sabatier, ed. *Theories of the policy process*. Boulder, CO: Westview Press.

Schelling, T.C., 1978. *Micromotives and macrobehavior*. New York: Norton.

Stinchcombe, A.L., 1991. The conditions of fruitfulness of theorizing about mechanisms in the social sciences. *The philosophy and social science*, 21 (36), 367–388. doi:10.1177/004839319102100305

Thelen, K., 2003. How institutions evolve. *In*: J. Mahoney and D. Rueschemeyer, eds. *Comparative historical analysis in the social sciences*. Cambridge: Cambridge University Press, 208–240.

Thelen, K., 2004. *How institutions evolve: the political economy of skills in Germany, Britain, the United States, and Japan*. New York: Cambridge.

Thelen, K. and Steinmo, S., 1992. *Structuring politics: historical institutionalism in comparative politics*. Cambridge: Cambridge University Press.

Tilly, C., 2001. Mechanisms in political processes. *Annual review of political science*, 4, 21–41. doi:10.1146/annurev.polisci.4.1.21

Tilly, C., 2002. *Stories identities, and political change*. Lanham, MD: Rowan and Littlefield.

Tilly, C., 2003. *Politics of collective*. Cambridge: Cambridge University Press.

Tilly, C., 2005. *Identities, boundaries, and social ties*. Boulder: Paradigm Press.

Toffler, A., 1984a. *Future shock*. New York: Bantam.

Toffler, A., 1984b. *The third wave*. New York: Bantam.

Toffler, A., 1991. *Powershift: knowledge, wealth, and violence at the edge of the 21st century*. New York: Bantam.

True, J., Jones, B., and Baumgartner, F., 1999. Punctuated equilibrium theory. Explaining stability and change in American policy making. *In*: P. Sabatier, ed. *Theories of the policy process*. Boulder, CO: Westview Press, 97–115.

Tsbelis, G., 2002. *Veto players: how political institutions work*. Princeton, NJ: Princeton University Press.

Tullock, G., 1965. *The politics of bureaucracy*. Washington, DC: Public Affairs Press.

Van Creveld, M., 1989. *Technology and war: from 2000 B.C. to the present*. New York: Free Press.

Van Creveld, M., 1991. *The transformation of war*. New York: Free Press.

Watts, B.D., 2007. *Six decades of guided munitions and battle networks: progress and prospects*. Washington, DC: Center for Strategic and Budgetary Assessments.

Wilson, J.Q., 1966. Innovation in organizations: notes toward a theory. *In*: J.D. Thompson, ed. *Approaches to organizational design pittsburgh*. Pittsburgh: University of Pittsburgh Press.

The US perspective on future war: why the US relies upon Ares rather than Athena

Jan Angstrom

ABSTRACT
This article addresses why the US in its military operations tends to focus on only one dimension in war – the military narrowly understood. More precisely, in the US case, its armed forces tend to be preoccupied with platforms and understand military capabilities as those that deliver death and destruction. I explain this one-sided understanding of the military dimension in war with how the US armed forces think about future war. How the US understands future war is, in turn, a reflection of how it organizes its long-term defense planning procedures. In particular, by approaching the concept of future as by and large structurally determined, a focus on platforms becomes natural. Investments in weapons systems, too, are more easily motivated to Congress since it is easier to attach a price to developing, for example, a new submarine than it is to attach a price to the cost of developing a military organization that is adaptive, learning and anticipating. The understanding of the future as something that happens whether you like it or not is particularly odd in the US context where of course a central tenet of the American dream is that the individual creates her own future.

Introduction

In his monumental book *Strategy*, Sir Lawrence Freedman (2013, pp. 22–41) reminds us that Greek mythology recognized that in war there is a tension between cunning and raw, brute force. *Mētis* was *Zeus'* first wife and the goddess of planning and anticipation. Early on in their marriage, *Zeus* realized that if *Mētis* ever gave birth to a son that combined the strength and power of *Zeus* and the guile and intelligence of *Mētis*, the son would be a great threat to *Zeus* and his leadership of the gods. Fearing to be ousted, *Zeus* killed *Mētis* and ate her. *Mētis*, however, had predicted this and was already pregnant. Later, *Zeus* had the rather unforgettable experience of giving birth to his daughter through his head. *Pallas Athena* – goddess of wisdom and war – was born. Later on, *Zeus* and his second wife, *Hera*, had a son – *Ares*. *Athena's* brother was also the god of war, but also the god of violence and rage. In Greek mythology, thus, war was understood to have two faces: one controlled, planned, reasoned, and calculated as well as one violent, uncontrolled, and hell-bent on death and destruction.

The dichotomy of war as symbolized by Athena and Ares is also a useful tool with which to approach current strategic affairs. In their pursuit of political ends, all states need to balance their strategy between restraint and unleashing large-scale violence as well as between the short-term use of force and the long-term creation and organization of military forces. Occasionally, however, states get this balance wrong. They develop military equipment that end up not being used the way they were intended, or the worst case, that end up being redundant. Indeed, sometimes they even use force in way that is counter-productive to the political ends that violence ought to serve. These are, arguably, the key concerns for strategists. Despite their best intentions and despite a wealth of documents proclaiming to be strategic that strategists dwell upon and carefully design, however, the balance end up being flawed. The question is why? What explains why states struggle with this balancing act?

In this article, I address this puzzle through a theory developing case study of US defense planning 2001–2016, i.e. the George W. Bush and Barack Obama presidencies. Although the problems face strategists everywhere, the post-Cold War US case is of special interest for mainly two reasons. First, during the period the US military supremacy was unparalleled at least since the birth of the modern state system. If the US with its global reach and superior military capabilities still face balancing difficulties, it is safe to assume that the problems is more acute in other states. Second, not least due to its dominance, the US is also a role model for other democratic states within a worldwide set of alliances and collaborative partnerships and its system of defense planning may therefore spread to others (e.g. Durell-Young 2018).

Many recent studies have concluded that the US tends to prioritize Ares rather than Athena. John Stone demonstrates that the US in all its might almost exclusively has focused on developing capabilities to further its "technique of war", rather than stressing how military means and methods can reach political ends. As such, Stone (2011) suggests that by focusing too much on the death and destruction in war, the US forgets the critical part of aligning military means with political ends. Colin Gray (2005, pp. 200–201) argues that US armed forces confuses military with strategic success, combat with war, and war for its own sake with war for a better peace. Antulio Echevarria (2004, 2014) reaches similar conclusions stressing that the US has a very distinct limited idea of "way of battle", rather than "way of war". Emile Simpson (2012), too, attributes US failure in Afghanistan to the US pre-occupation with seeking decisive military action and its military's attempt to uphold a sharp demarcation between military and political. Benjamin Buley (2008), finally, recognizes that there were attempts to align political and military goals during the Bush administration, but they proved to underestimate how deeply engrained the US strategic leadership was with the norms of war as a military undertaking. Even US military foreign basing – surely a sign of long-term planning – David Vine (2015) argues are developed first and foremost to serve as launch-pads for kinetic measures, long before any political aims of such use of force is developed.

Unfortunately, although many have criticized the US effort (e.g. Gray 2005, Ricks 2006, Hanley 2008, O'Hanlon 2009, Betts 2011), few have tried to explain the US problems of balancing its short-term use of force and its long-term defense planning. Some answers have been put forward. Hitherto, however, they suffer from various shortcomings. One answer is blunt and very obvious. It is precisely because the US is the world's most powerful state that it can ignore guile and anticipation and instead – by relying upon force – try to shape a system in which force decides outcomes. If the US can convince the world to play the game according to its rules, it will always end up on top. Consider David and Goliath. Goliath surely would like to continue to wage war in a way that enhances his strengths and not rely upon guile, deception, and new means and methods of war, which is difficult to plan for. David, meanwhile, needed to use guile, anticipation, and even some unorthodox means to bring Goliath down. We can also see this in how Virgil re-wrote the story of the siege of Troy and this time, Ulysses (Odysseys) was the villain, not the hero, since Ulysses was deceitful. (Freedman 2013, pp. 24–25) In the context of then-superpower Rome, it was Achilles that was the hero. Strength was heralded and appreciated, while intelligence to anticipate and plan was understood nearly as cheating and less honorable. Hence, by planning for, and reinforcing, that war is about the exchange of kinetic energy, the US is trying to shape the rest of the world in its mold. This would certainly imply a very significant master plan worthy of Athena herself. The problem with this explanation, however, is that it presupposes a conspiratorial mastermind somewhere in the US administration with the power to suppress talk of such a plan.

Another way to explain the seeming US failure to achieve long-term strategic success is that the process by which the US evaluates its military operations is flawed. According to this explanation, the strategic planning process feeds the decision-makers with the wrong kind of information and thus produces flawed decisions. (Brooks 2008) However, this would imply that all US wars would fail and since this is not the case, this explanation fails to account for variation in strategic outcome. Brennan and Kelly (2009) also suggest that US strategic procedures are to blame. In particular, they suggest that theorizing about conventional war gradually became routinized to a degree where Western planners forgot about the politics of war, instead focusing only on the fixed perceived enemy, the Soviet Union. The Cold War strait jacket thus made war militarized and in the mold of Ares. This latter explanation, however, does not take into account that the US seems to have understood war similarly before the Cold War. For example, Weighley (1973, cf. Sondhaus 2006) depicts the US military as relying upon overwhelming firepower, mass and technology stretching back to the Civil War.

By contrast and in similar fashion to Robert Egnell (2009) and Risa Brooks (2008), I draw upon how politics and military affairs are institutionalized. While they used a framework from civil-military relations theory to advance an explanation of, among others, the US behavior in the post-combat phase of wars, my empirical focus is rather ideational and more specifically on how military organizations consider the future and, in particular, the future of war and warfare. The sub-field civil-military relations usually stresses democratic control of the military and regularly approach the military organization from the perspective of distinct analytical categories of civilian and military (e.g. Feaver and Kohn 2001, Bruneau and Matei 2013). Instead of focusing on these two categories, I develop an original explanation that focuses specifically on how the state organizes and institutionalizes its long-term defense planning procedures. Occasionally, this coincides with the literature on the so-called civilian-military gap, but only rarely and by stressing planning procedures and how planning is organized, one avoids the sometimes heated and normatively laden civil-military divide.

My claim, in short, is that the way we organize our long-term planning procedures determines how we understand the concept of "future". This, in turn, determines the contents of our predictions on future war and the image of future war that we hold. Ideas do not exist and operate independently, though. As Jensen (2018) show they can be made important by epistemic communities within strategic elites. In addition, I suggest that ideas become important when they are institutionalized in decision-making processes. Ideas of future war are important since *how* we conceive of future war influences how we organize military forces, the capabilities that we develop and the ways in which we come to fight wars (Freedman 2017). Failure to align military means with political ends in for example Iraq, therefore, results from how long-term defense planning is organized. I develop this theoretical claim through a case study of US defense planning 2001–2016, i.e. the George W. Bush and Barack Obama presidencies. Case specific, by organizing long-term defense planning in an essentially apolitical process, the US understands future war as a narrowly military – a bureaucratic – undertaking rather than a political one. By not aligning politics and the image of future war, the US planning procedures and the resulting image of future war creates and continuously re-creates an understanding of the future as something that will happen regardless of our own actions. The future happens – whether you like it or not. This future, moreover, will consist of war in the shape of Ares – a military duel – since the planning process is essentially apolitical. The image of future war that follows is war without politics. War as rage, death and destruction. War in the shape of Ares.

By contrast, one could easily fathom planning systems and conceptions of the future that allow for agency in the process of creating the future in a dynamic interplay with other actors. A system in which, as Freedman (2013, p. *xi*) puts it, strategy "is fluid and flexible, governed by the starting point and not the end point". In the latter sense, the course of the future is dependent upon your actions as much as on those of others. Such a system would instead need to predict a much more active role of the subject in creating the future, but it would also entail a much clearer need to stress a political agency involved in war. Athena would be present.

The article not only contributes to the literature on US use of force, but also to the more narrow literature on defense planning. Typically, this literature attributes greatest explanatory power to the inherent problem of planning and developing military capabilities for an unknown future. Hence, it is not puzzling at all that some weapons systems are developed to counter what turns out to be a redundant threat. Defense planning, as Colin Gray (2014a, pp. 1–4) explains, is about meeting the challenge of uncertainty and its central dilemma is to prepare for a situation for which there is no knowledge, only estimates, predictions and, ultimately, guesses. (cf. Krepinevich 2010, Davis 2012) Those that still approach flaws in defense planning as puzzling usually focus on defense planning as a process. Due to the complexities of planning and manning a future military force, it usually entails several, only partly overlapping processes. Following the focus on processes of defense planning (e.g. Durell-Young 2018; Tama 2018; Davis 2012; Christiansson 2018), the argument advanced here stresses that it is the way we organize the defense planning that explains certain flawed outcomes. Admittedly, the literature recognizes that defense planning is political and that in especially in competitive political systems, defense planning issues can be politicized and highly conflictual (Gray 2014a, pp. 141–142). My argument, however, stresses that the US in its organization of defense planning processes reduces the impact of politics, thus putting Ares in front of Athena. This particular way of organization reveals two deep-seated ideational structures in the US democratic system: the Weberian ideal of a apolitical, rational bureaucracy and the basic division of legislative and executive powers.

It is important to recognize that the dichotomy of Ares and Athena is not synonymous with positivist and post-positivist, critical approaches to war and warfare. This latter larger epistemological and ontological debate has of lately become a centerpiece also in the study of war with the emergence of an entire field defining itself and positioning itself against traditional positivist strategic analysis. (e.g. Bousquet 2009, Barkawi 2011, Barkawi and Brighton 2011, Holmqvist 2014, Nordin and Oberg 2015) Typically, many (e.g. Paparone 2012, Zweibelson 2015) encourage the military to become more explicitly reflexive in its doctrines and in its education. Arguing in favor of the return of Athena in the US understanding of war, however, is not necessarily the same thing as calling for greater reflexivity. Planning, anticipation, and deception after all are all anchored also in rationalism. Indeed, one could even argue that rationalism is underpinned by the idea that predictions are possible.

The article proceeds as follows. I will first outline the causal story of the theory to explain exactly how a particular planning process will lead to a particular vision of the future. Second, I will provide empirical evidence of US planning procedures and demonstrate how a particular apolitical planning process leads to visions of future war in which there is a lack of political agency and one that stresses the technique of war.

Why planning procedures and decision-making procedures are important in creating a vision of war

In this section I develop the causal story explaining why and how planning procedures generate visions of future war. The logic draws upon how ideas become embedded in bureaucratic procedures that, in turn, determines how we approach future war. As such, the procedures produce certain documents that reinforce a particular understanding of the future, which leads to a particular vision of future war. More specifically, four institutional conditions are more likely to produce a representation of future war as apolitical: (1) separation of the power to wage war from the power to create, fund and organize military capabilities, (2) a separation of the processes for long-term planning, military acquisition, and the formulation of political ends, (3) a representation of future war as a narrowly understood military undertaking, and (4) a representation of the future as deterministic and without agency. Following among others Holsti (2004, pp. 18–27), I understand both formal decision-making structures as well as repeated patterns of practices and shared norms as "institutions".

First, separation of the power to wage war from the power to create, fund and organize military capabilities will encourage an understanding of apolitical war since the two key strategic processes are divorced from each other. Waging war will be understood as separate from creating and funding war, thus making the actor that wages war fight the war for different reasons and with different aims than the ones held by the actor that created the military capabilities. In turn, the actor creating military capabilities will not know of the future reasons to wage war thus making political ends less important in deciding exactly what military capabilities to develop. This separation of political ends creates a situation in which the politics of war does not come to the forefront. By contrast, parliamentarian political systems in which government controls all of these processes, politics can permeate both the creation of, and use of, force. In legal-technical terms, of course, even in parliamentary systems, it is the parliament rather than the executive branch that allocates the budget, but since the government consists of the parliamentary majority, the government can to a higher extent than in systems with separation of powers focus on the same political end.

Second, a separation of the processes for long-term planning, military acquisition, and the formulation of political ends will encourage an understanding of apolitical war since the future is planned without being connected to political ends and since the acquisition of military capabilities is done without a connection to the formulation of politics. There is a claim to be made that the separation of powers is especially acute in democracies. In democracies, the government is usually understood to be accountable to their voters in free and fair elections, while its bureaucracy is understood to be apolitical. When it comes to developing military capabilities, this accountability can be problematic since military hardware takes long time to develop. Strike fighters, for example, can see action for several decades which means that four-year elections cycles may not always have an impact. The long-term political context is impossible to predict and therefore one relies upon the default position of building platforms. Again, this is, however, not the case by definition. You can make institutional solutions that try to accommodate these challenges. For example, it is possible to integrate long-term planning with political ends and allow these to guide military acquisition.

Third, a representation of future war as a narrowly understood military undertaking encourages apolitical war since the representation of the future guides us in shaping that very future. As a structural condition, this factor very much works self-propelling, i.e. once in place, an understanding of future war as military, fosters and reinforces an understanding of war as apolitical. The main determinant of our understanding of the future is how we plan for it. In this case: the future of war is influenced by current long-term defense planning. Harry Yarger (2008, p. 52) suggests that "planning makes strategy actionable. It relies on a high degree of certainty – a world that is concrete and can be addressed in explicit terms. In essence, it takes a grey world and makes it black and white." We plan, therefore, to "reduce uncertainty". The world does not become more certain because of it, but it appears under control. As Hanley (2008, p. 1) suggests "War plans determine whom we fight, how we fight, where and under what provocation we fight – and to a large extent the peace that follows." The point, in short, is that if we imagine future war in a particular way, we will develop military capabilities that enable us to fight war in the way we imagine the future war. By developing these capabilities, however, we make this particular version of future war possible. As Freedman (2017) shows, ideas of future war as determined by decisive battles historically promoted standing armies. If we would have conceived of future war in a different way, then a different version of future would be more likely. Indeed, in order to develop capabilities for future war, the acquisition process will increase in pace. In order to develop systems for the future, you also inadvertently shorten the technical life span of the systems. This means that new projects need to be developed and thus military research and development will increase the pace of technological development (Buzan 1987, p. 96). Hence, an institutionalized representation of future war as military will stress the means of warfare, rather than the strategic, political dynamics of war.

Finally, a representation of the future as deterministic and without agency encourages apolitical war since it does not encourage the formulation of political ends that can permeate the conduct of war. If war happens regardless of what we do then producing the military capabilities ready to meet military challenges is logical behavior. When institutionalizing apolitical procedures where agency is not involved, we will automatically favor interpretations of the future reinforcing Ares in future war. Since we do not know the political context (since we do not plan it or take into consideration what we want), we end up stressing the means of war. The procedure sets the boundaries for our conception of the future, thus also setting the boundaries of how we consider future war. It is important to recognize that this does not mean that the future is fixed. It can vary to a high degree, but the actor understands thinks of the future as determined by others – be they structural factors or other powers. Conceiving of the future as deterministic, however, is not necessarily the only way to understand the future. The idea of the future was discovered during the Enlightenment almost by accident. When history was invented as an intellectual undertaking of not just re-telling the past but explaining it, it also became possible to explain past events through human agency. This leap of mind also implied that mankind could alter the future. When the idea of a non-cyclical, non-determinist history entered our minds, we could also start to think about the future as non-determined. We could influence its course. The enlightenment idea that mankind can intentionally shape the future through reason, knowledge and industry thus entered our understanding of the future. (Gaddis 2004, Giddens 1991, cf. Kuosa 2011, Holman 2001) In short, Athena was re-discovered.

Taken together, these four conditions create actors that are more or less "strategic illiterates".[1] They conceive of war as a narrow military business, conflating war with combat, thus waging war as Ares would. In the long run, it means actors that cannot use the necessary moderation and control of the use of force in order to guide the conduct of war to political ends. It is also important to recognize that variation is possible even in the US case. Admittedly, the US constitution with its strong division of powers is to some extent fixed, but the other variables differ. Freedman (2017), for example, shows that there has been great variation in how future war have been conceived of throughout history.

Research design and analytical tool

Intentionally, I approach the theory from the perspective of identifying conditions, rather than to try to treat them as separate independent variables. It is too early and it would require a different research design, if the ambition were to test these factors in order to identify the explanatory power of each of them. Most importantly, it would require a comparative design. However, in this article, I only expand on one case study in order to develop the causal mechanisms. Below I will develop the analytical tool and briefly elaborate on a few methodological issues.

First, as discussed above the four conditions considered in this article are (1) separation of the power to wage war from the power to create, fund and organize military capabilities, (2) a separation of the processes for long-term planning, military acquisition, and the formulation of political ends, (3) a representation of future war as a narrowly understood military undertaking, and (4) a representation of the future as deterministic and without agency. All of these conditions, as seen in Table 1, can be interpreted at least in binary terms, i. e. there are at least two possible outcomes for each of the conditions.

Second, the distribution of power in the decision-making process will be ascertained by an analysis of the formal decision-making procedures. This approach has its weakness considering that it cannot capture informal decision-making processes or the impact of political culture. The approach, however, is not without merits since the formal rules still set the stage for the decision-making.

Third, the representation of future war is ascertained through contents analysis of the key strategic futures documents such as DoD:s *Quadrennial Defense Review*, Joint Chiefs' *Joint Visions* as well as the National Intelligence Council's so-called *Global Trends*. Although there are far more documents that are important in the US defense planning process, these documents, arguably, cover key issues relating to how US strategic elites conceive the future of war. An in-depth reading of these documents thus reveals how the "future" is understood and how this idea shapes the understanding of future war. The *Quadrennial Defense Review* as Tama (2018) outlines in great detail, was issued by the DoD every four years during the Bush and Obama presidencies aiming to present to the Congress, the administration's overall strategy and explain how political ends were met with certain demands of force structure and acquisition plans. As such, the document series was important for the short-term defense planning process, although it should be noted that some long-term modernization and acquisition programs ran almost independently of the QDR since development of significant platforms such as main battle tanks, destroyers or fighters takes longer than four year cycles. Even if there is also planning in the different services, the Joint Chiefs' documents on future war, the so-called *Joint Vision* is an authoritative source for how US armed forces understand and represent future war. The Joint Vision considers the future of war in the 10–20 year future, which means that it both considers war fighting done with current weapons systems, but it also factors in and projects that ongoing development programs are concluded successfully. Finally, the concept of the future will be ascertained through analyzing the long-term planning documents, the so-called *Global Trends* issued every fourth year by the National Intelligence Council (NIC). The Global Trends-series consider the future of war and future threats in the 30-year and beyond future. Hence, in this context, most of the current weapon platforms have been replaced. The role of the document is to provide one basis for the long-term defense programs and defense planning.

Table 1. The analytical tool outlined.

Conditions		
Distribution of power	Separated	Unified
Planning processes	Divided	Integrated
Representation of future war	Means	Ends
Concept of future	Deterministic	Indeterministic
Outcome	Apolitical war of Ares	Political war of Athena

Fourth, considering that this paper consists of an analysis of open-source documents, some words of caution are necessary. It may, for example, be the case that planning procedures are highly politicized and have clear political agendas and premeditated outcomes, but this will not be visible in seemingly apolitical and public processes that are supposed to produce objective threat assessments allowing for rational, unbiased decision-making. Moreover, military acquisition processes can be laden with inter-service rivalries, bureaucratic politics, partisan competition, and influences from defense industries (Builder 1988, McAllister Linn 2007, Mahnken 2008). None of these influences can be expected to be visible in open-source documents. Furthermore, considering that military organizations – as other bureaucracies – mainly are able to do what they have planned for, it creates incentives to be secretive in order not to give rivals too many advantages. In particular, since war according to Athena would rely upon flexibility, moderation, calculation, and deception – rather than raw, brute force – it may be the case that the US will not be open about its powers to deceive (e.g. Gooch and Perlmutter 1982). Finally, due to the so-called civil-military relations gap in the specific US context, it cannot perhaps be expected to be political judgments and political alignment in military open-source documents.

Finally, engaging with representations of future as pathways to the future is not simply about conceiving a certain future, which then emerges out of itself as a self-fulfilling prophecy. When we think of the future, we should think of it as one being created by multiple patterns of agency. The future is created in the present by planning a desired end-state and then back-casting to the present. Here, we can talk, in Holman's (2001) terms, of *prospective* causality. It is by no means certain that a future will develop because it is planned for. The reason, of course, is that other actors also plan for certain futures and provided that resources are scarce, not everyone will be able to reach their preferred outcomes. Defense planning is therefore, as Echevarria (2010) reminds us, fraught with inherent difficulties such as occasionally planning for one war, but getting another. The tale of the supersonic fighter jet F-22 Raptor is notable. Development of the Raptor began in 1981 in response to the then threatening Soviet Union. It was finally operational in 2005 and the only combat missions it has done is against Daesh targets in Syria, anything but the Soviet fighters it was developed to beat.

Case study: US defense planning 2001–2016

In this section, I will demonstrate that the US long-term defense planning procedures follows an essentially apolitical process. By not recognizing, indeed by being prevented from explicitly addressing the US role in the world in the future, the process produces documents that reinforce the image that the future will just happen. The fact that the US in and of itself probably will have an impact on the future is not recognized. Hidden, in this conception of war, of course, are still important political and ethical judgments on the composition of war. War itself does not become apolitical just because one actor describes it as such. But this is at the core of the problem. Because the US does not include agency in its vision of future war, it does not recognize that war is political, and it therefore ignores Athena and focuses only on the military, kinetic dimension of war – Ares. The section is structured according to the four key conditions earlier identified: (1) separation of the power to wage war from the power to create, fund and organize military capabilities, (2) a separation of the processes for long-term planning, military acquisition, and the formulation of political ends, (3) a representation of future war as a narrowly understood military undertaking, and (4) a representation of the future as deterministic and without agency.

Together these four conditions shape defense planning and influence it to lean towards either Athena or Ares. In particular, since the processes work in different temporal dimensions, some platforms that are developed are redundant and some threats never materialize, while others, unforeseen, occur. Due to the complexities and multitude of actors involved, defense planning could be understood as a battle of the future, rather than developing the means for future battle.

The separation of the power to wage war from the power to create forces

In the US case, there is a strong separation of powers between the actor waging war and the actor with the power to create the armed forces. Indeed, separation of powers is the fundamental principle permeating the entire US constitution. At the federal level, the Presidency is responsible for the conduct of war, while the Congress is responsible for declaring war and financing war.

The US constitution is based on a separation of the executive and legislative branches. The executive, the Presidency, is also commander-in-chief of the armed forces (article 2, section 2) and is thus the body that is entrusted to wage war. The legislative branch, meanwhile, has the power to declare war (article 1, section 8) as well as the budgetary power, i.e. it controls acquisition and defense spending. Although this suggests a seemingly straightforward division of power, there is a vast grey area since the Presidency was afforded the power to wage war without a Congressional declaration of war to repel an immediately impending attack on the US. This pragmatic solution created space of political contention between the Presidency and the Congress. Where do you, for example, draw the line between a threat against US interests abroad and the constitutional arrangement? Indeed, many presidents have understood this as it does not need Congressional support to wage war abroad, while the Congress has tried to infringe these rights (Hays, Vallance and van Tassell 1997, pp. 73–100).

In 1974, Congress passed the War Powers Act in an attempt to curb Presidential self-proclaimed powers to wage war abroad. Although the President (in this case Richard Nixon) tried to use his veto powers to stop the law, the Congress passed it anyway. Effectively, the War Powers Act has not been a major infringement on Presidential powers, but it requires the Presidency to report to the Congress, within 48 hours of the beginning of hostilities, about the reasons of the use of force. It also stipulates that the President shall consult with Congress before committing troops abroad even if there is no declaration of war. The Act also provides to the Congress the powers to stop ongoing wars. Through the Act, the Congress tried to ensure that it had a say in the use of force even in cases where it did not declare war (Nathan and Oliver 1994, p. 79). There is thus a distinction between the power to wage war and declare war in the US.

Moreover, there is also a separation of powers regarding the power to create forces and organize forces and the power to use force. The Congress has virtually all of the formal powers regarding defense spending and organizing the armed forces. The US armed forces are organized through two major pieces of legislation, the 1947 National Security Act outlining the four services – the Army, the Air Force, the Navy, and the Marine Corps – as well as institutionalizing the National Security Council (NSC) – the body tasked to integrate foreign and defense policies. The next major legislation, the 1986 Goldwater-Nichols Act, institutionalized the Joint Chiefs of Staff and a joint staff at the Pentagon to integrate the services. Hence, it is the Congress that decides upon the organization of the armed forces. Naturally, the executive branch can suggest changes to the Congress, but the decision rests with the Congress. The problem is not only the separation of powers in the strategic process, it is also the fact that such a system promotes a division of interests. Members of the House of Representatives, in particular, are in need of near-constant election campaigning since they are elected bi-annually. This creates pressures to fund projects beneficial for the economy of their constituencies, i.e. platforms and industry employment will be prioritized (Auerswald and Campbell 2017). This logic also makes Congress vulnerable from industry and lobbyists (Warburg 2017).

Meanwhile, the annual budget as well as military procurement is also decided by the Congress, but in practice the executive branch also plays a role. The Department of Defense (DoD) is tasked to regularly update Congress on its spending as well as its future projects spending in both a five-year estimate and the so-called future years defense program. Within the executive branch, the DoD is tasked to develop a budget proposal to the Congress based on the *National Security Strategy* (published by the National Security Agency (NSA)) that usually is signed by the President. Within the DoD, the Joint Chiefs is tasked to develop a *National Military Strategy* that then is operationalized into a Guidance for Development of Force and Joint Programming Guidance that is the key document engaging particular military missions and which begins to translate strategy into capabilities. The four services can then develop force composition and acquisition plans that inform the budget as well as the future years' defense program. (O'Hanlon 2009, Hays *et al.* 1997, pp. 205–233, Hodgson 2010, Gunziger 2013).

Even within the military, there are two separate chains of command for the use of force and the creation of force. The employment and deployment of force is steered through the different theatre commands, while the processes of developing and creating force is implemented by the service chiefs and Defense Planning Guidance. The division of powers regarding the power to wage war, declare war, and finance war effectively means that the Presidency has to wage war with whatever resources the Congress has afforded it. Moreover, the military resources created, will not be related to the executive branch's political aims. There is, thus, in the US case a condition set to favor Ares rather than Athena. War will be understood as apolitical.

The separation of the planning processes

During the Bush and Obama presidencies, there was a strong separation of the key planning processes in war planning. First, the long-term future planning was carried out by the National Intelligence Council, which produced its Global Trends reports to the President every four years. Second, military procurement was decided in interplay between Congress and the Presidency in ten-year plans. Third, the Presidency issued so-called Quadrennial Defense Reviews (QDR:s) together with National Security Strategies to try to outline in the short term how political aims and military means were aligned. Finally, the war planning was done exclusively within the Pentagon and the DoD.

Up until the 1880s, the US military did no serious war planning. Instead, when called upon by Congress or the President volunteers quickly amassed to the armed forces with little or no training (Hanley 2008, p. 3). At the turn of the century, then US secretary of war, Elihu Root influenced by the emergence of General Staffs in Europe and their planning capabilities, introduced operational planning in the US army. Still, this planning was rather undeveloped and heavily permeated by the then US isolationism. For example, even during the First World War, the US planning consisted of two plans where Japan attacked the pacific coastline (Plan Orange) or Germany invaded the US over the Atlantic (Plan Black). (Hanley 2008, pp. 5–6) Clearly, the idea that US forces would go to war abroad was not, apart from the Marine Corps, an obvious option.

With the US engagement in the First World War, this gradually changed and US war planning became gradually more detailed and sought to develop planning for a full range of strategic options. With this as well as the rapid development of the mass army and increased focus on development of gradually increasingly advanced complex military technology planning also became harder to institutionalize in a rational way. War planning gradually became separated in several different strands.

First, operational war planning is conducted by the DoD and the Pentagon, i.e. the armed forces. This planning, as all military operational planning, is challenged by three major uncertainties: from uncertainty of future enemies and allies, uncertainty about the nature of future war, and uncertainty about the timing of the future war. (Imlay and Toft 2006, p. 1, Gray 2010, 2014b) In order to manage these challenges, operational planning consists of method development in planning as well as both generic and more specific future war plans. Crucial for this paper, however, the operational planning is secretive, which means that there are difficulties to ascertain the degree to which politics are allowed to guide the military planning. What we do know from previous US wars such as the Vietnam War or the Second World War is that the operational planning was shaped by developing different scenarios. "Scenarios are stories about how the world changes and how it will be changing at some future time." (Hopkins and Zapata 2001, p. 8) Scenarios are about thinking about different futures without necessarily predicting them. The scenario approach was developed during the mid-1950s among long-term defense planners in the US, in particular to try to identify relevant developments of weapons technology. Using scenarios, however, have the downside that they limit our capability to envision other futures. It can also imply an understanding of the future as something that will just happen regardless of present action. We also know that contemporary operational planning tools rely, at least partly, on a causal, linear logic in which planning and predictions are understood to be constituent parts (Kem 2009, Erdeniz 2016). In this respect, planning serves to create order and focusing on platforms essentially serve the same function as planning. It seemingly reduces uncertainty. It makes an uncertain future appear manageable and thus avoids difficult political issues.

Second, during the Bush and Obama presidencies the short-term strategic planning was guided by the National Security Strategy as well as the QDR:s. (DoD 2001, 2006,

2010, 2014, Flournoy 2001) In 2001, the QDR introduced capabilities-based planning, rather than the traditional threat-based planning (Quester 1992). Regardless, the process was separated from both the more long-term military procurement processes as well as the immediate operational planning processes. Admittedly, the QDR goes to great length to anchor its ideas of the use of force with US interests. It therefore seems clear that the QDR projects future war as clearly political. The problem, however, is that the military means and methods are already set within the four-year process till the next QDR. The means are present and one could, cynically, claim that the main task of the QDR is to find suitable use of an already existing tool box. The problems addressed here are thus still prevalent. The planning procedures are separate and therefore, war in the mold of Ares will permeate the US understanding of future war.

Third, defense spending, furthermore, follows yet another process. Here, the President and Congress agree upon ten-year plans that do not necessarily follow presidential elections. This seemingly undermines an integration of both presidential and congressional visions of US future, but this is to take it a bit too far. In 2016, the Obama administration outlined cut-backs of up to one trillion USD over the coming decade. Much of it is "natural savings" coming from the withdrawal from the wars in Iraq and Afghanistan, but there are also "real" budget cuts that will lower US defense spending. Historically, US defense spending as percentage of GDP is low at around 4.5% in 2016. During the Cold War, it varied between 6 and 10%. These figures are not necessarily a result of lack of political involvement. On the contrary, politics – even intra-service politics – is heavily involved in choosing various long-term military procurement projects (e.g. Karlsson 2002). As explained above, moreover, there is a great deal of interaction between the executive and legislative branches when it comes to defense spending. Rather than a clean – once-every-ten-years' master plan – defense procurement was updated annually.

Although this seems like a way to set up the processes of military acquisition to be continuously in line with the strategic aims of the US, plenty of reports suggests otherwise. The year-to-year updates, for example, creates a situation of funding instability coupled with expectations gaps on the pace of technological development that creates incentives to follow procedure and therefore promotes short-term solutions. (Riposo, McKernan and Duran 2014, McKernan et al. 2015) This incremental decision-making occasionally creates tension between President and Congress, the logic of their respective electoral cycles and has, according to Auerswald (2001), hampered the development of American missile defense programs for decades. Others have also warned that too elaborate planning procedures, in and of themselves, create strong bureaucratic interests that in particular in times of shrinking defense budgets create incentives for inertia and a particular focus on the means of war, platforms, rather than a focus on what political ends that should be met. (Nelson 2001, Meese 2014) The fact remains, though, that the formal powers rest with the body that will not decide the strategy of any future war.

Finally, the long-term defense planning, more specifically, involves forecasting future war in a 20–30 years perspective. Again, upholding the analytical distinction, this process is separate from the operational planning, military procurement as well as the short-term strategy planning. Rather than integrated with the other necessary planning processes, the National Intelligence Council issues quadrennial futures reports that focus on the 20–30 year perspective. Summarizing, the various different necessary war planning procedures are not integrated in the US case. Thus, the condition of separated procedures is upheld and this separation makes it difficult for politics to permeate war.

Representation of future war as a narrowly understood military undertaking

Combined, the separation of constitutional powers and separation of different war planning procedures creates the foundation for the operational war planning to represent the future in a particular way. The US case 2001–2016 is no different. Because the conditions are set in a particular way, the military planners tend to focus on the means of war in their planning. On top of these conditions, the way civil-military relations are understood in the US case, military planners rarely venture outside of the military domain (e.g. Huntington 1957, Nielsen and Snider 2009). In the Joint Chiefs' planning documents future war is represented in the shape of a military undertaking. This sets the conditions for what I referred to as a self-propelling effect, i.e. if we think of future war as a military undertaking dominated by platforms, the likelihood of such a future increases.

From the National Security Strategy of the National Security Council and the QDR, the Joint Chiefs of Staff develops the US National Military Strategy (Lovelace and Durell-Young 2018). The Joint Chiefs also plan for future war in their Joint Visions-documents that are supposed to identify military capabilities for future wars. The documents, Joint Visions 2010 and 2020 respectively, are not totally void of strategic deliberations. Indeed, both identify certain elements of a future strategic context and identify some US interests and derived from it, key military tasks. For example, adversaries are portrayed as being adaptable to US strengths and being in possession of modern communications technology (Joint Chiefs of Staff 1996, p. 11, 2000, p. 4). However, this picture is very generic and arguably you would not need to develop a representation of future threats for reaching a conclusion that the US armed forces are supposed to successfully deter enemies or, if push comes to shove, "fight and win the nation's wars".

If the representation of future war is far too generic when it comes to the politics of war, it is much more detailed when it comes to the military dimension of war. Here, the Joint Chiefs identify key operational requirements and operational lines. It is, for example, suggested that full-spectrum dominance, i.e. "the ability of US forces, operating unilaterally or in combination with multinational and interagency partners, to defeat any adversary and control any situation across the full range of military operations" is the aim of US forces (Joint Chiefs of Staff 2000, p. 6). It suggests, moreover, that future war will be more lethal as a symptom of rapidly improving military technology (Joint Chiefs of Staff 2000, p. 11). Furthermore, mass and concentration of force are still believed to represent future warfare. In effect, the representation of future war in the documents portrays future war as a military undertaking characterized by more precision-guided munitions.

Still, this representation of future war also entails the standard defense planning paradox. It is aptly captured by Hanley (2008, p. 16): "Active duty officers are discouraged from commenting on policy, for the time-honored and compelling reason that service members must not be seen as challenging the supremacy of civilian leadership on such matters. Even so, military officers are duty-bound to recommend to political authorities the best means of employing military force in the service of national, strategic aims." This is in many respects a perfect depiction of the schizophrenic nature of documents such as the Joint Visions. While they have to relate to politics in order to make certain choices reasonable and certain selected procurements possible to motivate through the Congress, they cannot involve too much politics.

It is this latter argument that also shows the promise of this condition as an explanation of why the US understands future war in a particular way, focusing on the trademarks of Ares. Because it cannot be too explicit when it comes to political ends, these documents tend to focus on the military dimension of war – much like Ares. It also shows how and builds upon how easily planning in a particular process shapes and creates what Jeffrey Michaels (2013, cf. Noreen et al. 2017) has called a "discourse trap" where decision-makers are locked into certain choices due to how one frames the strategic challenge at hand.

Representation of the future as deterministic and without agency

In the final part of the analysis, I assess the extent to which the US planning procedures includes agency in its concept of the future. Above I argued that this final condition is important in the overall explanation of US failure to understand war as political (instead favoring an understanding of war as narrowly military) since a future void of agency would automatically imply that the US does not think it has a say – a political end – with its wars. Even if Echevarria (2014) moderates Weighley's (1973) image that the US way of war is about overwhelming firepower, reliance upon mass and concentration as well as technology, the image of future war in the US as shown above, still focuses on kinetic energy. The vision of future war is heavily influenced by deductions from current, developing, or futuristic technologies. It is technically possible to perform system-of-system warfare, where you can remove human decision-making if desirable. Sensors can alert other systems that go for the kill within minutes of discovery and from a whole range of automated responses – from submarines, drones or regular fixed-wing aircraft. (e.g. Berntsen *et al.* 2016, Kreps 2016, Johansson forthcoming) Developing the platforms to perform these tasks becomes the task. The purposes for which you would want to apply such force are ignored. Naturally, this may not be a problem at all. It only poses a problem if the political aim is neglected – if Athena is forgotten in favor of Ares. Harmony (or at least balance) between them seems necessary and even in such cases there are no guarantees of victory since the adversary may either be more clever or more powerful.

The NIC has used several different methodologies for its long-term future planning over the last few decades. For example, the roles of government and non-government experts have varied over the years and estimates of the future have varied. Still, the least common denominator in the different methodologies is that the representation of the future is derived from extrapolations of current trends. The future, then, is understood to be deterministic and can be acquired through mechanical analysis. The role of informed estimates on a series of factors that are contingent on political decisions in the upcoming decades has varied. For example, in *Global Trends 2015*, there is considerable weight attached to a series of expert opinions on how quick scientific progress will be during the upcoming 20 year-period (NIC 2000).

Most importantly for the argument advanced here, the US is clearly considered to possess agency in the early 2000s, but gradually this agency disappears. In *Global Trends 2015*, it is stated as a natural fact that: "The United States will continue to be a major force in the world community. US global economic, technological, military, and diplomatic influence will be unparalleled among nations as well as regional and international organizations in 2015." (NIC 2000, p. 12) Meanwhile, in *Mapping the Global Futures 2020*, it is recognized that "The role of the United States will be an important variable in how the world is shaped, influencing the path that states and nonstate actors to follow." (NIC 2004, p. 9) But this is more or less it. In the report, the US is more systematically examined from outside. The US is treated as an object, rather than a subject or an "imperial we". Still, US agency is not altogether forgotten. For example, a new section on how the US is perceived abroad is introduced. There is also an ensuing section on policy recommendations if the US wants to change how the world looks upon it. Again in *Global Trends 2025*, the US is objectified. (NIC 2008, p. xi) The report talks of the US in third person, rather than first, but this time there are no policy recommendations and there are uncertainties surrounding the role of the US in the future. Finally, in *Global Trends 2030*, there are grave concerns of whether or not the US will be able to maintain its technological superiority. In the midst of deducing from global megatrends (demography, access to raw material, trade flows, energy scarcity, the climate change), identifying game-changers and black swans to develop four different scenarios, the *Global Trends 2030*, treats the US as an object in a future destined to emerge as a result from the megatrends. (NIC 2012) Oddly, for a US government product on the future, it does not ascribe agency to the US.

To summarize, US long-term planning is remarkably void of agency. For the greater part of the post-Cold War period, the planning tool considers the US as an object – a third person – involved in the story, but also one that can influence the future to a lesser and lesser degree. This is far from what we would expect especially in this period of time where the US, arguably, is the only superpower. The really odd thing about the agency-less defense planning process is that it utterly lacks allusions to the American dream in which one creates your own destiny and fortune. It also goes against the grain of the idea of manifest destiny in US foreign policy. Much like the then idea that the US had a manifest destiny (and indeed an obligation) to colonize and culture the American West in the nineteenth century, it has been suggested that the US in its foreign policy identity is driven by an idea to spread its Enlightenment values world-wide (Pfaff 2010).

Conclusions: why athena should matter more than ares

Why do states struggle to balance short-term use of force with long-term defense planning? In this article, I have argued – through a case study of US defense planning 2001–2016 – that the way we organize our long-term planning procedures determines how we understand the concept of "future". This, in turn, determines the contents of our predictions on future war and the image of future war that we hold. Case specific, by organizing long-term defense planning in an essentially apolitical process, the US understands future war as a military – a bureaucratic – undertaking rather than politics.

By not aligning politics and the image of future war, the US planning procedures and the resulting image of future war creates and continuously re-create an understanding of the future as something that will happen regardless of our own actions. The future happens – whether you like it or not. This future, moreover, will consist of war in the shape of Ares – a military duel – since the planning process is essentially apolitical. The image of future war that follows is war without politics. War as rage, death and destruction. War in the shape of Ares.

This understanding of the US difficulties to align military means and political ends contributes to other rivaling explanations, rather than replacing them. There are still issues of civil-military relations and still issues of the inherent problems of strategizing as they expressed in doctrine, but to this picture, we also ought to add that *how* we think and organize ourselves to meet the challenge of future war, influences the war we then come to wage.

Through a case study on US defense planning 2001–2016 structured according to the four theoretical conditions: (1) separation of the power to wage war from the power to create, fund and organize military capabilities, (2) a separation of the processes for long-term planning, military acquisition, and the formulation of political ends, (3) a representation of future war as a narrowly understood military undertaking, and (4) a representation of the future as deterministic and without agency, the article has demonstrated that the way we plan for future war has an impact on how we pursue it. Based on the case study, thus, the theory seems valid. However, it is not necessarily certain that the results will be able to travel. To some extent, the United States is an outlier as a state in the modern state system. No other state has accumulated so much wealth or possessed such an overwhelming military superiority. Still, the theoretical conditions are not unique to the US. Virtually all states conduct, however small in comparison, defense planning – and must therefore organize this planning according to some procedure. Moreover, many democracies rely upon a strong ideal division between a Weberian apolitical bureaucracy and the elected political decision-makers. There is thus a potential that the theory can explain other cases too.

Why, then, would a stronger emphasis on Athena be advantageous? And how should such a strategy be devised? Instead of platform-centric warfare, we should approach future war as being about identifying and building certain key strategic capabilities. Perhaps a greater investment could be made in creating generic organizational skills and characteristics: learning, adapting, recruitment, planning and "shaping". The strict focus on Ares, moreover, has other problems. If we only, in short, focus on the technique of war, we fail to consider how our adversaries understand future war. It is, for example, exceedingly difficult to create and maintain a strategic narrative of war as understood as exchange of kinetic energy, while maintaining ideals of wars for humanitarian purposes. For adversaries and bystanders such claims will ring hollow. Thinking about war as Athena would, however, solve a series of issues. Instead of just focusing on the use of force, we are forced to consider how force is created and organized. An apt illustration of this twin problem is the decision to dissolve the Iraqi Army in 2003. Instead of just focusing on the Iraqi Army as an adversary and a threat, it should have been recognized that in order to create a stable, democratic Iraq, there had to be a hierarchical state. And, as Tilly (1975) as taught us, the state and its armed forces is in a mutually dependent relationship.

Moreover, approaching war as Athena also redirects strategic planning processes. Instead of just focusing on military means and separating operational planning from long-term defense planning and be satisfied with a division of labor within the military organization, Athena would have us to continuously and critically think through how the processes are interlinked. This is no small endeavor since it would rearrange how military organizations understand the relationship between hierarchy, obedience, and criticism. In this way, the problems associated with differing time-lines could at least partly be solved.

Conceiving of war as Athena, however, is hardly a panacea to all strategic problems, nor is it easily achievable. First, as the Greek forces in the siege of Troy understood, the mere deception and the small band of soldiers hidden within the wooden horse was only sufficient to open the city gates. In order to conquer Troy, the larger Greek Army was necessary. Force and the threat to use force is sometimes needed to an extent that surpasses the effects of deception. Second, it is easy to claim that wisdom, judgment, and flexibility ought to be the hallmarks of any military organization, but it is easier said than done. The reasons are many, but at one level there is huge issues of bureaucratic inertia. As all big organizations, the military is dependent on a division of labor to be efficient. The problem, of course, is that such divisions of labor create vested interests and thus resistance to change.

Note

1. Isabelle Duyvesteyn (2013) has rejuvenated Bernard Brodie's (1949) term "strategic illiteracy" and called for increased strategic awareness in Western military operations.

Disclosure statement

No potential conflict of interest was reported by the author.

References

Auerswald, D.P., 2001. The President, the Congress and American Missile Defence Policy. *Defence studies*, 1 (2), 57–82. doi:10.1080/714000032

Auerswald, D.P. and Campbell, C.C., 2017. Congress: the Other Branch. In: R.Z. George and H. Rishikof, eds. *The National Security Enterprise: navigating the Labyrinth*. Washington, DC: Georgetown University Press.

Barkawi, T., 2011. From war to security: security studies, the wider agenda, and the fate of the study of war. *Millennium*, 39 (3), 701–716. doi:10.1177/0305829811400656

Barkawi, T. and Brighton, S., 2011. Powers of war: fighting, knowledge, and critique. *International political sociology*, 5 (2), 126–143. doi:10.1111/ips.2011.5.issue-2

Berntsen, T.A., Dyndal, G.L., and Johansen, S.R., eds., 2016. *Når dronene våkner*. Oslo, Norway: Cappelen Damm.

Betts, R., 2011. *American force: dangers, delusions, and dilemmas in National Security*. New York: Columbia University Press.
Bousquet, A., 2009. *The scientific way of warfare: order and chaos on the battlefield of modernity*. London: Hurst.
Brennan, M. and Kelly, J., 2009. *Alien: how operational art devoured strategy*. Carlisle, PA: Strategic Studies Institute.
Brodie, B., 1949. Strategy as a science. *World politics*, 1 (4), 467–488. doi:10.2307/2008833
Brooks, R., 2008. *Shaping strategy: the civil military politics of strategic assessment*. Princeton, NJ: Princeton University Press.
Bruneau, T.C. and Matei, F.C., eds., 2013. *The Routledge handbook of civil-military relations*. London: Routledge.
Builder, C., 1988. *The masks of war: American styles in strategy and analysis*. Baltimore, MD: The Johns Hopkins University Press.
Buley, B., 2008. *The new American way of war: military culture and the political utility of force*. London: Routledge.
Buzan, B., 1987. *An introduction to strategic studies: military technology and international relations*. London: MacMillan.
Christiansson, M., 2018. Defense planning beyond rationalism: the third offset strategy as a case of metagovernance. *Defence studies*, 18 (3), 262–278.
Davis, P.K., 2012. *Lessons from Rand's work on planning under uncertainty for national security*. Santa Monica: RAND.
Department of Defense, 2001. *Quadrennial defense review 2001*. Washington, DC: Department of Defense.
Department of Defense, 2006. *Quadrennial defense review 2006*. Washington, DC: Department of Defense.
Department of Defense, 2010. *Quadrennial defense review 2010*. Washington, DC: Department of Defense.
Department of Defense, 2014. *Quadrennial defense review 2014*. Washington, DC: Department of Defense.
Duyvesteyn, I., 2013. *Strategic illiteracy: the art of strategic thinking in modern military operations*. The Netherlands: Universiteit Leiden.
Durell-Young, T., 2018. Questioning the "sanctity" of Long-Term Defense Planning as practiced in Central and Eastern Europe. *Defence studies*, 18 (3), 357–373.
Echevarria, A., 2004. *Toward an American way of war*. Carlisle, PA: Strategic Studies Institute.
Echevarria, A., 2010. *Preparing for one war and getting another?*. Carlisle, PA: Strategic Studies Institute.
Echevarria, A., 2014. *Reconsidering the American way of war: US military practice from the revolution to Afghanistan*. Washington, DC: Georgetown University Press.
Egnell, R., 2009. *Complex peace operations and civil-military relations: winning the peace*. London: Routledge.
Erdeniz, R., 2016. Operations planning revisited: theoretical and practical implications of methodology. *Defence studies*, 16 (3), 248–269. doi:10.1080/14702436.2016.1187567
Feaver, P.D. and Kohn, R.H., eds., 2001. *Soldiers and civilians: the civil-military gap and American national security*. Cambridge, MA: MIT Press.
Flournoy, M.A., 2001. *QDR 2001: strategy driven choices for America's security*. Washington, DC: National Defense University Press.
Freedman, L., 2013. *Strategy: a history*. New York: Oxford University Press.
Freedman, L., 2017. *The future of war: a history*. New York: Public Affairs.
Gaddis, J.L., 2004. *The landscape of history: how historians map the past*. Oxford: Oxford University Press.
Giddens, A., 1991. *The consequences of modernity*. Stanford, CA: Stanford University Press.
Gooch, J. and Perlmutter, A., eds., 1982. *Military deception and strategic surprise*. London: Frank Cass.
Gray, C., 2005. *Another bloody century: future warfare*. London: Cassell.

Gray, C., 2010. Strategic thoughts for defence planners. *Survival*, 52 (3), 159–178. doi:10.1080/00396338.2010.494883

Gray, C., 2014a. *Strategy and defence planning: meeting the challenge of uncertainty*. Oxford: Oxford University Press.

Gray, C., 2014b. *Defense planning for national security: navigation aids for the mystery tour*. Carlisle, PA: Strategic Studies Institute.

Gunziger, M., 2013. *Shaping America's future military: toward a new force planning construct*. Washington, DC: CSBA.

Hanley, B., 2008. *Planning for conflict in the twenty-first century*. Westport, CT: Praeger.

Hays, P.L., Vallance, B.J., and Van Tassel, A.R., eds.., 1997. *American defense policy*. 7th ed. Baltimore, MD: The Johns Hopkins University Press.

Hodgson, Q.E., 2010. *Deciding to buy: civil-military relations and major weapons programs*. Carlisle, PA: Strategic Studies Institute.

Holman, R., 2001. The imagination of the future: a hidden concept in the study of consumer decision-making. *Advances in consumer research*, 8, 187–191.

Holmqvist, C., 2014. *Policing wars: on military intervention in the twenty-first century*. London: Palgrave.

Holsti, K.J., 2004. *Taming the sovereigns: institutional change in international politics*. Cambridge: Cambridge University Press.

Hopkins, L. and Zapata, M., 2001. *Engaging the future: forecasts, scenarios, plans and projects*. Cambridge, MA: Lincoln Institute of Land Policy.

Huntington, S., 1957. *The soldier and the state: the theory and politics of civil-military relations*. Cambridge, MA: Belknap Press.

Imlay, T.C. and Toft, M.D., ed., 2006. *The fog of war and peace planning*. London: Frank Cass.

Jensen, B., 2018. The role of ideas in defense planning: revisiting the revolution in military affairs. *Defence studies*, 18 (3), 302–317.

Johansson, L., forthcoming. Ethical aspects on military maritime and aerial autonomous systems. *Journal of military ethics*.

Joint Chiefs of Staff, 1996. *Joint vision 2010*. Washington, DC: Department of Defense.

Joint Chiefs of Staff, 2000. *Joint vision 2020*. Washington, DC: Department of Defense.

Karlsson, H., 2002. *Bureaucratic politics and weapons acquisition: the case of the MX ICBM program, 2 vol: s*. Stockholm: Stockholm University.

Kem, J.D., 2009. *Campaign planning: tools of the trade*. Fort Leavenworth, KS: Department of Joint, Interagency and Multinational Operations.

Krepinevich, A.F., 2010. *7 deadly scenarios: a military futurist explores war in the 21st century*. New York: Bantam Books.

Kreps, S., 2016. *Drones: what everyone needs to know*. Oxford: Oxford University Press.

Kuosa, T., 2011. Evolution of futures studies. *Futures*, 43, 327–336. doi:10.1016/j.futures.2010.04.001

Lovelace, D.C. and Durell-Young, T., 1995. *US department of defense strategic planning: the missing nexus*. Carlisle, PA: Strategic Studies Institute.

Mahnken, T., 2008. *Technology and the American way of war*. New York: Columbia University Press.

McAllister Linn, B., 2007. *The echo of battle: the army's way of war*. Cambridge, MA: Harvard University Press.

McKernan, M., Drezner, J.A., and Sollinger, J.M., 2015. *Tailoring the acquisition process in the US department of defense*. Santa Monica, CA: RAND.

Meese, M.J., 2014. Strategy and force planning in a time of austerity. *Strategic studies quarterly*, 8 (3), 19–29.

Michaels, J., 2013. *The discourse trap and the US military: from the war on terror to the surge*. London: Palgrave.

Nathan, J.A. and Oliver, J.K., 1994. *Foreign policy making and the American political system*. Baltimore, MD: The Johns Hopkins University Press.

National Intelligence Council, 2000. *Global trends 2015: a dialogue about the future with non-government experts*. Washington, DC: National Intelligence Council.
National Intelligence Council, 2004. *Global Trends 2020: mapping the global future*. Washington, DC: National Intelligence Council.
National Intelligence Council, 2008. *Global trends 2025: a transformed world*. Washington, DC: National Intelligence Council.
National Intelligence Council, 2012. *Global trends 2030: alternative worlds*. Washington, DC: National Intelligence Council.
Nelson, D.N., 2001. Beyond defence planning. *Defence studies*, 1 (3), 25–36. doi:10.1080/714000042
Nielsen, S. and Snider, D.M., ed., 2009. *American civil-military relations: the soldier and the state in a new era*. Baltimore, MD: The Johns Hopkins University Press.
Nordin, A. and Öberg, D., 2015. Targeting the ontology of war: from Clausewitz to Baudrillard. *Millennium*, 43 (2), 392–410. doi:10.1177/0305829814552435
Noreen, E., Sjöstedt, R., and Ångström, J., 2017. Why small states join big wars: the case of Sweden in Afghanistan 2002-2014. *International relations*, 31 (2), 145–168. doi:10.1177/0047117816651125
O'Hanlon, M., 2009. *The science of war*. Princeton, NJ: Princeton University Press.
Paparone, C., 2012. *The sociology of military science: prospects for postinstitutional military design*. New York: Continuum.
Pfaff, W., 2010. *The irony of manifest identity: the tragedy of America's foreign policy*. New York: Walker.
Quester, G.H., 1992. Evolving Determinants of US Strategic Policy-Making. In: J.C. Gaston, ed. *Grand strategy and the decision-making process*. Washington, DC: National Defense University Press.
Ricks, T., 2006. *Fiasco: the American military adventure in Iraq*. New York: Penguin.
Riposo, J., McKernan, M., and Kaihoi Duran, C., 2014. *Prolonged cycle times and schedule growth in defense acquisition*. Santa Monica, CA: RAND.
Simpson, E., 2012. *War from the ground up: twenty-first century combat as politics*. Oxford: Oxford University Press.
Sondhaus, L., 2006. *Strategic culture and ways of war*. London: Routledge.
Stone, J., 2011. *Military strategy: the politics and technique of war*. London: Continuum.
Tama, J., 2018. Tradeoffs in defense strategic planning: lessons from the U.S. Quadrennial Defense Review. *Defence studies*, 18 (3), 279–301.
Tilly, C., 1975. Reflections on the history of European state-making. In: C. Tilly, ed. *The formation of national states in Western Europe*. Princeton: Princeton University Press.
Vine, D., 2015. *Base nation: how US military bases abroad harm America and the world*. New York: Metropolitan Books.
Warburg, G.F., 2017. Lobbyists: when US National Security and Special Interests Compete. In: R. Z. George and H. Rishikof, ed. *The National security enterprise: navigating the labyrinth*. Washington, DC: Georgetown University Press.
Weighley, R., 1973. *The American way of war: a history of United States military strategy and policy*. New York: Macmillan.
Yarger, H.R., 2008. *Strategy and the national security professional: strategic thinking and strategy formulation in the 21st century*. Westport, CT: Praeger.
Zweibelson, B., 2015. One piece at a time: why linear planning and institutionalisms promote military campaign failures. *Defence studies*, 15 (4), 360–374. doi:10.1080/14702436.2015.1113667

Rediscovering geography in NATO defence planning

Alexander Mattelaer

ABSTRACT
This article explores the relevance of geography in NATO defence planning. Historical analysis of strategic concepts and other planning documents suggests a pendulum movement from treating geography as the central organising principle within the alliance, to downplaying its role in favour of functional considerations, and back. In view of mounting tensions alongside Europe's eastern and southern flanks, this argument acquires contemporary relevance with regards to how alliance responsibilities can be (re)distributed. Rediscovering the early principle that allies should concentrate on those tasks for which they are the most geographically suited offers a promising approach for a new division of labour.

Introduction

Geography is key to military strategy. By definition, military conflict must unfold in one or several geospatial domains, be it land, sea, air, space or cyberspace (Peltier and Pearcy 1966, Gray 1991, Collins 1998). Preparing defence establishments for future conflict entails anticipating how these different domains may constrain operations and enable new concepts for gaining an advantage over an expected adversary. Answering the question *where* a conflict may take place immediately provides a certain direction as to how this conflict may be fought. This is not to say that other factors – such as time or psychology – play no meaningful role in military strategy. They most certainly do, as Robert Leonhard (1994) has for instance demonstrated with regards to the role of time. Yet geography, if for no other reason than its material unavoidability, has always assumed a central role in shaping strategic culture, military theory and the education of future military leaders.

It comes as no surprise that geography has historically been central to NATO defence planning, and intimately tied to burden-sharing discussions. The Cold War confrontation between NATO and the Warsaw Pact involved possible conflict in a wide range of localities, but it was recognised that the central effort was to be found on the European plain. It would therefore be dominated by massed formations of heavy armour on land and supporting fires delivered from the air. In addition, nuclear deterrence cast a long shadow over the probability of conflict and the way it would evolve, should deterrence ever fail. Geography provided the conceptual anchor point for organising allied defence planning in all its aspects. It provided a practical basis for a division of labour amongst allies – answering the question who should do what – and infused the alliance with an intuitive sense of organising its activities around areas of regional focus and responsibility. Drawing inspiration from the prescient analysis of Mackinder (1943), NATO got its bearings from the compass rose it carried in its emblem, so to speak.

What is more of a surprise is the extent to which the importance of geography was reduced as NATO adapted to the post-Cold War environment. As the alliance evolved in the 1990s and 2000s into a more globally-oriented security organisation and conducted counterinsurgency operations beyond the Hindu Kush, defence planning could not help but follow the political agenda. This resulted in frequent contestation and – to a certain extent – a loss of direction. Instead of planning for specific threats, the alliance started pursuing a more functional approach to the development of military capabilities. Yet faced with a revanchist Russia, turmoil throughout its extended southern neighbourhood and intensifying US pressure on allies to do more for their own defence, the alliance is now forced to think hard about how it goes about its core tasks. This re-emergence of threats close to home raises profound questions about both the content and methodology of defence planning.

Can geography once more provide the conceptual anchor point for alliance planners? This article puts forward an affirmative response. In suggesting such continuity between the past and the future, the aim is not to predict what is yet to come, but rather to highlight possible ways of responding to contemporary challenges that build on what the alliance was able achieve in the past. Encouraging nations to undertake the tasks for which they are the most suited because of their geography and capabilities – to paraphrase NATO's very first Strategic Concept – may also be the most pragmatic way forward in the twenty-first century. Going back to the basic principles of the alliance offers contemporary defence planners with some much-needed respite by assigning clearly designated regional responsibilities. This admittedly poses a risk of fragmenting the alliance, which needs to be overcome by cementing trust amongst the US and its key allies. Yet even if the transatlantic link were ever to be stretched beyond breaking point, this argument retains substantial validity as a basis for conceiving complementary force structures amongst European nations. In this sense, focusing on the content of defence planning efforts allows one to look beyond the institutional debates that often plague discussions about European security.

This argument proceeds in four parts. The first section focuses on the central role geographical factors played in the founding of the alliance and the way it was set up to deter conflict and to ensure a common defence in the event of war with the Soviet Union. Geography inspired not only the political *raison d'être* of the alliance and its early strategic concepts, it also infused its organisational command and control architecture as well as the joint military doctrine it generated. Armed with this historical background, the second section discusses the relative drift away from specific geographical considerations and the emergence of functional approaches to defence planning. As the alliance awkwardly embraced a global political agenda, uncertainty about future risks produced capability-based approaches to defence planning as a substitute for geography-inspired threat analysis.

When NATO leaders gathered in Wales in 2014, however, they agreed that "a pivotal moment in Euro-Atlantic security" was reached (NATO 2014). Faced with so-called hybrid conflict in Ukraine, the Russian annexation of Crimea and deepening instability throughout its southern neighbourhood, NATO adopted an ambitious adaptation agenda. The third section reviews the implicit comeback of geography this engendered. The decisions announced at the 2016 Warsaw Summit – in particular those relating to the defence of the geographically most vulnerable Baltic states – constitute the clearest expression thereof. As force requirements started growing significantly, the difficulty of matching political ambitions with adequate financial resources is set to persist. The fourth and final section suggests a set of policy recommendations by considering how a geography-inspired division of labour can offer an acceptable way of surmounting those challenges. Such a division of labour would boil down to a hub-and-spokes model in which different European allies pursue broadly complementary force structures along geographical lines. This implies a key role for Germany in the land-centric, territorial defence of the eastern flank, French leadership in joint expeditionary operations along the southern flank, and a more global and maritime-centric role for the United Kingdom. As such, the United States can both underwrite European security and recalibrate its strategic focus across the Eurasian landmass in function of competing requirements. The more the US retreats from its longstanding role as underwriter of European security, the more these burden-sharing questions re-emerge in a European context, with all consequences these entail in terms of military requirements.

A brief note on methodology is in order. This article draws heavily on archival research on declassified NATO documents from the Cold War period (compiled by Pedlow 1997) and more recent unclassified primary documents. One point of potential confusion concerns the evolving meaning of the term "defence planning". Historically, there existed no clear distinction between defence policy, planning and defence plans. Today the term "defence planning" in a NATO context is reserved for the process of building the force pool designed to meet the level of ambition as codified in the NATO defence planning process (Mattelaer 2014). This practice followed the post-Cold War introduction of a conceptual distinction between force planning and operational planning. Throughout this analysis, the term "defence planning" is used *in its respective historical context and meaning*. As such, this article also traces how alliance defence planning has conceptually evolved over time.

The role of geography in NATO's early defence planning

Throughout the Cold War, geography made itself felt in all aspects of the alliance. Not only stood geography central in the very identity of the alliance, it also informed the way in which the core objectives of preparing for a common defence and deterring conflict were pursued. As far as defence planning was concerned, the original Strategic Concept for the defence of the North Atlantic area constituted ample evidence thereof. The vision this document put forward subsequently inspired the organisational development of the alliance as well as the doctrinal foundations for imagining a possible conflict with the Soviet Union. Right until the Berlin Wall came down, defence planners could not but engage in their work but through this geography-inspired prism.

From its very inception, the NATO alliance itself constituted a geopolitical project. The transatlantic link provided not only the basis for protecting Europe from a communist take-over, it also constituted the foundation for anchoring the United States in European affairs and enabling the project of European integration to flourish – not in the least by keeping a watchful eye over a divided Germany (cf. Rühle and Williams 1997, Rynning 2013). The collective defence commitment enshrined in Article 5 of the North Atlantic Treaty hinged upon the condition of an armed attack on the territory of any of the parties or their forces, vessels, or aircraft operating in the North Atlantic area, which includes not only NATO territory and airspace but also the Mediterranean Sea and the Atlantic Ocean north of the Tropic of Cancer. These definitions and political inspirations infused the alliance with an innate appreciation of the idea that geography matters at the level of grand strategy.

The original NATO Strategic Concept from 1949 treated geography as key to the internal organisation of the alliance. First and foremost, it did so by codifying a list of agreed principles for guiding defence planning (Mattelaer 2016). Among those is the following: "each nation should undertake the task, or tasks, for which it is best suited. Certain nations, *because of geographic location* or because of their capabilities, will appropriate specific missions" (NATO 1949, §5.f, emphasis added). In turn, this principle constituted the foundation for distributing the tasks and requirements posed by NATO's defence plans. Strategic bombing was labelled "primarily a U.S. responsibility" whereas European nations were tasked to provide "the hard core of ground forces" and "the bulk of tactical air support". The United Kingdom would share responsibility with the U.S. in the "organization and control of ocean lines of communication" (NATO 1949, §7.a-f). This division of labour effectively remained in place throughout the Cold War. Its geographical inspiration is plain to see: the closer the nation was located to the central front, the more emphasis was put on heavy armour and short-range air support, whereas the Anglo-Saxon nations would provide seaborne reinforcements and support wherever needed. In operational terms, this approach was meant to arrest a hypothetical Soviet advance, allow for the launch of a strategic air offensive and the full mobilisation of alliance resources. In effect, this elaborated on Mackinder's (1943) earlier vision of France as a continental bridgehead, Britain as a moated aerodrome and North America as a reserve of manpower and industry.

In order to facilitate detailed defence planning, additional strategic guidance was issued to five Regional Planning Groups: Northern Europe, Western Europe, Southern Europe/Western Mediterranean, United States/Canada, and the North Atlantic Ocean (NATO 1950). Defence planning was organised around geographical sectors with distinct strategic roles: to hold Soviet forces at bay in the three interconnected European regions; to generate reinforcements for regions under attack and to launch the strategic air offensive from Canada and the United States; and to control the sea lines of communication for shipping reinforcements across the Atlantic. Subsequent updates of this strategic guidance added more detailed estimates of the relative importance of different regions, the main factors influencing their defence and a regional concept of operations taking topographical considerations into account (see e.g. NATO 1952). Relying on the transatlantic bargain that the US would underwrite NATO's collective defence if and only if sufficiently offset by European contributions, the Military Committee methodically established a geography-inspired common basis for coherent defence plans. By the time that the most detailed discussions on nuclear strategy unfolded – most emblematically codified in the "flexible response" Strategic Concept (NATO 1968) – these foundations were firmly in place.

When NATO established its command structure in the early 1950s, which over time would grow into the organisational backbone of the alliance, it replicated this regional division of the North Atlantic area. Having been appointed as the first Supreme Allied Commander Europe (SACEUR), General Dwight D. Eisenhower proposed that each region would be given a Commander-in-Chief, supported by separate Land, Air and Naval Commanders for each region (Pedlow 2009). Because of political compromises, the eventual structure for Allied Command Europe became more convoluted and evolved repeatedly over time. Throughout the Cold War, however, the division into regional areas of responsibility and geospatial focus per service (land/air/navy) was maintained.

The development of Allied doctrine followed the established trend. While much intellectual energy went to nuclear matters and deterrence theories, preparations for combined arms operations in Western Europe continued throughout the coldest parts of the East-West standoff (cf. Hoffenaar and Krüger 2012). The best example thereof is the formulation of the AirLand Battle concept codified in the 1982 *US Army Field Manual 100–5 Operations*. As argued by Richard Lock-Pullan (2005), AirLand Battle "grew out of concern with the European Central Front" and sought to transform operational manoeuvre by expanding the battlefield in terms of space, time and depth (cf. Doerfel 1982). While much has been made about the subsequent extension of the concept to other theatres, this line of thought was deeply rooted in European geography and the German experience of fighting defensive battles across the steppe in 1943–1944. It was geared, *inter alia*, towards the goal of avoiding heavy fighting on NATO soil and surrendering German terrain (Mearsheimer 1982). Moreover, its bi-dimensional focus meshed well with the emphasis put on the development of land forces and tactical air support by the European allies.

In sum, the consideration of geographical factors was paramount for NATO defence planning during the Cold War. The 1957 Strategic Concept went as far as listing "considerations of geographic position" as the first foundation of collective plans (NATO 1957, §2). Frequent concern over the "defence of the flanks" illustrated this mindset. In the words of Admiral Horacio Rivero (1972), Commander-in-Chief Allied Forces Southern Europe, "it is well to look first at the geography of the area. Geography has a great impact on the strategic considerations that we need to discuss." NATO defence ministers accordingly commissioned detailed studies for informing regional force plans (NATO 1967, §3). This was particularly true for the southern region, where "geography and national prerogatives constrain allied contingency planning ... more than anywhere in the alliance" (Ruiz Palmer 1990, p. 276). One generation later, however, opinions would starkly differ.

Post 1991: capability planning in an age of geographical uncertainty

The fall of the Berlin Wall and the removal of the Iron Curtain constituted a turning point in the evolution of the European security landscape (cf. Webber *et al.* 2012). Once NATO as an organisation embarked on its post-Cold War trajectory the influence of geography on defence planning efforts sharply decreased. Geographical considerations were effectively downplayed in favour of a global agenda and so-called "out-of-area" missions. Defence planners sought and found new methodological bearings in the notion of capability-based approaches to defence planning (cf. Davis and Finch 1993). The campaigns undertaken in Bosnia, Kosovo and Afghanistan ended up setting new expectations of what military power was all about. While geography was never fully discarded, NATO successfully reinvented itself as a sprawling security network (Mattelaer 2011). In the absence of a clear-cut adversary, the alliance became a provider of military command and support services tailored to various coalitions with a view to addressing security challenges that emerged not so much from great power rivalry, but rather from lack of state capacity and so-called rogue states. These problems tended to unfold over a longer range and in less predictable ways than anything the alliance had become accustomed to.

The 1991 Strategic Concept charted the course for NATO's organisational evolution: "In contrast with the predominant threat of the past, the risks to Allied security that remain are multi-faceted in nature and multi-directional, which makes them hard to predict and assess" (NATO 1991, §8). While the Strategic Concept confirmed the collective defence clause of the Washington Treaty, it redirected attention to the global context and security challenges such as the proliferation of weapons of mass destruction, terrorism and the potential disruption of the flow of vital resources. The operational capability to manage crises affecting the security of its members started to emerge as the principal benchmark for the alliance's defence planning system. While regional considerations still lingered, the conventional force posture was numerically reduced and geared towards greater flexibility and mobility of deployment. Nuclear strategy was correspondingly downgraded in terms of its relative prominence. The 1999 Strategic Concept reinforced this reorientation toward unpredictable security risks, notably by introducing the Combined Joint Task Force concept for conducting non-Article 5 crisis response operations.

This transformation of the alliance caused considerable debate. The proposition that NATO had to go "out of area or out of business" was met by scepticism about what such a switch from collective defence to collective security would imply (see e.g. Rupp 2000). On the one hand, considerable unease existed over the idea of NATO enlargement. While the alliance did accept several former members of the Soviet block as new members, a growing concern over antagonising Russia caused France and Germany to block Ukraine and Georgia from joining the Membership Action Plan at the Bucharest Summit in 2008. On the other hand, strong support emerged in the US for the idea of a "global NATO". As eloquently put by Daalder and Goldgeier (2006): "If the point of the alliance is no longer territorial defense but bringing together countries with similar values and interests to combat global problems, then NATO no longer needs to have an exclusive transatlantic character". However, such proposals prompted widespread European fears, not only about the possible dilution of the Article 5 security guarantee, but also about the way in which the US exercised its power during the age of unipolarity. Widespread European opposition to the US-led invasion of Iraq in 2003 underscored such fears (cf. Daalder 2003, Andréani 2006).

Even if the notion of "global NATO" was politically contested, the practical corollary of downplaying geography in defence planning was broadly accepted. As an otherwise sceptical Karl-Heinz Kamp (1999) noted, "Conflict can no longer be regionalized. Technological progress tends to abolish geographical distance; ... Hence NATO allies are likely to face future military threats from regions far beyond the borders of traditional NATO defense planning". Soon after the 11 September 2001 attacks, the "out of area" debate was sealed "by the simple statement that our forces needed to be able to operate where necessary, as decided by the Council" (Pfeiffer 2008, p. 119). When NATO assumed command of the International Security Assistance Force in Afghanistan, which went on to become the largest operation NATO has ever undertaken, the shift towards an alliance based on a variable geometry model was complete.

The methodological consequences for defence planning were wide-ranging. First, the switch from collective defence scenarios to crisis response planning precipitated the introduction of the force generation process. As it could no longer be assumed that allies would automatically provide NATO commanders with the forces they required for conducting expeditionary operations, force generation would need to provide the new link between the alliance's force posture and operational planning activities (Pfeiffer 2008, p. 106). Second, a corresponding shift materialised from a threat-based to a capability-based approach to defence planning. In the light of widespread uncertainty about when or where future crisis management operations would unfold, the alliance switched to using an operational "level of ambition" as the principal yardstick for defence planning (Pfeiffer 2008, p. 119). The codification of such a level of ambition drew inspiration from US force planning constructs adopted in earlier years (Khalilzad and Ochmanek 1997, Gunzinger 2013). The NATO level of ambition was correspondingly built around the ability to sustain concurrent major joint operations and several smaller operations for collective defence and crisis response. On this basis, "minimum capability requirements" could be apportioned to individual allies, based on what could be deemed a "reasonable challenge." While NATO defence planners still attempted to match specific areas of national interest with capability targets, the explicit division of labour that was present in the Cold War gradually evaporated.

As capability-based planning was glorified as the new gold standard for defence planning, new challenges started to appear (De Spiegeleire 2011, cf. also Ångström 2018). Given that the notion of capability-based planning was predicated on the claim that future military contingencies are uncertain in their nature and whereabouts, hypothetical scenarios were needed to provide methodological rigour. In turn this led to much debate over how flexible or rigid such scenarios must be, and whether long-term planning could ever break away from the "dictatorship of the present" (De Spiegeleire 2011, p. 23, cf. Fitzsimmons 2006). The most fundamental consequence was that the fading of clear-cut threats from the defence planning debate entailed a loss of recognisability and therefore of broad political support for resourcing defence establishments. Simply put, military requirements formulated in abstract terms did not resonate with domestic publics keen to cash in on the peace dividend of the post-Cold War era. Despite the intellectual rigour that undergirded many capability-based approaches, it proved impossible to address the persistent capability shortfalls plaguing NATO defence planners (see e.g. Yost 2000).

While this relative downgrading of geographical considerations remained somewhat abstract in the defence planning discussion in a narrow sense, it manifested itself in a more tangible way in the 2003 reform of the NATO Command Structure. The radical reorganisation decided upon by the ministerial meeting of the Defence Planning Committee in June 2003 effectively ended the regional distribution of command responsibilities (see NATO 2003, Pedlow 2009). Supreme Allied Command Atlantic (SACLANT) became Allied Command Transformation (ACT), responsible for expediting alliance capability development processes in line with the shift to capability-based planning. In turn, Allied Command Europe became Allied Command Operations, tasked with directing all NATO operations at the strategic level. While subordinate headquarters continued to be organised per geospatial dimension at the tactical level (land, air, maritime), these entities were stripped from having a designated regional focus. "At the heart of this organisational metamorphosis", explained Air Vice-Marshal Andrew Vallance (2003) in *NATO Review*, "has been the concept of *using functionality rather than geography as the basic rationale for Alliance command arrangements*. (...) in today's far more dynamic, fluid and resource-conscious strategic environment, in which secure, real-time, global, mass data transfer is readily available, such an approach is essential" (emphasis added).

The above is not meant to suggest that geographical considerations disappeared from the NATO debate altogether. The tyranny of distance made itself acutely felt in terms of expeditionary logistics – a problem set that was hitherto relatively unknown to most European allies. The more out-of-area NATO wanted to go, the greater the requirement for strategic air and sealift. The larger an area of operations was delineated, the more pressing tactical mobility became, a requirement usually associated with transport helicopters. Heavy weaponry such as main battle tanks was often deemed exceedingly difficult to transport, and therefore considered to have become unusable. This trend effectively culminated in the decision of several smaller allies to scrap heavy armour from their force structure altogether. In sum, geographical considerations were downgraded in the defence planning debate from the level of organising principle to that of being a practical nuisance that technology would someday be able to overcome. Again, this situation was not to last.

The road from Wales to Warsaw

By the end of the previous decade, the trend of downplaying geography started topping out. The decisive break, however, materialised at the Wales Summit in 2014. The Russian annexation of Crimea and the war in eastern Ukraine prompted NATO heads of state and government to change course and initiate a process of alliance adaptation. As such, defence planners received a strong impetus to refocus significant efforts on the core task of collective defence (Deni 2017). While confronting the newly identified threats, however, they could not avoid discovering various puzzles in which geographical factors returned with a vengeance. The defence of the Baltic states arguably constituted the best case in point. Once Russia is seen as a possible adversary, the geographical vulnerability of the Baltic states becomes impossible to ignore, and the requirements for providing for European security increase exponentially. Yet the delicate balancing act between catering to the eastern and southern flanks of the alliance became a more strategic problem for defence planners, as available resources fell far short of what was required. The decisions announced at the 2016 Warsaw Summit consolidated the new trend of re-emphasising geography. Yet it also raised contentious questions with respect to the future evolution of the alliance's force posture, and the mutual trust amongst allies it requires.

Already before 2014, early signs could be detected that the drift away from geography was reaching its limits. The 2010 Strategic Concept, which remains in force to the present day, still built on the notion of non-territorial security challenges and global effects. "Unique in its history, NATO is a security Alliance that fields military forces able to operate together *in any environment*; that can control operations *anywhere...*" (NATO 2010, §36, emphasis added). At the same time, it codified three core tasks: collective defence, crisis management and cooperative security. These tasks formed concentric circles, with territorial defence constituting the alliance's "greatest responsibility". Yet its force planning construct remained welded around the notion of "the ability to sustain concurrent major joint operations and several smaller operations for collective defence and crisis response, including at strategic distance" (NATO 2010, §19).

At the same time, the financial crisis that had hit the Western world from 2008 onwards left its mark on the alliance. The Strategic Concept stressed that resources must be sufficient, but put a premium on maximising efficiency and cost effectiveness. In 2011, this made itself felt in another round of NATO Command Structure reform, which reduced command staff posts by more than 30 per cent as part of a political drive to cut costs. Interestingly, the operational-level joint force headquarters in Brunssum and Napels were set to regain their regional focus with respect to knowledge development (on the eastern and southern periphery, respectively) that they had lost in previous reforms (Wouters 2011). While not meant to be exclusive – in the sense that SACEUR could assign command of any operation to either of the joint force commanders – nations were keen to have headquarters dedicated to their own region of interest.

The 2014 Wales Summit Declaration *de facto* amended the Strategic Concept in important ways. First, the ongoing instability in the alliance's neighbourhood took precedence over other threats. NATO leaders expressed deep concern over Russian actions in Ukraine and its "breaking the trust at the core of our cooperation" (NATO 2014, § 21). In parallel, growing instability in the Middle East and North Africa region – in particular the emergence of the so-called Islamic State – was perceived to constitute another threat to the security of the alliance. Second, a Readiness Action Plan was put forward to respond the threats that were identified (cf. Arnold 2016). This included so-called assurance measures as well as adaptation measures. The former consisted in the generation of a continuous air, land, and maritime presence in the eastern part of the alliance by means of rotational deployments and exercises. The latter concentrated on the establishment of the Very High Readiness Joint Task Force (VJTF) and the desire to increase the size and responsiveness of the NATO Response Force. Notable was also the fact that the regional focus for the NATO Command Structure was explicitly underscored "to exploit regional expertise and enhance situational awareness" (NATO 2014, §9). Third, NATO leaders realised that this new security environment implied increasing force requirements. To that purpose, they agreed to reverse the trend of declining defence expenditure, which in many nations had continued unabated for three decades (expressed as percentage of gross domestic product, see e.g. Marrone *et al.* 2016). The combination of these three considerations implied that NATO as an organisation was poised for experiencing a proverbial rebirth (cf. Deni 2014).

Supplementing the Wales Summit Declaration, the NATO defence ministerial meeting in June 2015 issued new political guidance to alliance defence planners. While this guidance left the force planning construct unchanged, it significantly amended the underlying scenarios and accepted the use of representative geography instead of artificial terrain. As these underlying scenarios are driving resource demands and the composition of the combined force pool, this exercise implied careful trade-off between the different core tasks of the alliance that meshed with different geographical focal points (i.e., collective defence in the east versus crisis management and cooperative security in the south). Within the desired force mix the share of high-end capabilities started to grow markedly so as to boost the conventional deterrence posture. New shortfalls in long-range artillery and ground based air defences were identified, and issues such as the expected rate of combat attrition were hotly debated. The subsequent process of thinking through this new guidance in operational detail only amplified the awareness of how geography brought about new constraints and opportunities.

No debate illustrated the return of geographical considerations more starkly than that over the defence of the Baltic region. The newly established VJTF was meant to provide a mobile tripwire that could be put in place as a guarantee of alliance solidarity when and where needed. Yet planners were quick to point out that Russia could make use of its anti-access and area denial capabilities in Kaliningrad to hamper or block NATO reinforcements such as the VJTF arriving in the most exposed parts of allied territory (cf. Frühling and Lasconjarias 2016, Glatz and Zapfe 2016). A series of widely publicised wargames suggested that Russian forces would be able to mass quickly and reach the outskirts of Talinn and Riga in less than 60 hours – thus presenting the alliance with a sudden *fait accompli* (Shlapak and Johnson 2016). Given that any hypothetical counteroffensive to liberate the Baltic states would be enormously costly and fraught with escalatory risks, the call for establishing forward-based defences quickly became overwhelming (Clem 2016, Kramer and Craddock 2016). This would also provide the necessary assurances that the Baltic states – or even Poland – would not be abandoned in case of conflict.

While the details of such a forward presence were the subject of heated debate, the methodological consequence was that defence planning for such Baltic contingencies started to resemble operational planning again. At a higher level, the case of the Baltic states was only a small part of a broader debate on defending NATO's eastern and southern flanks – terminology which made a remarkable popular come-back since 2014 (cf. Simon 2014, Rogers and Romanovs 2015b). Taken together, this implied a gradual shift back from capability-based planning to threat-informed, requirements-based planning approaches. Along NATO's eastern flank, nations started to contemplate how to adopt sufficiently "prickly" hedgehog postures to deter the adversary they faced, and to what extent this required support from the larger and more geographically sheltered allies (cf. Rogers and Romanovs 2015a).

The 2016 Warsaw Summit took stock of NATO's adaptation since Wales and announced a series of major decisions. Most importantly, the alliance agreed to establish an "enhanced forward presence" in Estonia, Latvia, Lithuania and Poland (NATO 2016, §40). This presence would consist of four battalion-sized battlegroups, led by the UK, Canada, Germany and the US, respectively. These would be present at all times (relying on a heel-to-toe rotation schedule) and underpinned by a viable reinforcement strategy. More generally, NATO conceptualised the Russian challenge in terms of three regions that each required a tailored response. In keeping with geography, these centred around the Baltic Sea, the Black Sea and the North Atlantic Ocean. With respect to organisational matters, the summit commissioned an assessment of the NATO Command Structure, "(in) light of the changed and evolving security environment and the increased overall requirements" (NATO 2016, §46). Needless to say, the alliance also paid considerable attention to the threats emanating from its southern neighbourhood and the global threat of terrorism, which "knows no border, nationality, or religion" (NATO 2016, §8).

While some elements of the previous paradigm thus still lingered in the NATO debate, the most substantive decisions and resourcing commitments all had a distinctly geographical flavour. In their June 2018 meeting, NATO defence ministers approved the creation of a new Joint Force Command for the Atlantic in Norfolk, Virginia (responsible for moving forces quickly and safely across the Atlantic), a Joint Support and Enabling Command in Ulm (responsible for organising and protecting movements of troops and equipment within Europe) and a Cyber Operations Centre (integrating cyberspace alongside the land, sea and air domains). Under the heading of the "enablement of SACEUR's Area of Responsibility", defence ministers listed measures to improve military mobility by means of intensified cross-departmental cooperation. As such, the geography of one conflict scenario – that of the Maximum Level of Effort – imposes itself on the organization of the alliance as a whole once again.

Throughout these debates, the aggregate volume of defence budgets constituted a strategic challenge provoking heated debate (cf. Hoffman 2017). To the present day, a yawning gap exists between the actual level of defence spending and the level required for maintaining the level of ambition and meeting political ambitions. At the Warsaw Summit, NATO leaders could claim that the alliance has turned a corner in terms of reversing the decline, but only with some difficulty. Most budget increases displayed a distinct geographical pattern, with sharp increases occurring in Eastern and Northern Europe and mere stagnation across Western and Southern Europe. Furthermore, expressing defence spending as a percentage of GDP hides the fact that the trend in absolute terms is determined overwhelmingly by the large nations. After all, the combined defence budgets of France, Germany, Italy and the United Kingdom constitute 69 percent of the European NATO total. This implies that the overall picture is – at least so far – one of arrested decline instead of real growth. For the years ahead, however, major budget increases are projected in France, Germany and various other allies.

At the same time, the existing NATO force pool falls far short of what is required in terms of force readiness and availability – especially when the US cannot be fully relied upon for doing much of the heavy lifting. The requirements of deterrence (as embodied in the enhanced forward presence debate), the need for a sufficiently large pool of follow-on-forces (in case reinforcements would be called upon) and the potential simultaneity between the core tasks of collective defence and crisis management all suggest that European allies confront a major challenge. When taking into account how hollow the force structures of many European allies have become, the situation looks nothing but alarming. Sustained investment will be required merely to avoid internal collapse (cf. Barry and Binnendijk 2012). In the light of the deteriorating security environment and rising requirements, one single question therefore dominates the landscape of European security: how to make ends meet?

Towards a new regional division of labour

The pendulum movement of NATO's evolution over the past decades is widely understood. Yet the specific focus on the role of geography in defence planning allows one to discern a logical answer to the most pressing concern facing the alliance today. Uncoordinated budget cuts have initiated "a creeping process of specialization by default" (Barry and Binnendijk 2012, p. 7). Looking to the future, what could be more fitting than a return to the 1949 defence planning principle stating that each nation should undertake the tasks for which it is best suited because of its geographic location or capabilities? Not only would this give a sense of direction in terms of setting priorities for force structure development. Crucially, a distribution of geographical responsibilities will help to ensure that the idea of specialisation is not misused for security free riding. The crucial challenge therefore becomes to understand the shape that such a new division of labour may assume, and explore in what ways it resembles or differs from the one that existed during the Cold War.

At the most basic level, the alliance could re-envisage the defence of the European continent on the basis of a hub-and-spokes model resembling the compass the organisation carries as its emblem. Multiple threats emanate from different geographical vectors and nations are most likely to respond to those threats they consider most immediate or disproportionately affecting their national security. As such, one can easily conceive a division of labour in which the geographical frontier states – along the northern, eastern and southern edges of the alliance – concentrate their security resources on defending their territory and neighbourhood, whereas geographically-sheltered Western European allies retain a more expeditionary mindset along with a responsibility for those non-territorial security threats that concern them immediately, of which islamist terrorism is the prime example. This squares well with the US interest in recalibrating its strategic engagement across the European and Asia-Pacific theatres and devolving a greater share of the defence burden to its allies. At the same time, it is important to remember that the US remains the anchor for the Western alliance in its entirety (Mitchell 2018).

In a practical sense, this hub-and-spokes model would suggest the development of broadly complementary force structures for different allies. The Baltics States and Poland would understandably focus on territorial defence and the hardening of their armed forces that this entails, to the detriment of strategic mobility. Turkey, Greece and Italy would remain more in crisis-management mode with regards to their tumultuous neighbourhood and dealing with the refugee-related dynamics this entails. While Germany would provide the principal pool of reserve land and air-defence forces for meeting a collective defence contingency in Eastern Europe, France would remain engaged in joint expeditionary operations along a far-flung southern and south-eastern axis. A maritime-oriented United Kingdom would remain the most globally oriented of the European allies. The protection of the global commons and the ability to rapidly project military power alongside the US stands at the centre of British defence planning (cf. Blount 2013, Childs 2016). With such an arrangement in place the United

States can focus on the provision of key enablers and reserves forces as required by different regional contingencies. Apart from its longstanding leadership in areas such as command and control, ISTAR and cyber-security, it can shift its resources in function of its evolving international context.

Multiple signs exist that indicate that such a regionally inspired division of labour – or "nodal defence" – is already in the process of emerging irrespective of intentional design (cf. Simon 2015, p. 166). While various allies have been cutting their national force structures without serious attempt at coordination, they have individually engaged in formulating their own threat perception. By taking their own geographical position on the map into account, generic investment and capability priorities emerge that would presumably line up relatively well with what the old NATO defence planning system would have generated. Crucially, most allies are increasingly aware of the fact that the gap between their own political ambitions and their level of defence resourcing is becoming untenable. The principal contemporary challenge for NATO defence planners may therefore reside in the task to ensure overall consistency between these national planning cycles and alliance strategy, and to disseminate awareness of common challenges and best practices.

By doing what comes naturally, the European NATO allies are already well underway in returning to the time-honoured principle of letting their geographical position and related capability preferences inspire their national defence plans. The principal difference between the division of labour as it existed during the Cold War and the present concerns not so much the principles of alliance defence planning, but rather than new geographical boundaries of the alliance and the wider spectrum of threats it faces. The challenges of ensuring consistency between the national defence planning cycles and overall NATO strategy is essentially similar to the one that the alliance has faced over and over again in previous decades, namely the calibration of scarce resources across different areas of responsibility. In this light, a formal return to the regionalisation of alliance defence planning is a straightforward way for meeting the threats that NATO faces today. By itself it will not constitute a panacea to the long-standing problem of under-resourcing in European security, but it will shed much greater clarity about defence requirements and incentive policy action to address the shortfalls.

Conclusion

The rediscovering of geography offers secure ground for anchoring European national as well as NATO defence planning. The present analysis has surveyed how this claim manifested itself like a pendulum throughout the history of the alliance. During the Cold War, the Soviet threat focused the minds of NATO planners on geographical factors. From 1991 onwards, the relative absence of threats to vital interests infused and enabled capability-based approaches to defence planning. Following the dramatic deterioration of the European security environment in 2014, NATO was forced to return to the hard business of defending European territory. While some may lament the direction of this trend, the historical track record offers some comfort in the sense that the transatlantic community has been through trying times before. Studying this historical pendulum process is therefore one mechanism of rising to the challenge.

The principle that allies should concentrate on the defence tasks for which they are the most suited constitutes the analytical key to defining a new division of labour. One key element thereof is that all individual allies can recognise their own interests in the defence tasks they are tasked to undertake. This may prove to be an indispensable argument in terms of building up support for the political will that increasing defence resources requires. This type of broad specialisation is also driven by operational necessity. Any hope that this will prove to be a cost-saving measure that will allow the under-resourcing of Europe's defences to continue must be abandoned. But it may be just enough to sharpen minds about what is required for meeting the present challenges that the alliance faces.

Such a division of labour amongst European allies has one major downside, namely that it embeds a degree of fragmentation into the alliance. The cohesion of the Euro-Atlantic political architecture is already being sorely tested by intra-European as well as transatlantic policy disputes. After all, even the German Chancellor Angela Merkel has repeatedly stated the US can no longer by fully relied upon (Reuters 2017). Would a formal division of roles along geographical lines not undermine the shaky consensus within the alliance even further? While this concern is not to be discarded lightly, the tyranny of geography does make the division easy enough to explain. When compared to the difficulty of explaining that European security is being defended in theatres as far away as Afghanistan, this intellectual simplicity exercises a significant appeal. A new division of labour along such lines also speaks to existing national strategic cultures. The concept has the merit of having been tested under particularly challenging circumstances, namely in the shadow of potential nuclear conflict.

The best possible answer to the objection raised above, however, relates to the fundamental nature of any alliance: to share the burden over many shoulders. A division of roles and responsibilities amongst allies must be part of a greater plan. Individual allies must assume the burden for their area of responsibility, but their forces will also be part of a wider pool. This brings about significant advantages in terms of military proficiency and resources management. In addition, some allies like the United States, Canada and the United Kingdom will continue to focus on their role as nations being able to reinforce whatever front that needs to be supported by mobile reserves. Even if one has doubts about whether the US can be relied upon to provide such reinforcements, the same questions about burden-sharing would continue to apply amongst Europeans – the difference being that capability shortfalls would increase exponentially if Europeans would need to fend for themselves. These shortfalls manifest themselves not only in the nuclear and cyber dimensions, but also with respect to critical mass thresholds in land, sea and air capabilities. One could even wonder to what extent decreasing US commitment to European security would foster European unity, or instead contribute the re-emergence of a "Westphalian Europe" (Simon 2018).

In short, the rediscovering of geography can be exploited to increase the coherence of the alliance's multiple challenges and to communicate to domestic audience what is being defended against. The suggested vision of an emerging division of labour for shoring up NATO defences in the twenty first century is of course rudimentary and incomplete. More in-depth analysis is required for turning this into a practical reality. It can be argued that this constitutes a programme for research as much as a task for NATO defence planners. Identifying what tasks any individual nation is most suited for is not as straightforward as it sounds. Like any elegant and parsimonious principle in international politics, this will require scholarly reflection and debate. Across the alliance, civil-military relations have much to gain from such an exercise.

Acknowledgments

This research was financially enabled through the generous support of the Fulbright Commission for Educational Exchange. The author is also much indebted to Birthe Anders, Frank Hoffman, Manuel Muñiz, Luis Simon, Patrick Wouters, the editors of this special issue and the two anonymous reviewers for commenting on earlier drafts of this text. Last but not least, the ideas contained in this argument have grown organically through numerous off-the-record discussions with NATO planners. Many thanks are due to these interlocutors for their time and candour. The responsibility for any errors is of course the author's alone.

Disclosure statement

No potential conflict of interest was reported by the author.

Funding

This work was supported by the Commission for Educational Exchange between the United States of America, Belgium & Luxembourg [Fulbright Schuman award].

References

Andréani, G., 2006. De la dérive au divorce: les relations transatlantiques après la guerre d'Irak. *Commentaire*, 113, 55–66. doi:10.3917/comm.113.0055.

Ångström, J., 2018. The US perspective on future war: why the US relies upon Ares rather than Athena. *Defence studies*, 18 (3), 318–338.

Arnold, J.-M., 2016. NATO's readiness action plan: strategic benefits and outstanding challenges. *Strategic studies quarterly*, 10 (1), 74–105.

Barry, C. and Binnendijk, H., 2012. *Widening gaps in U.S. and European defense capabilities and cooperation*. Washington DC: Institute for National Strategic Studies.

Blount, C., 2013. Staying in step: the US "Pivot" and UK strategic choices. *Strategic studies quarterly*, 7 (2), 137–150.

Childs, N., 2016. The measure of britain's new maritime ambition. *Survival*, 58 (1), 131–150. doi:10.1080/00396338.2016.1142143.

Clem, R.S., 2016. Geopolitics and planning for a high-end fight: NATO and the baltic region. *Air & space power journal*, 30 (1), 74–85.

Collins, J.M., 1998. *Military geography for professionals and the public*. Washington DC: National Defense University Press.
Daalder, I., 2003. The end of atlanticism. *Survival*, 45 (2), 147–166. doi:10.1080/00396330312331343536.
Daalder, I. and Goldgeier, J., 2006. Global NATO. *Foreign affairs*, 85 (5), 105–113. doi:10.2307/20032073.
Davis, P.K. and Finch, L., 1993. *Defense planning for the post-cold war era: giving meaning to flexibility, adaptiveness, and robustness of capability*. Santa Monica, CA: RAND Corporation.
De Spiegeleire, S., 2011. Ten trends in capability planning for defence and security. *RUSI journal*, 156 (5), 20–28. doi:10.1080/03071847.2011.626270.
Deni, J.R., 2014. NATO's new trajectories after the wales summit. *Parameters*, 44 (3), 57–65.
Deni, J.R., 2017. *NATO and article 5: the transatlantic alliance and the twenty-first-century challenges of collective defense*. Lanham, MD: Rowman & Littlefield.
Doerfel, J.S., 1982. The operational art of the AirLand battle. *Military review*, LXII (5), 3–10.
Fitzsimmons, M., 2006. The problem of uncertainty in strategic planning. *Survival*, 48 (4), 131–146. doi:10.1080/00396330601062808.
Frühling, S. and Lasconjarias, G., 2016. NATO, A2/AD and the Kaliningrad challenge. *Survival*, 58 (2), 95–116. doi:10.1080/00396338.2016.1161906.
Glatz, R.L. and Zapfe, M., 2016. *NATO defence planning between Wales and Warsaw: politico-military challenges of a credible assurance against Russia*. Berlin: Stiftung Wissenschaft und Politik.
Gray, C.S., 1991. Geography and grand strategy. *Comparative strategy*, 10 (4), 311–329. doi:10.1080/01495939108402853.
Gunzinger, M., 2013. *Shaping america's future military: toward a new force planning construct*. Washington DC: Center for Strategic and Budgetary Assessments.
Hoffenaar, J. and Krüger, D., eds., 2012. *Blueprints for battle: planning for war in central Europe, 1948-1968*. Lexington, KY: University Press of Kentucky.
Hoffman, F.G., 2017. *Making NATO Less 'Obsolete'*. Philadelphia, PA: Foreign Policy Research Institute.
Kamp, K.-H., 1999. A global role for NATO? *The washington quarterly*, 22 (1), 7–11. doi:10.1080/01636609909550362.
Khalilzad, Z. and Ochmanek, D., 1997. Rethinking US defence planning. *Survival*, 39 (1), 43–64. doi:10.1080/00396339708442896.
Kramer, F.D. and Craddock, B.J., 2016. *Effective defense of the Baltics*. Washington DC: Atlantic Council.
Leonhard, R.R., 1994. *Fighting by minutes: time and the art of war*. Westport, CT: Prager.
Lock-Pullan, R., 2005. How to rethink war: conceptual innovation and AirLand battle doctrine. *Journal of strategic studies*, 28 (4), 679–702. doi:10.1080/01402390500301087.
Mackinder, H.J., 1943. The round world and the winning of the peace. *Foreign affairs*, 21 (4), 595–605. doi:10.2307/20029780.
Marrone, A., De France, O., and Fattibene, D., eds., 2016. *Defence budgets and cooperation in Europe: developments, trends and drivers*. Rome: Istituto Affari Internazionali.
Mattelaer, A., 2011. How Afghanistan has Strengthened NATO. *Survival*, 53 (6), 127–140. doi:10.1080/00396338.2011.636517.
Mattelaer, A., 2014. Preparing NATO for the next defence-planning cycle. *RUSI journal*, 159 (3), 30–35. doi:10.1080/03071847.2014.927995.
Mattelaer, A., 2016. Revisiting the principles of NATO burden-sharing. *Parameters*, 46 (1), 25–33.
Mearsheimer, J.J., 1982. Maneuver, mobile defense, and the NATO central front. *International security*, 6 (3), 104–122. doi:10.2307/2538609.
Mitchell, A.W., 2018. *Anchoring the western alliance. Speech delivered at the heritage foundation*. Washington, DC: U.S. Department of State, 5 June.
NATO, 1949. Strategic concept for the defence of the North Atlantic area. *NATO, DC 6/1*, 1 December 1949.

NATO, 1950. Strategic guidance for North Atlantic regional planning. *NATO, MC 14*, 28 March 1950.
NATO, 1952. NATO strategic guidance. *NATO, MC 14/1*, 9 December 1952.
NATO, 1957. Overall strategic concept for the defense of the North Atlantic treaty organization area. *NATO, MC 14/2*, 21 February 1957.
NATO, 1967. Decisions of defence planning committee in ministerial session. *NATO, DPC/D (67) 23*, 11 May 1967.
NATO, 1968. Overall strategic concept for the defense of the North Atlantic treaty area. *NATO, MC 14/3*, 16 January 1968. doi:10.1055/s-0028-1105114.
NATO, 1991. The alliance's new strategic concept. *NATO*, 8 November 1991. Available from: https://www.nato.int/cps/ua/natohq/official_texts_23847.htm
NATO, 2003. Final communique: ministerial meeting of the defence planning committee and the nuclear planning group. *NATO*, 12 June 2003. Available from: https://www.nato.int/docu/pr/2003/p03-064e.htm
NATO, 2010. Active engagement, modern defence: strategic concept for the defence and security of the members of the North Atlantic treaty organisation. *NATO*, 19 November 2010. Available from: https://www.nato.int/cps/ua/natohq/official_texts_68580.htm
NATO, 2014. Wales summit declaration. *NATO*, 5 September 2014. Available from: https://www.nato.int/cps/ic/natohq/official_texts_112964.htm
NATO, 2016. Warsaw summit communiqué. *NATO*, 9 July 2016. Available from: https://www.nato.int/cps/ic/natohq/official_texts_133169.htm
Pedlow, G.W., 1997. *NATO strategy documents 1949-1969*. Brussels: NATO.
Pedlow, G.W., 2009. *The evolution of NATO's command structure, 1951-2009*. Mons: Allied Command Operations.
Peltier, L.C. and Pearcy, G.E., 1966. *Military geography*. Princeton, NJ: Van Nostrand.
Pfeiffer, H., 2008. Defence and force planning in historical perspective: NATO as a case study. *Baltic security & defence review*, 10, 103–120.
Reuters, 2017. After summits with trump, merkel says Europe must take fate into own hands. *Reuters*, 28 May. Available from: https://www.reuters.com/article/us-germany-politics-merkel-idUSKBN18O0JK
Rivero, H., 1972. The defence of NATO's Southern Flank. *RUSI journal*, 117 (666), 3–10. doi:10.1080/03071847209429768.
Rogers, J. and Romanovs, U., 2015a. Baltic military preparations after Ukraine: a sufficiently 'prickly' deterrent? *RUSI newsbrief*, 35 (2), 8–10.
Rogers, J. and Romanovs, U., 2015b. NATO's Eastern Flank: rebuilding deterrence? *RUSI newsbrief*, 35 (3), 14–16.
Rühle, M. and Williams, M., 1997. Why NATO will survive. *Comparative strategy*, 16 (1), 109–115. doi:10.1080/01495939708403093.
Ruiz Palmer, D.A., 1990. Paradigms lost: A retrospective assessment of the NATO Warsaw pact military competition in the Alliance's Southern Region. *Comparative strategy*, 9 (3), 265–286. doi:10.1080/01495939008402814.
Rupp, R., 2000. NATO 1949 and NATO 2000: from collective defense toward collective security. *Journal of strategic studies*, 23 (3), 154–176. doi:10.1080/01402390008437804.
Rynning, S., 2013. Germany is more than Europe can handle: or, why NATO remains a pacifier. Rome: NATO Defense College (Research Paper No. 96).
Shlapak, D.A. and Johnson, M., 2016. *Reinforcing deterrence on NATO's Eastern Flank: wargaming the defense of the Baltics*. Santa Monica, CA: RAND Corporation.
Simon, L., 2014. Assessing NATO's Eastern European "Flank". *Parameters*, 44 (3), 67–79.
Simon, L., 2015. Understanding US retrenchment in Europe. *Survival*, 52 (2), 157–172. doi:10.1080/00396338.2015.1026093.
Simon, L., 2018. *The spectre of a Westphalian Europe*. London: Royal United Services Institute (Whitehall Paper 90).

Vallance, A., 2003. A radically new command structure for NATO. *NATO review*, Autumn issue. Available from: https://www.nato.int/docu/review/2003/NATO-Strategic-Partners/Radically-new-Command-Structure-NATO/EN/index.htm

Webber, M., Sperling, J., and Smith, M.A., 2012. *NATO's post-cold war trajectory: decline or regeneration?* Basingstoke: Palgrave Macmillan.

Wouters, P., 2011. Technical background briefing on NATO command structure. *Brussels: NATO*, 9 June 2011. Available from: https://www.nato.int/cps/ic/natohq/opinions_75353.htm

Yost, D.S., 2000. The NATO capabilities gap and the European Union. *Survival*, 42 (4), 97–128. doi:10.1080/713869441.

Questioning the "Sanctity" of long-term defense planning as practiced in Central and Eastern Europe

Thomas-Durell Young

ABSTRACT

It is an article of faith amongst many defense officials that long-term defense planning constitutes the gold standard in the development and management of modern armed forces. That such a method has become central to the U.S. and other countries' defense planning systems it is surprising that there is so little questioning of its contemporary relevance, let alone an understanding of its provenance, original intent, and its highly nuanced nature. Rather, what one finds on closer examination of long-term defense planning methods is that they have contributed to producing sub-optimal defense plans. In order to provide greater clarity and understanding of the utility of long-term defense plans, this essay argues that as a key element of PPBS, this planning method has been a failure when measured against the ability of defense institutions in Central and Eastern Europe to produce viable defense plans. To produce cost-informed and implementable defense plans, these defense institutions need to return to the original intend of this planning tool: to inform officials of long-term financial obligations and to enable informed decision-making to fund the current force.

It is an article of faith amongst many defense officials that long-term defense planning constitutes the gold standard in the development and management of modern armed forces. In the case of the U.S. Department of Defense this is manifested in the Future Year Defense Program (FYDP). Indeed, one is schooled in its inviolate nature: staff and war college graduates will "fondly" recall briefings on the "rolling donuts" representing circles of the intersection of planning, programming, and acquisition. Likewise, authoritative sources simply assert that long-term defense planning is a critical and needed element of modern defense planning. To wit: "Long term planning (LTP) is essential to organisations facing the combined impact of uncertainty of the future and little flexibility with regards to resource employment" (NATO 2003, p. iii). As an essential aspect of programming within the U.S. Department of Defense (i.e. the

---

The views expressed in this article are those solely of the author and do not reflect the policy or views of the Naval Postgraduate School, Department of the Navy, or the Department of Defense. The writer would like to express his sincere gratitude to Dr Bence Nemeth, Messrs. Glen Grant, Fred LaBarre, Vladimir Milenski, Jaan Murumets, Bostjan Mocnik, and Mihail Naydenov for their insightful comments made on earlier drafts of this paper.

Planning, Programming, Budgeting, and Execution system – PPBE; often named PPBS where it has been adopted by other defense institutions), it is seen as being managed by the high priests of programming, and heretical questioning of the programming liturgy is simply not countenanced. Indeed, the method of PPBE (and its assumption of the necessity of long-term planning) has been exported abroad, notably to former communist states in Central and Eastern Europe (Vance and Hinkle 2010, pp. B-1 thru B5). With the encouragement of NATO nations and the International Staff, these countries have followed U.S. practices and, *inter alia*, dutifully develop long-term defense plans, albeit not as ambitious as their American counterparts' military departments, e.g. the U. S. Navy's Thirty-year Ship Building Plan (O'Rourke 2017).

That such a method has become central to the U.S. and other countries' defense planning systems it is surprising that there is so little questioning of its contemporary relevance, let alone a broader understanding of its provenance, original intent, and its highly nuanced nature. This is not even to address how relevant such a concept can be in the contemporary fluid security environment, not to mention how this planning process can address in a timely fashion disruptive technological innovation. Rather, what one finds on closer examination of long-term defense planning methods is that they have contributed to producing sub-optimal defense plans which are rarely executed. All the while this process is typically managed by its proponents in a needlessly highly complex manner which obviates against planning clarity and transparency, e.g. '[Long-term defense planning] is a complicated process fraught with significant and perhaps dire consequences for nations' (NATO 2003, p. 1). Indeed, arguably in its worst manifestations when it is employed as an essential element of PPBS, it contributes to isolating policy priorities from financial execution (Young 2016b).

This essay constitutes a continuation of a series of writings by the current writer that endeavours to analyze the utility of the PPBS in the context of defense institutions in Central and Eastern Europe. This particular work will assess the utility of long-term defense planning in its current usage and within its proper context as constituting one of the key assumptions of PPBS. As such, this essay is organized accordingly. First, it is important for planners and analysts to know the unique historical provenance and institutional context of the assertion that long-term planning is essential to producing viable defense plans, e.g. 'To deal with an increasingly complex security environment producing disparate competing demands, decision-makers need increasingly sophisticated support in the LTDP [long-term defense planning] process' (NATO 2003, p. iii). Critically related to this question is to understand the exceptional *American* historical and lingering contemporary institutional context behind the unquestioning need for long-term defense planning. Second, it is essential to analyze how this concept has been adopted and implemented in both the United States, as well as Central and Eastern Europe. The result of this review demonstrates that the method of long-term defense planning is plagued with muddled concepts and imprecisions in nomenclature, all of which has led to confusion and continues to impedethe development of viable defense plans. Third, it is necessary to enquire whether this method has been shown actually to *work*. Despite its wide-spread use, particularly for instance amongst "new" members of NATO, it is difficult to find many instances (despite a plethora of documents) of cases where these plans have ever been actually implemented as intended. Fourth, the essay will examine in light of the foregoing analysis whether there is any demonstrable utility for defense institutions to adopt long-term defense planning methods. Fifth, the conclusion will include recommendations to aid defense official and planners gain greater clarity of defense planning and how certain aspects of long-planning can be re-conceptualized to be utilized to greater benefit and utility. At the heart of these recommendations is the need for officials to return to the original intention for creating long-term defense plans and redoubling their efforts to created costed priorities that are essential to *drive* effective defense planning, and forego the illusion that somehow long-term defense planning can ever provide a solution to the reality of budgeting uncertainty.

Origins of modern long-term defense planning

The origins of modern, formal long-term defense planning arguably can be traced to the introduction of the process in the U.S. Department of Defense in the early years of the Kennedy Administration when the president gave the task to his Secretary of Defense, Robert McNamara, to bring greater unity of effort to the sprawling and uncoordinated department. A key starting point was the appointment of Charles Hitch as Assistant Secretary of Defense (Comptroller). Hitch, along with Roland N. McKean, were the authors of a well-regarded work, published in 1960, that took the then novel approach of looking at defense planning as an economic, vice solely a military, challenge (Hitch and McKean 1960, p. 105). In other words, they endeavoured to conceptualize the challenge of defense planning as an economic problem, which needed to be solved through the efficient allocation of resources and reconciling conflicting views amongst organizations. In what is arguably the most persuasive treatise on the programming method, Alain C. Enthoven and K. Wayne Smith; both of whom helped introduce programming to the U.S. Department of Defense, best identified the challenges facing the administration as it attempted to bring unity of effort amongst three independent military departments (i.e. departments of the army, navy, and air force):

> Perhaps the key reason for the limited usefulness of the defense budget was the fact that defense budgeting was, in effect, conceived as being largely unrelated to military strategy. The two were treated as almost independent activities. They were carried out by different people, at different times, with different terms of reference, and without a method for integrating their activities. The strategy and forces were thought to be essentially military matters, while the budget was thought to be mainly a civilian matter. Force planning was done for several years into the future, by military men, on a mission-oriented basis, by the Services with attempts at coordination by the JCS organization. Financial planning was done one year at a time, largely by civilians, in terms of object classes of expenditures such as personnel and procurement, through the Service and DoD Comptroller organizations. This gap between strategy and forces, on the one hand, and budgets, on the other, posed a serious obstacle to rational defense planning (Enthoven and Smith 2005, p. 13).

The situation in which the new administration found itself was unenviable. The seminal 1947 National Security Act, whilst creating the Department of Defense, in reality only merged loosely a 'confederation of the three military departments' and where the secretary of defense exercised only limited powers (Hitch 1967, p. 15). Until the early 1960s defense planning consisted of the secretary of defense dividing the defense budget amongst the three military departments, essentially leaving to these organizations how to decide best to spend their respective budgets. This was the case, in large part, due to the Department of Defense's lack of management structures and techniques. This *de facto* budget-driven process predictably produced sub-optimization since the military departments recognized only their own priorities; and in consequence, jointness suffered (Hitch 1967, pp. 18, 23–4).

With a mandate from President Kennedy to bring greater coherence to defense, Secretary McNamara put the services on notice that he expected to see, *inter alia*, the full life-cycle costs of all new proposed acquisitions. It needs to be recalled that this was during a period of high peacetime defense expenditures, conscription, conventional modernization, as well as each service developing and attempting to field their own expensive nuclear delivery platforms (Hitch and McKean 1960, pp. 23–83). To create the planning and management methods to achieve these objectives, McNamara directed Hitch and his team to implement "programming" for Fiscal Year 1963, giving them only 6 months to accomplish this task (Enthoven and Smith 2005, pp. 27–9). The Planning, Programming, and Budgeting System (PPBS) created in 1962 was designed to give the department a single method to prepare its annual defense budget, as well as establishing guidance for *future* planning in the form of costed capability proposals. Yet, given limited time and fierce opposition from the military departments a little-known accord was agreed which has, in effect, obviated against achieving the objectives of programming. By this, Hitch obscuficated this critically important point when he later wrote, 'Thus, the SECDEF now has the tools he needs to take the initiative in the planning and direction of the entire defense effort on a truly unified basis' (Hitch 1967, p. 58). Yet the fact of the matter is that the new programming system left *untouched* the existing budget structure (and thereby ensuring the military department's continuing autonomy) and connecting planning to budgeting via the new programming structure (Hitch 1967, p. 30). In short, Hitch allowed to remain stand one of the key weaknesses in the planning system that predated programming as identified by Enthoven and Smith (2005, p. 13).

Recounting the above historical record is critical to understanding the origins of long-term defense planning as a basic tenet of PPBS because the military departments had to produce detailed financial projections for the fiscal year in which funds were being planned, plus the following four years for review by the Office of the Secretary of Defense. These data were compiled to constitute a five-year plan. This practice was further institutionalized in law (U.S) when Congress directed the Department of Defense to compile these figures and submit a five-year defense program, i.e. the FYDP (*U.S. Code*, Title 10, Subtitle A, Part I, Chapter 9 § 221), which is used by the Secretary of Defense to project expenditures and proposed budget requests.[1] The submission of the FYDP annually to Congress meets the requirements of this legislation (U.S. Government Accountability Office 2004, pp. 4–5).

To the credit of those officials who attempted to bring reform to the Department of Defense through creating greater unity of effort and to produce financial efficiencies, there are benefits to elements of assessing the full financial implications of decision-making. As one U.S. government report notes, "leading practices in capital decision-making include developing a long-term capital plan to guide implementation of organizational goals and objectives and help decision-makers establish priorities over the long term" (U.S. General Accounting Office 1998). All too often prior to the McNamara era, the long-term financial liabilities being assumed by the military departments (and by extension, U.S. tax-payers), often went unacknowledged. This situation resulted in military planners being *freed* from having to consider the financial consequences of their plans, whereas budgeting planning which lives within the context of yearly budget-cycles, *had* to be accurate. Worse yet, as Hitch noted, this led to military requirements being represented in absolute terms, disconnected from its cost implications (Hitch 1967, pp. 25–6). Clearly, a solution to this conundrum needed to be found. As an element to bring greater understanding of the financial implications of defense plans, officials realized that planning in a one-year timeframe was simply too short at the national-level. What was needed by senior defense officials was an understanding not only of future financial obligations of proposed draft plans, but also an accurate data-base of past financial costs to create an informed perspective of trends. In consequence, the fifth pillar of PPBS comprised a plan for combining forces and their costs projected into the future to provide officials with financial data of their decisions. Yet importantly, the authors of PPBS claimed that their long-term plan was never envisaged to be inflexible. Rather it was seen as providing officials with a projection of the financial implications of past decisions and planning assumptions, all with the objective of providing needed financial context by which defense plans could be developed. It was envisaged that a long-term plan would encourage officials to be mindful that today's decisions have long-term financial implications and these needed to be factored into current and future-year plans. Once implemented the initiative would force services to provide accurate financial projections of decisions (i.e. full life-cycle costs). Portrayed in this light, the authors argued that a long-term defense plan would not bind future officials to past decision-making. Rather, they argued that it would provide officials in future years with *flexibility* to shift priorities as they would have a full appreciation of the potential financial consequences of a decision to change directions (Enthoven and Smith 2005, pp. 20, 44–5, 48, 50).

There are a number of salient implications from this brief recounting of the original intent of the U.S. Department of Defense's concept of long-term defense planning. First, it is important to acknowledge that long-term "planning"; that is to say, multi-year force and supporting financial planning, was seen as constituting an essential element of PPBS. Second, PPBS was designed explicitly to meet the then prevailing rigid bureaucratic structures and political realities within the U.S. government. Uniquely different from other Western ministries of defense, the U.S. Department of Defense remains a confederacy of independent organizations, and critically, each with their own jealously guarded budgetary *autonomy* and legally-defined institutional responsibilities and functions. As Haynes so presciently writes, "The process [PPBE] became the essential means by which the US military services protected their respective identities, preferred weapons systems, and relevance" (Haynes, 2013, p. 7). And, as the military departments' individual PPBE systems have evolved, they have succeeded in isolating administrations' policy priorities from financial execution precisely in a way unforeseen or intended by its originators, i.e. the inability of secretaries of defense to change quickly priorities. No better example of this fact can be seen in Secretary of Defense Robert Gates's battle against his own Department of Defense to procure mine-resistant, ambush-protected vehicles (MRAPs) during the war in Iraq. "The hidebound and unresponsive bureaucratic structure that the Defense Department uses to acquire equipment performs poorly in peacetime. As I saw, it did so horribly in wartime" (2014, p. 126).

Additionally, notwithstanding public "strategy" documents published by administrations, the development of major force programs via PPBE and which are enshrined in the FYDP, all are a result of the intention of successive Congresses that the military departments are to remain largely independent from the Office of the Secretary of Defense.[2] One does not find such similar bureaucratic structures and supporting political realities in Central and Eastern Europe; the situation is to the contrary as ministries of defense are firmly under the control of cabinet/councils of ministers and powerful ministries of finance. Establishing government financial priorities are greatly complicated in the case of coalition governments with many political parties: a political reality in many of these countries. Furthermore, many ministries of finance in Central and Eastern Europe, e.g. Slovakia (Simon 2004, p. 200) and Georgia (Akubardia 2010, pp. 31–2) have been reluctant to recognize the concept of programming as a legitimate financial management technique as it is perceived as constituting future financial obligations. Third, unless carefully managed and controlled; all of which is manpower-intensive, experience demonstrates that programming can devolve into "strategic budgeting" which has the effect of isolating endorsed policy and priorities from budgetary execution. Evidence of this reality can be found in numerous defense institutions in Central and Eastern Europe (argued in Young 2017b), as well as in the case of the U.S. Department of the Navy (Young 2016c). Thus, if only at the conceptual level, it is clear that the conditions which produced PPBS and what has become known as the FYDP are unique and it is highly unlikely that any defense institution in Central and Eastern Europe would have developed such complex methods on their own. It is, therefore, a legitimate question to pose: why was this highly complicated, nuanced, and U.S.-centric methodology exported extensively to the region?

Conflated concepts and nomenclature and muddled thinking

A review of the historical antecedents of programming and the creation of long-term defense planning in the United States demonstrates that the creators of this methodology went to great lengths to try to bring order to an incoherent process by which the Department of Defense conducted what can only be described as disaggregated budgeting. Thus, whilst perhaps the "theory" was valid, its application and subsequent transmutations have proven that programming has not been successful. The record demonstrates that it has led to conditions whereby it has contributed to isolating policy from financial execution. Thus, it is instructive to compare the original intent of employing long-term planning with its current application and usage by defense institutions in Central and Eastern Europe.

Most importantly, the creators of programming never intended the original five-year defense plan to be a rigid, unchangeable plan, which one sees all too often in Central and Eastern Europe, where the institutional memory of communist 5-year plans is inevitably still very strong in many countries. Rather, it was created to solve two problems in bringing coherence to defense planning in the Department of Defense. First, in advocating new acquisitions, the military departments often did not present the full costs of new equipment, i.e. their full life-cycle costs. Thus, it was not unusual that prospective procurements would be over budget. Second, in addition to insisting on accurate costings of defense, McNamara's officials insisted that the military departments provide both the full cost of the procurement (which, in itself, proved to be challenging), as well as an eight-year projection of forces and a five-year projection of costs of associated personnel in all mission-oriented programs. This was judged as necessary to enable the Office of the Secretary of Defense to transition from one-year budgeting ceilings which were seen as being inappropriate for managing and financing large acquisitions over multiple years.

Critically, Enthoven and Smith argued that their long-term defense plan was never intended to obligate future governments to fund previous decisions. Rather than constituting an inflexible plan to be followed blindly and without question, it was envisaged to provide defense planners with a road-map of the costs to be used in creating future plans and programs. In fact, in its earliest versions, it did not appear as a plan, but rather as a series of force tables. Thus, the original purpose of long-term defense planning was seen as providing planners with a guide to understand future financial obligations associated with past decision-making. In fact, Enthoven and Smith argued that, in lieu of limiting the decision-making abilities of the Secretaries of Defense, a long-term defense plan would provide officials with needed *flexibility* to *change* directions as dictated by policy and events, given that it was known what the costs would be associated with alternative options (Enthoven and Smith 2005, pp. 48, 52–3).

The adoption of PPBS and other Western defense planning concepts in legacy defense institutions in Central and Eastern Europe has faced two key challenges. First, there has been the practice by Western officials of an infelicitous usage of nomenclature which has led to confused thinking and understanding of how to plan using Western methods. One distraction to providing clarity has been the practice of conflating planning, programming, and acquisition as if they were one process; whereby history has demonstrated that the former activity is all too often ignored by programming bureaucracies, and the separation of these three activities provides the opportunity to solve the antagonism in the requirements and responsibilities of each one against the other two. To be sure, the decision to introduce a new capability into an armed force needs to be assessed holistically, particularly related to its full life-cycle costs. However, as the experience of the U.S. Department of the Navy has demonstrated, without continuous strong policy control (articulated with costed plans), there is a tendency for the process to devolve into "strategic budgeting", with a strong emphasis on funding existing platforms, vice weapon systems and new technologies.[3] All of these defense institutions for years following the end of the Cold War lacked empowered policy directorates. Absent a cadre of civilian defense experts with a deep knowledge of the Western concept of "policy", recommendations of general staffs have often gone unchallenged, and hence unrestrained by financial realities. The record of these defense institutions demonstrates that in many cases long-term defense plans are perceived as being synonymous with acquisition and procurement, as well as the plans being immutable, thereby restricting officials' ability to change priorities after they have been approved. Seemingly lost has been the logic that all aspects of the defense budget need to be relevant to delivering "defense". After all, if an existing capability is not needed on the modern battlefield, there is no military logic that could possibly dictate that it should remain in the order of battle. Yet all too often officials and analysts have twisted the purpose of these plans to argue that once approved, long-term defense plans cannot be changed and are unassailable later for review by policy, e.g. Ukraine (Young 2017a, pp. 76–7).

Second, in the context of Central and Eastern European defense institutions, the concept of long-term defense plans was inappropriately introduced and poorly adopted and has become in many cases a bureaucratic pathology that has served to inhibit the development of coherent defense planning. Evidently, the experts who exported PPBS were not fully aware of the conceptual basis of the post-communist environment in which they were operating. This environment, most of which still remains intact today, operates in a militarized setting, based on a high degree of centralized control, which still adheres to communist-inspired legacy military concepts, impervious to revision. At its heart, leggacy "military doctrine" (Donnelly 1988, pp. 106) remains part of many institutions' mental operating systems. Due to its highly coherent nature, it remains as an unstated "theology" over which the entire armed forces are subjected to the highest degree of centralized control imaginable. Complicating the adoption of Western defense concepts is both the pernicious character of legacy military concepts and the fact that they are antithetical to the former (Young 2016a). Other legacy planning assumptions include an obsession with procuring new platforms and systems in large number, as opposed to optimizing the current force, as well as a cost blindness to such realities as long-term financial liabilities, life-cycle costs, inflation, and the amortization of the current system. Finally, it should not be ignored that until recently these were societies which had been ruled and dominated by Soviet-inspired ubiquitous five-year plans (the first covering 1928–32), which were ruthlessly implemented and which had the effect of centralizing communist control over an entire economy and society: down to the very last person. The prevalence of "military doctrine"; which, indeed 25-years after the Cold War can still be "felt" throughout these armed forces (Young 2017a, pp. 16, 59), and the continued utilization of antithetical legacy planning concepts and assumptions, like the indisputable "plan", have all combined to forestall the adoption of Western defense concepts.

One can observe in official planning documents produced by defense institutions in the region, and indeed in the writings on the subject of long-term planning, widespread confusion and misunderstanding of the original intent of this method that has inhibited the development of viable (i.e. executable) defense plans. Long-term defense plans drafted in legacy-burdened ministries of defense and general staffs inevitably are premised on the problematic assumption that if an activity, formation, or platform is *in* the plan, it implies that it *will be* funded and therefore the plan will be executed. The best example of this fallacious thinking can be found in the troubled history of the series of Ukrainian *strategic bulletins* that have been produced with five-year regularity after extensive periods of analysis and study; none of the efforts have succeeded in tying these plans with the defense budget (Young 2017a, 76–7). As a result, they have all failed to provide any coherent direction to the armed forces, and once shown to be ineffectual, produce planning stasis, but without any negative consequences for any civilian or military officials, as responsibility is collectivized in almost all of these defense institutions (Young 2017c). By focusing on producing the "plan", officials have abjured what should be their first responsibility as planners: to make defense *fit* the existing budget. Examples can be found in such ministries of defense that present detailed force modernization and ambitious acquisition plans, but then explain how these objectives are financially impossible to achieve, e.g. Bulgaria (2015), or obsess over future growth in GDP and assume that economic growth will be translated directly into a larger defense budget, e.g. Macedonia (2014, pp. 38–40). Indeed, a good indicator of whether a long-term defense plan was developed using legacy concepts is where they do not start with an understanding of financial realities. Often, "money", if it is discussed at all, is relegated to the end of the document and not addressed in a meaningful manner. One sees this lack of financial realism even in those defense institutions which some might consider to be quite developed by "Western" standards, e.g. Slovenia (Slovenia 2009, Katič 2016).

Contributing to these conceptual misunderstandings has been muddled thinking about long-term defense planning that can be found in the literature, limited as it is (e.g. Håkenstad and Larsen). A representative example is provided by Ball and Le Roux (2006, pp. 41, 23), "As already stated, strategic situations change rapidly whilst the building of defence capabilities and expertise takes time. All strategic defence planning must therefore take the long-term view". They proceed to advocate the development of medium-term expenditure frameworks that tie policies and objectives, improve transparency, focus on outputs, and increase "ownership" by sectorial ministries. Stojkovic and Dahl (2007, p. 11) have written the rare essay that attempts to define and explain the nature and advantages of long-term planning.

> The general purpose of LTDP [long-term defense plan] is to (re)consider the mission of the Defence and to establish realistic long term goals and objectives consistent with that mission, as well as to define strategies for their fulfilment. Also, LTDP will promote [sic] desirable development of the Defence and to avoid unwanted effects.

Long-term defense planning, they claim, encourages planners to consider contingencies and develop the means to address them, whilst also "providing insights into future risks". They go on to claim that long-term defense planning establishes a link to financial challenges; albeit on the latter point they do not explain how this is the case (Stojkovic and Dahl 2007, p. 11). Finally, a NATO handbook on long-term defense planning writes of the need 'to balance defence expenditures with assumptions about future defence budgets' (NATO 2003, p. 7).

All of these works, implicitly or otherwise, are attempting to provide planners with a solution to the central challenge that bedevils all defense planners: how can one predict future defense budgets, and build a viable defense plan within these parameters? Ball and Le Roux even claim that absent a governmental commitment to achieve certain expenditure levels, no meaningful planning or programming can take place (Ball and Le Roux 2006, 47). Yet, in the end, their understanding of the nature of planning and the realities of democratic defense governance are not supportive of their assertions. In short, these arguments are weak on four key points. First, they perpetuate the misunderstanding that long-term defense planning, by definition, must be linear and perforce static. As one NATO report states: "Given the significant period it takes to implement a new force structure, partly due to lengthy development and acquisition times, Long Term Defence Planning (LTDP) usually focuses ten to thirty years into the future" (NATO 2003, p. x). What they are advocating is that by creating these plans, planning will be more predictable and in the worst misunderstanding of them, are implicitly contracts between the defense institution and government and somehow will be funded; after all, in most countries long-term defense plans are enshrined in law. Second, as will be discussed below in the context of NATO policies regarding

PfP Partner countries, attempting to obtain from governments or ministries of finance assurances of future defense expenditure levels is simply a fool's errand, and dwelling on obtaining such assurances distracts from the most important task of a defense planner: executing the one responsibility that is the most powerful instrument that they possess: to produce *costed priorities*. Third, none of these works define long-term defense planning within its proper originating context as proving a critical tool for managing today's defense force, i.e. creating an understanding of future financial projection of current obligations. Unfortunately, they represent a common misunderstanding of the original nature of long-term defense planning in the limited literature, which can be observed in the many failures to implement long-term defense plans by defense institutions in Central and Eastern Europe. Fourth, implicit in these arguments in favor of long-term defense planning is an implied assumption that they are successful in foretelling future requirements of the armed forces. Unfortunately, this is simply not the case as the "enemy" does have a vote. After all, if the U.S. FYDP constitutes a best practice, then one has the challenge of explaining why, for instance, it had not predicted the need for up-armoured vehicles (i.e. MRAPs) in Afghanistan and Iraq and that they had to be procured out-of-cycle.

Does long-term defense planning (actually) work? The case of Central and Eastern Europe

In order that the current writer not to be open to the charge of "navel gazing" over methodology at the expense of practicality, it is essential that the fundamental question of whether long-term defense planning has any proven *utility* needs to be addressed. As seen, notable analysts and NATO itself have argued the value of using this technique in producing defense outcomes. However, these arguments must be "tested" to actual defense planning situations to ascertain whether this technique actually delivers its intended outcome, i.e. do they create and maintain defense policy-determined defense capabilities? Indeed, one obscure report cited by Stojkovic and Dahl argues that many long-term plans are never fully implemented, or they prove to lack utility in cases of changing and unpredictable environments (The Voluntary Sector Knowledge Network 2007). Since it is hard to imagine what could be a more unpredictable environment than that which relates to defence, this reality suggests confirmation of LTDP's lack of utility for defense.

If one returns to the context of "new" NATO allies and PfP Partners with legacy heritage, it is the rare defense institution in the region which does not dutifully draft long-term defense plans with an almost religious-like expectation that these plans will be executed by the very "power" of having been approved. Traditionally, long-term defense plans had been envisaged to span a five-year timeframe; however, following the international financial crisis, with advice provided by Western nations and NATO International Staff, these plans now mirror NATO's ten-year planning cycle introduced in 2008 (Kordowski et al. n.d., p. 49) and in at least one country, the plan is twelve-years (Latvia), based on the PPBS-inspired assumption of a viable multi-year force and financial planning. Yet all the while that these defense institutions have been diligently developing long-term defense plans, they have all universally struggled to implement PPBS, failing to see this conceptual disconnect. There is now another trend which is to develop modern sounding and apparently NATO compatible, "capability plans".

However absent developing fully cost-informed plans (that include their long-term financial obligations) premised on a defense budget divided into thirds (i.e. personnel, operations and maintenance, and investment), these are likely to be just another long-term defense plan by another name, and equally ignored by governments and ministries of finance. In point of fact, the general norm in the region is that defense planning is largely conducted absent full costing data. For instance, as late as 2016, the Estonian defense institution *still* did not possess a methodology to provide estimated costs of generic capability options (Murumets 2016, p. 1). Another example can be seen by studying the past practices of the Polish defense institution. The general staff created the 'Army 2006' modernization plan, which in the end proved to be neither politically, nor financially, supportable (Gogolewska 2006, p. 112). In recent years, Polish planning methods again failed in the case of the development of the ten-year technical modernization program launched in 2012. By the end of 2015, it was reported that this plan had not met its acquisition objectives due to the fact that the plan had not been properly *costed* (Paszewski 2016, pp. 126–7). One can only hope that the Polish government's 2017 defense review and recommended force structure (which was subjected to an extensive series of analytical studies and war games) is fully costed and therefore proves to be viable over time (Poland 2017, pp. 13, 62–5). As a result, as the current writer has argued in another forum, the record of defense planning amongst "new" NATO members, almost all of them are attempting to use programming and draft extensive long-term defense plans, is clearly one of abject failure (Young 2016b, pp. 68–77). Put another way, tabling the argument that not one of the countries have been able to produce a viable long-term defense plan that has been executed, one is challenged to cite a case (using objective data and not assertion) where one *has* been implemented as planned.[4]

When examining the defense planning methods employed by these countries, it is clear that the imported programming methodology has not performed to expectation. At worse, programming combines with national and organizational cultural norms, e.g. high power-distance (Hofstede 2011 and Hofstede *et al.* 2010) to isolate government-endorsed policy from financial execution. Left unaddressed is that the concept of "money" remains defined by these defense institutions in legacy terms as a given, and all existing problems would be solved if only there were *more* (often articulated in the context of an aspired certain percentage of GDP). For instance, this very line of argument is found in the 2010 Serbian Defense White Paper, which states authoritatively (and nonsensically) that to implement the methods provided by the International Monetary Fund (the precise source not being cited), defense requires at least 2 percent of GDP (Serbia 2010, pp. 128–9). This representative example illustrates that these defense institutions continue to struggle to adopt the basic concept that in a democracy existing finances must be optimized to produce defense outcomes and that ministries have no authority to dictate to parliaments their financial aspirations.

The final question of the utility of long-term defense planning relates to the method's ability successfully to effect planning continuity in periods of financial uncertainty and throughout periods of escalation. As to the former point, during the early years of this decade, the U.S. Congressional mandated sequestration of the federal budget under the terms of the Budget Control Act (which had the aim of reducing the federal government's deficit), stressed both the U.S. Departments of the Navy and Air Force's PPBE to the point that they collapsed due uncertainty of their budgets (Young 2016c, pp. 942, 946). This experience alone suggests that programming as a method may well be only appropriate in financial environments where there is budgetary certainty and/or strategic stability, i.e. conditions which existed during the Cold War.[5]

Second, it must be judged as problematic that long-term defense planning methods are sufficiently robust to survive the stress that inevitably would befall policy officials and planners should a defense institution have to respond militarily amidst a state of escalation. By this, it is unclear; to say the least, that long-term defense planning methods have been explicitly designed with the objective of ensuring methodological *continuity* and functionality of planning in peace, tension, crisis, and war. If one accepts the Western concept that one prepares the defense institution with the objective of being able to conduct effective military operations under wartime conditions, logic therefore dictates that planning methods must be applicable throughout the *entire* spectrum of escalation. Whilst this point has not been widely discussed by officials or analysts, given the wide use of ineffectual programming and long-term defense plans by countries throughout the region, one is left with the suspicion that such considerations have not been fully understood by defense officials, or those foreign experts assisting in introducing PPBS, let alone addressed sufficiently. Therefore, one fears that existing programming methods, expressed in long-term defense plans in Central and Eastern Europe, as well as in the United States,[6] remain in idyllic isolation from confronting this reality. This precise methodological weakness can be witnessed very clearly in the case of the US PPBE which has proven itself impervious to being relevant during periods of war, notwithstanding Enthoven and Smith's lengthy, but unconvincing, argument related to the Vietnam war, to the contrary (2005, pp. 267–9). It is arguable that the U.S. Department of Defense has sufficiently robust institutional capability and enough money to enable it to maintain, in effect, two different planning systems; i.e. PPBE and Operations and Overseas Contingency funding (Williams and Epstein 2017), albeit this has not been without severe criticism by some influential members of Congress (Bender and Herb 2015). Yet, one would be imprudent to assume that any of these legacy defense institutions have such institutional planning and programming redundancy, let alone political support for such a solution. Instead, one suspects that in a case of escalation, existing programming and multi-year funding assumptions will be quickly jettisoned and less complex planning methods tied to operations would have to be quickly developed: if there is sufficient time.

Unfortunately, Western political officials and the NATO International Staff have not been able to develop a sharp and consistent message to convince defense officials in the region that their planning methods need to make "defense" fit the existing defense budget. For example, Partnership Goal General (PG) 0022 is defined as stable budget planning and has been adopted (alas) by too many PfP members' defense institutions (Boland 2014). The problem with encouraging ministries of finance to develop stable medium-term expenditure plans (three years) is that it has given ministries of defense false expectations of predictable budgeting into the future. Leaving aside that it is highly problematic that any parliament, or ministry of finance, would agree (let alone carry out) such a commitment; simply on the grounds of national sovereignty, the fact of the matter is that such assumptions have acted to encourage defense officials to accept the planning assumption of multi-year force and supporting financial planning without any assurances that the funds will ever come to hand. This has enabled defense officials to avoid facing the all-too-often harsh reality that their current budget is too small in relation to the existing legacy mindset-driven force structure ambitions, and thus forcing the development of long over-due *costed* priorities. There is no shortage of examples of ambitious long-term defense plans, which sometimes are even endorsed by government and parliament, and which nevertheless remained underfunded, at which point they are innocently declared un-implementable, e.g. Slovenia (2010) and have produced institutional stasis. As a result of this prevailing conceptual miasma, planning, budgeting and financial management in all of these defense institutions, to varying degrees, remains isolated, and even in some cases impervious to the realities facing the rest of the organization.

Conclusion

The record of long-term defense planning in Central and Eastern European defense institutions is far from constituting a successful technique that ties defense policy priorities to financial execution. More specifically, long-term defense planning has encouraged defense officials to plan modernization far in the future without regard to financial realities, let alone addressing current defense needs *today*. But with minor exception, this "future" never arrives, whilst all the while ignoring the need to fund short-term operational requirements. In its worst manifestations in the region, the imported version of long-term defense planning embraces the US practice of reinforcing the autonomy of military planners as they create future year plans, 2 to 3 years in advance of the current budget year. Once developed, following U.S. practice it is not unusual that such plans are declared to be "baked" and immune from subsequent policy changes. This conceptual dissonance holds that multi-year force and supporting financial planning are expectations, whilst they should be more accurately described as constituting merely institutional aspirations at best, and manpower-intensive "science projects" in the worst cases. Moreover, in lieu of producing predictable defense outcomes, the use of programming and long-term defense plans has had the pernicious effect in many countries of facilitating the hyper-centralization of financial decision-making within ministries of defense, as opposed to being delegated to commanders who are responsible for producing capabilities. It is equally clear that programming and long-term defense plans have not been able to assist ministries of defense plan effectively during periods of financial uncertainty and budget cuts. Lastly, it must be assessed as problematic whether programming and particularly the use of long-term defense planning methods can support a defense institution to respond with military forces in a period of escalation, let alone during war.

Methodologically speaking, the original purpose of long-term defense plans has apparently been lost to, or never understood by, many defense institutions in Central and Eastern Europe, just it has subsequently evolved in the case of the U.S. Department of Defense's FYDP. As this essay has demonstrated by reviewing the origins of long-term defense planning, it was initially envisaged to enhance policy flexibility and not inhibit it. As programming has proven itself difficult to implement in these countries, considerable effort has been placed on the all but forlorn hope that developing long-term defense plans would provide *he* silver bullet to produce predictable and perhaps even greater defense expenditures. Yet, an inability in the case of many of these countries to cost properly the existing force, let alone to define capabilities in terms of their life-cycle costs, has made these "plans" little more than dreams generating unsubstantiated, and thus harmful expectations.

The solution to this conundrum facing defense planners in the region is the need to review comprehensively the role of "policy" in developing priorities. Fundamentally, in essentially all of these countries, bureaucratic powers need to be rebalanced to reinforce the authority and scope of responsibilities of defense policy directorates. The empowerment of policy directorates to develop and oversee the execution of policy priorities will enable these defense institutions to escape the current planning trap in which they find themselves: developing long-term defense plans which are almost always not costed and therefore not executable at the expense of creating viable defense options that can aligned with their contemporary security environment. As such, PPBS directorates, many of which have been incapable of carrying out something as basic as costing the current force or even acquisitions (i.e. using life-cycle costing) need to be dismantled as independent directorates. Policy directorates need to be reinforced to include a defense planning branch where planning does not currently already fall under policy, as well as another branch responsible for managing finances. All proposed plans must be costed by the planning branch (ergo, they must "own" cost models) and only once that they have been approved by policy will the financial branch manage execution, to include maintaining a full appreciation of all future financial obligations. On this very point, it is regrettable to note that the recent reorganization of the Hungarian Ministry of Defense has shuttered its planning branch and merged it with the Department of Economic Planning and which stands in direct contradiction to the findings and recommendations of this paper (A honvédelmi miniszter 33/2017).

Such reforms will return the function of long-term defense planning to its original purpose of providing officials with a data-base of projected costs associated with the current and planned force, as opposed to limiting their ability to shift priorities. In fact, the utility of these financial projections should be judged by how much *flexibility* they can provide ministers and senior defense officials to change the way money is being spent to produce relevant defense outcomes. Critically, plans may well be approved that extend financial obligations into the future, but this in no way implies that current or future year plans are in any way "baked" and isolated from the policy directorate, and hence from the operating defence and security environment. These organizational reforms will link costed policy priorities closer to financial execution, and will enable the policy directorate to make changes quickly to respond to the operational requirements of the armed forces.

These recommendations will prove themselves challenging to adopt and fully implement as they must be accompanied by the thorough retirement of the existing conceptual logic of long-term defense planning and replaced by one that empowers policy directorates to determine where and *when* the defense budget is to be spent. Therefore, it can be expected that bureaucracies will be seriously unsettled, which should be of concern in that many of Central and East European defense institutions remain in various phases of development and sophistication. But, the one commonality that they do share is an inability to produce and execute viable defense plans, all the while their armed forces slowly rust away. As such, senior political officials in these countries must take responsibility to ensure that these reforms are fully implemented: institutional self-evaluations (i.e. "grading one's own homework") needs to be rejected to ensure that these deep reforms are appropriately prescribed and fully executed. And all of which needs to be executed against a backdrop of immediacy as the other commonality they share is to prepare their armed forces to respond, if necessary, to an aggressive Russia which has militarized its policy towards the West and new democracies in Central and Eastern Europe (Sherr 2017).

Notes

1. U.S. legislation requires the FYDP covers the fiscal year with respect to which the budget is submitted and at least the four succeeding fiscal years. For each fiscal year of the period in question, it must also include estimated expenditures and the proposed appropriations, as well as for procurement of equipment, military construction for the reserve components of the armed forces. U.S. Code 10 § 10,543 (2004).
2. Another weakness in the development of PPBS was the blind and uncritical acceptance by Hitch of the Joint Staff's annual Joint Strategic Objectives Plan (JSOP) which was used to initiate the programming process. Hitch writes of his acceptance of the valid initiation starting point by the JSOP as the it initiates PPBS; whereas with the benefit of additional years of experience of implementing PPBS, Einhoven and Smith excoriate the document. They write that it was solely a wish-list of the military departments, way over budgetary projections, and the Joint Staff consistently failed to force the Military Departments to find efficiencies and produce great jointness. *Cf.*, (Hitch 1967), p. 31 and (Enthoven and Smith 2005), pp. 94–5.
3. See then-Secretary of Defense Ashton Carter's letter critical of navy priorities to then-Secretary of the Navy Ray Maybus, 14 December 2015 (Maucione 2015).
4. In this respect, it is instructive to compare the two Croatian long-term defense plans, 2006 and 2013 where the latter actually advocated the need for defense cuts if the defense institution were to be able to meet policy objectives: honesty in policy planning that is almost unheard of in defense planning documents found in the region. (*Cf.*, Croatia 2006), with (Croatia 2013).
5. This point would underscore the argument made by the influential Henry Mintzberg who writes that the development and adoption of PPBS constitutes one of the greatest efforts and failures of all time in public finance (1994, p. 19).
6. Secretary of Defense Robert Gates complained that the Department of Defense was reluctant to meet a current battlefield requirement with purchasing MRAPs as it was seen as being at the expense of long-term procurement programs. In the end, the vehicles were purchased outside of the normal services' budgets averting a bureaucratic "blood bath", which should be seen as constituting a salient lesson for defense institutions in Central and Eastern Europe (Gates 2014, p. 121).

Disclosure statement

No potential conflict of interest was reported by the author.

References

Akubardia, T., 2010. Overview of the legislation facilitating the civil democratic oversight of armed forces in Georgia. *In*: T. Pataraia, ed. *Democratic control over the Georgian armed forces since the august 2008 war*. Geneva: Geneva Centre for the Democratic Control of Armed Forces,

Ball, N. and Le Roux, L., 2006. A model for good practice in budgeting for the military sector. *In*: W. Omitoogun and E. Hutchful, eds. *Budgeting for the military sector in Africa: the process and mechanism of control*. Oxford: Oxford University Press,

Bender, B. and Herb, J., 2015. 'War budget might be permanent "slush fund", *Politico*. http://www.politico.com/story/2015/03/war-budget-might-be-permanent-slush-fund-116367.

Boland, F., 2014. 'Capability development', briefing. Brussels: Defense Policy and Planning Division, NATO International Staff.

Bulgaria, 2015. *'Programme for the development of the defence capabilities of the Bulgarian armed forces 2020'*. Sofia: Council of Ministers.

Croatia, 2006. Croatian armed forces long-term development plan 2006-2015. *adopted in the Croatian parliament on 7 july 2006*. published in the Official Gazette, No.81. Zagreb: Ministry of Defense,

Croatia, 2013. *Strategic defence review*. Zagreb: Ministry of Defence.

Donnelly, C., 1988. *Red banner: the Soviet military system in peace and war*. Coulsdon, Surrey: Jane's Information Group.

Enthoven, A.C. and Smith, K.W., 2005. *How much is enough? shaping the defense program, 1961–1969*. Santa Monica, CA: RAND.

Gates, R.M., 2014. *Duty: memoirs of a secretary at war*. New York: Alfred A. Knopf.

Gogolewska, A., 2006. Problems confronting civilian democratic control in Poland. *In*: H. Born, et al., eds. *Civil-military relations in Europe: learning from crisis and institutional change*. New York: Routledge,

Haynes, P.D., 2013. 'American Naval thinking in the post-cold war era: the U.S. navy and the emergence of a maritime strategy, 1989–2007'. Thesis (Ph.D.) Naval Postgraduate School.

Hitch, C.J., 1967. *Decision-making for Defense*. Berkeley: University of California Press.

Hitch, C.J. and McKean, R.N., 1960. *The economics of defense in the nuclear age*. Cambridge, MA: Harvard University Press.

Hofstede, G., 2011. *Culture's consequences: comparing values, behaviors, institutions and organizations across nations*. 2nd ed. Thousand Oaks, CA: Sage.

Hofstede, G., Hofstede, G.J., and Minkov, M., 2010. *Cultures and organizations: software of the mind*. 3rd. New York: McGraw-Hill.

A honvédelmi miniszter 33/2017. (VI. 30.) HM utasítása a honvédelmi minisztérium átalakításának 2017. évi egyes szervezési feladatairól és egyes honvédelmi miniszteri utasítások módosításáról [translation: 33/2017. (VI.30.) 'Order of the minister of defence on the organizational tasks of the reorganization of the ministry of defence in 2017 and on the amendments of certain defence ministerial orders', 30 july 2017], http://www.kozlonyok.hu/kozlonyok/Kozlonyok/13/PDF/2017/7.pdf. The writer is grateful to Bence Nemeth for raising this point and providing the translation.

Katič, A., 2016. *'Increasing sSlovenia's defence capacity'; strategic defence review 2016*. Ljubljana: Ministry of Defence.

Kordowski, M., et al., n.d. *Defence resources management system in Visegrad group*. Warsaw: National Centre for Strategic Studies (NCSS).

Macedonia, January, 2014. *Long-term development plan, 2014-2023*. Skopje: Ministry of Defense.

Magnus, H. and Larsen, K.K., 2012. Long-term defence planning: a comparative study of seven countries. *In*: *Oslo File 5*. Oslo: Institutt for forsvarsstudier,

Maucione, S. 2015. 'Carter scolds Navy Secretary over spending priorities', *Federal News Radio*, https://federalnewsradio.com/defense/2015/12/carter-scolds-mabus-spending-priorities/

Mintzberg, H., 1994. *The rise and fall of strategic planning: reconceiving roles for planning, plans, planners*. New York: Free Press.

Murumets, J., 2016. *Estonian maritime security: executive summary.* Tartu: Kaitsevӓe Ühendatud Õppeasutused.
NATO, 2003. *Handbook on Long Term Defence Planning,* RTO technical report 69, AC/323 (SAS-025)TP/41. Paris: Research and Technology Organisation.
O'Rourke, R., 2017. 'Navy Force Structure and Shipbuilding Plans: background and Issues for Congress', RL32665. Washington, DC: Congressional Research Service.
Paszewski, T., 2016. Can Poland defend itself? *Survival,* 58 (2), 126–127. doi:10.1080/00396338.2016.1161907
Poland, 2017. *The defense concept of the republic of Poland.* Warsaw: Ministry of National Defense.
Serbia, Strategic Planning Department, Defence Policy Sector. 2010. *White paper on defence of the republic of Serbia.* Belgrade: Ministry of Defense.
Sherr, J., 2017. *The militarization of Russian policy.* Washington, DC: Transatlantic Academy. Paper Series No. 10.
Simon, J., 2004. *NATO and the Czech and Slovak republics: comparative study in civil-military relations.* Lanham: Rowman and Littlefield.
Slovenia, 2009. Defence sector strategic review 2009 (DSSR): summary of key DSSR 2009 conclusions. *In: No. 800-1/2009-189.* Ljubljana: Ministry of Defence,
Slovenia, 2010. Resolution on general long-term development and equipping programme of the Slovenian armed forces up to 2025. *In: Official Gazette of the Republic of Slovenia no. 99/2010.* Ljubljana: Ministry of Defence,
Stojkovic, D. and Dahl, B.R., 2007. Methodology for long term defence planning. *In: FFI-rapport 2007/00600.* Kjeller: Norwegian Defence Research Establishment,
U.S. Code title 10, § 10543 (2004).
U.S. Code, Title 10, Subtitle A, Part 1, Chapter 9 § 221. *National Defense Authorization Act for Fiscal Years 1988 and 1989* (Pub. L. No. 100-180, Sec. 1203; Dec. 4, 1987). 'Future-years defense program: submission to Congress; consistency in budgeting'.
U.S. General Accounting Office, 1998. Executive guide: leading practices in capital decision-making. *In: GAO/AIMD-99-32.* Washington, D.C:
U.S. Government Accountability Office, 2004. Future years defense program: actions needed to improve transparency of DoD's projected resource needs. *In: GAO-04-514.* Washington, DC: GAO.
Vance, G.C. and Hinkle, W., January, 2011. Best practices in defense resource management. *IDA document D-4137.* Washington, DC: Institute for Defense Analysis,
The Voluntary Sector Knowledge Network, 2007. *Leadership: strategic planning and strategic management.* http://vskn.ca/lead/strategy.htm. accessed.
Williams, L.M. and Epstein, S.B., 2017. Overseas contingency operations funding: background and status. *In: R44519.* Washington, DC: Congressional Research Service,
Young, T.-D., 2016a. Impediment to reform in European post-communist defense institutions: addressing the conceptual divide. *Problems in post-communism,* http://www.tandfonline.com/doi/full/10.1080/10758216.2016.1220256.
Young, T.-D., 2016b. Is PPBS applicable to European post-communist defense institutions'? *RUSI journal,* 161 (October/November 2016), 68–77. no. 5. doi:10.1080/03071847.2016.1253382
Young, T.-D., 2016c. When programming trumps policy and plans: the case of the U.S. Department of the Navy. *Journal of strategic studies,* 39 (7), 2016. http://www.tandfonline.com/doi/abs/10.1080/01402390.2016.1176564?needAccess=true
Young, T.-D., 2017a. *Anatomy of post-communist European defense institutions: the mirage of military modernity.* London: Bloomsbury Academic.
Young, T.-D., 2017b. The failure of defense planning in Eeuropean communist legacy defense institutions: ascertaining causation and determining solutions. *Journal of strategic studies,* http://www.tandfonline.com/doi/full/10.1080/01402390.2017.1307743.
Young, T.-D., 2017c. Mission command: strategic implications—legacy concepts: a sociology of command in Central and Eastern Europe. *Parameters,* 47 (1), 31–42. https://ssi.armywarcollege.edu/pubs/parameters/issues/Spring_2017/6_Young_MissionCommand-CentralAndEasternEurope.pdf

Defense planning when major changes are needed

Paul K. Davis

ABSTRACT
The principles and formalities of modern U.S. Defence planning stem from the 1960s and have largely served well. This paper, however, is about the special challenges that arise when major changes have been needed, some even transformational in character. It discusses how changing realities, independent studies and analysis, events, leaders, and political processes have led to changes not easily instigated within normal processes. Several examples are discussed for the period 1976–2016. Today, the United States and allies again face major challenges that require major military changes. Those have not yet been decided, much less accomplished. The paper draws on lessons from earlier periods to identify obstacles to and mechanisms for change. The last section focuses on defence *analysis*, which has sometimes been an obstacle but can be part of the solution. The paper urges a new ethic for analysis and the analysts who perform it.

Introduction

This paper stems from an invited presentation in 2017 to a workshop on defence planning held at the Centre for Military Studies in Copenhagen. The paper is drawn from the author's experiences as a planner in the U.S. Department of Defence (DoD) and observations from many subsequent years of research, often conducting studies for senior DoD planners and other officials (Davis 1994, 2014). Supporting detail can be found in the publications cited.

The paper's first theme is that in thinking about defence planning we should recognize the special needs associated with major changes, e.g., with changes that are against the grain and are sometimes even accompanied by such adjectives as "transformational" or "revolutionary." A second theme is that the changes should often emphasize planning for adaptiveness rather for a particular vision of the future.

The paper's structure is as follows. Section 2 reviews basic elements of defence planning. Section 3 discusses four instances in which major changes have been needed, which could not easily be accommodated by the normal processes. A number of unusual mechanisms were then used to deal with obstacles. Section 4 focuses on the particular obstacles created by normal analysis processes and methods for doing better.

Core elements of defence planning

Basics

Defence planning, the DoD's version of strategic planning, is the deliberate process of deciding on a nation's future military forces, force postures, and force capabilities. It is distinct from operations planning, about how to employ forces in war. The core elements of defence planning trace back to Robert McNamara's reforms introduced in 1961. A major contributor was Alain Enthoven, who headed McNamara's new Systems Analysis office. Enthoven expressed tenets of defence planning and analysis that were rooted in rational-choice theory.[1] They have endured for more than a half century, as evidenced by their endorsement by officials in 2005 when Enthoven's book was reissued (Enthoven and Smith 2005).

Enduring Tenets about Analysis and Planning

(1) Decisions should be based on explicit criteria of national interest, not on compromises among institutional forces.
(2) Needs and costs should be considered simultaneously.
(3) Major decisions should be made by choices among explicit, balanced, feasible alternatives.
(4) The Secretary of Defense should have an active analytic staff to provide him with relevant data and unbiased perspectives.
(5) A multiyear force and financial plan should project the consequences of present decisions into the future.
(6) Open and explicit analysis (including transparent data and assumptions) available to all parties, should form the basis for major decisions.

The U.S. Planning, Programming, Budgeting, and Execution system (PPBE) is the procedural element of defence planning and is similar to the system that it replaced (Grimes 2008, Tulkoff et al. 2010). It is the process by which the U.S. Department of Defence (DoD) allocates resources. The process attempts to be goal oriented with decisions guided by objectives, strategy, and policy. Alternative ways of achieving these objectives are evaluated, their costs estimated, and choices made on a portfolio of programs. Budgeting then maps the decisions into a multiyear timeline of expenditures consistent with the Department's resource stream. Execution refers not just to conducting the programs, but also to monitoring results and adjusting.

The DoD's PPBE has been criticized for decades and its effectiveness reviewed skeptically (Rosen 1984, Mintzberg 1994, Tama 2015). Complex processes are natural targets for critics, both petty and serious. Interestingly, however, thoughtful reviews have typically concluded that Enthoven's *tenets* are more important than details of process and that the DoD's process has proven adaptive to the preferences of successive Secretaries (Chu and Bernstein, 1983). Further, senior executives inside and outside government have commonly claimed that – despite its many imperfections in practice – the PPBE is the most effective planning system in the U.S. government.[1] For ordinary purposes, that may well be. Nonetheless, this paper discusses some particular chronic shortcomings of *mainstream* aspects of the PPBE. DoD leaders have managed to cope, but the paper argues that defense planning should be understood to include not only "mainstream processes" but also the kinds of special mechanisms described below. Recognizing this, and lessons from the past, may make future coping easier.

Characteristics of defence planning as practiced

As a student of management theory would expect, DoD's complexity necessitates establishing order through such mechanisms as doctrine, routine processes, standards, metrics, rules, and requirements. These features help greatly in establishing coherence and promoting predictability, efficiency, and effectiveness. They can also cause problems, however, as discussed in the scholarly literature on strategic planning generally (Quinn 1980, Pascale 1991, Mintzberg 1994, March 1996, Mintzberg *et al.* 2005). The troubles include increased organizational inertia and sluggishness even when change is needed. Ultimately, there is a constant tension between continuity and change. The present paper illustrates several types of problem, but then focuses on some particular culprits related to over-standardizing planning scenarios, models, and data, and on over-valuing organizational consensus.

When defence planning has special problems

Cases considered

Most aspects of defence planning can be treated straightforwardly with normal mainstream processes, but special challenges arise (more so in some periods than others, but arguably in all periods). These may come about because of, e.g., (1) new or newly recognized threats; (2) technological changes; or (3) shocks, such as failures in war.

This paper uses examples from various periods as indicated in Figure 1. They involve (1) building overseas contingency capability with rapid deployment forces (early 1980s); (2) introducing precision fires, precision navigation, and the information era (accelerating in the late 1990s) (Era A); (3) building capabilities for counterterrorism and counterinsurgency (2001-); and (4) today's era (Era B). Not all of these were "transformational," but all involved big changes difficult to accomplish.

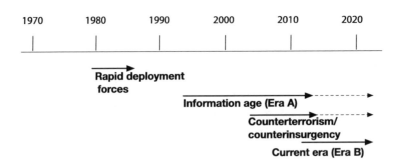

Figure 1. Selected Periods of Change.

Rapid deployment forces

President Jimmy Carter's National Security Council (NSC) reviewed strategic issues in 1977 and, as part of that, observed a military vacuum in the Persian Gulf region, i.e., Southwest Asia.[2] A Presidential Review Memorandum (PRM 10) and a subsequent Presidential Directive (PD 18) included a call for a DoD study to address the vacuum. PD 18 (originally Top Secret, but now available on the web) stated that the United States "will maintain a deployment force of light divisions with strategic mobility independent of overseas bases and logistical support...for use against both local forces and forces projected by the Soviet Union..." This led to a two year effort, the "Wolfowitz Report."[3]

Doing something about the problems identified in PD 18 proved challenging. Those involved in the Wolfowtiz report saw the problems as including (Davis 1982):

(1) *Preexisting problems and related inertia.* The DoD had long focused on Europe's Central Region and Korea. Conventional defence of both were very difficult and available resources were inadequate for these preexisting demands.
(2) *Lack of immediacy.* Persian Gulf problems were abstract. The last thing that most officials or officers wanted to hear about was a new problem area, especially one that seemed to pose no imminent threat.
(3) *Organizational resistance to seeing new strategic problems.* Many senior and most officials did not see potential threat in the region.
(4) *Vested interests and incentives.* Most military officers saw their leadership opportunities as connected with the Central Region (i.e., preparing for the battle in the Fulda Gap) or perhaps Korea, but not in some backwater called Southwest Asia.
(5) *Standard analysis processes and methods.* Mainstream analysis focused on standardized Central Region and Korean scenarios with large-scale head-on-head attrition warfare in which only tanks appeared to have value. Such analysis of standard scenarios saw little value in the kinds of forces and mobility capabilities emphasized in the Wolfowitz study.

The study was issued in 1979, not long after the Iranian revolution and embassy seizure had shaken some of the complacency about the region. The study laid out relatively modest initiatives for improving capabilities for *whatever* military contingencies might arise in the region. Most responses to the study were initially tepid, including those of Secretary Harold Brown, who disliked the report having highlighted an Iraqi invasion of Kuwait as one possible scenario (the other primary scenario involved a Soviet invasion of Iran). Brown saw Iran as the bigger regional threat (Keefer 2017, 334). The Soviets then invaded Afghanistan in December 1979 and attitudes changed discontinuously. Because of the invasion of Afghanistan and other indicators, the perceived plausibility of a Soviet threat to Iran and the Persian Gulf went up – so much so that conventional wisdom at high level focused exclusively on the Soviet threat. This was in contrast to the 1979 study, which had considered both Iraqi and Soviet invasion threats without regarding either as "likely." The study had emphasized having broad expeditionary capabilities for both deterrence and coping with whatever events arose.

The politics had also changed (for other reasons), making more money available to the DoD. Real growth began again toward the end of the Carter administration and accelerated thereafter. Because of the prior staff work and cooperation among top officials,[4] it proved possible quickly to move a number of program initiatives into the 1980 budget. Some were relatively incremental (e.g., some improved strategic mobility), but one was anything but: creation of a new military command. This was the Rapid Deployment Joint Task Force (RDJTF), which in 1983 become U.S. Central Command (USCENTCOM) (Bliddal 2011). Establishing the new command was exceptionally important. It indicated seriousness and created a new constituency for the capabilities. The RDJTF was led by Lt. General Paul X. Kelley of the Marine Corps, who later became Commandant of the Marine Corps. That was significant because the Marine Corps had competed for leadership in the mission, promising significant changes in doctrine to establish credibility.

The new capabilities paid off a decade later. The Soviet threat never materialized, but Saddam Hussein invaded Kuwait. By then, the United States had military forces and a military command able to deter further aggression against Saudi Arabia, to launch a counteroffensive, and to defeat Saddam's forces handily. Ironically, this was despite the fact that during most of the 1980s the "normal processes" of defence planning and operations planning had led USCENTOM to focus almost exclusively on the Soviet threat. Only in 1990 did it begin to plan for an Iraqi threat, after being directed to do so by the Chairman of the Joint Chiefs of Staff, who was himself being prodded by Under Secretary Wolfowitz (Department of Defense 1992). Planning was in its early stages and Saddam's invasion was a big surprise, but U.S. capabilities permitted rapid adaptation as described in an official command history (Hines 1999).

In summary, the changes that occurred involved (1) top-down strategic guidance; (2) non-standard scenarios and analysis in a study driven by a single organization (OSD's Office of Program Analysis and Evaluation) concerned with uncertainty and largely unencumbered by department-wide processes and committees; (3) accidents of politics; and (4) civilian officials getting "out of their lane" by urging changes of the command system. The normal routines of defence planning played little role initially, but the changes – once decided by policymakers – were accommodated by the PPBS, in part because OSD(PA&E) led the PPBS process. The related programs flowed into the budgeting process and were largely enacted as intended. Further, after review, they were embraced and expanded by the Reagan administration – remarkable in itself because incoming administrations usually look quite negatively upon programs that they inherit.

Transformation efforts of the late 1990s and early 2000s

In the 1991 Gulf War, the United States Air Force conducted some strikes with precision weapons, demonstrating to those who watched (including the Soviets) that a revolution in military affairs was occurring (Lambeth 1992). Remarkably, however, much of the defence establishment barely noticed. Much of defence planning went on as usual with the same standard forces, scenarios, and models. These called for large head-on-head attrition battles of ground forces, governed by models designed and calibrated from the experiences of World War II. As of 1996, the Department's senior leaders were largely somewhat smug about the suitability of the forces they already possessed: their primary concern was the need for recapitalization after a period of underfunding.[5]

Advocates for change certainly existed both inside and outside government, but they were sometimes seen as radical or technology-captured.[6] With some justification, the term "transformation" was often criticized as hype. The DoD's policy report in 1993 (Aspin 1993) gave no hint of major changes; the first Quadrennial Review (Cohen 1997) had a chapter on transformation but little guidance or funding – a shortcoming quickly criticized by an independent review panel (National Defense Panel 1997). After the election of 2001, President George Bush and Secretary of Defence Donald Rumsfeld championed transformation efforts.

Although this is not always recognized because so many events occurred in the 2000s, the transformation was largely successful, although implemented incrementally, consistent with discussion of Quinn years ago (Quinn 1978). After the decisions were made, programs and initiatives followed reasonably well, although defence secretaries had to exert personal pressure to accelerate introduction of unmanned aerial vehicles, cancel programs (e.g., *Comanche*), and to reduce the size of legacy programs (e.g., the F-22).

How did the changes occur? It was not because of routine defence planning or defence analysis. For example, *mainsteam* analyses throughout most of the 1990s included but underestimated the future effectiveness of precision fires; it ignored special operations forces and mostly continued to focus on classic attrition battles of ground forces. The impetus for change came from independent analyses, some special in-government studies (Bexfield 2001), and some leaders. Further, mainstream PPBS analysis sometimes failed to pick up on opportunities because of artificial boundaries in the budgeting process. For example, since precision weapons were expensive compared with "dumb bombs," the routine budget processes allowed only modest purchases – a sub optimization that persisted for some time.

Major changes, then, were introduced in a short period of time. The 2003 invasion of Iraq demonstrated U.S. military prowess in then-modern manoeuvre warfare. It culminated years of development and training (Jensen 2018). The changes were remarkable, whether or not the wars themselves were good ideas or disasters, whether or not the ideas were fully and consistently implemented, and whether or not the changes were sufficient for war winning.

Counterterrorism and counterinsurgency

The third period of major change occurred in the 2000's. Some of the changes extended information-age developments, but others were of a different character.

Late in 2001, after al-Qaeda's attack on the Twin Towers and the Pentagon, the United States found itself in war deep within Afghanistan. This was a war like none other, with special operations forces playing a prominent role, sometimes famously from horseback but with real-time connections to aircraft with precision weapons as well as to local tribal forces. There had been no planning scenarios akin to the operation. Nor was there suitable doctrine. Instead, military officers developed tactics ad hoc, with some Air Force commanders awed by what they saw as an emerging new mission allowed by the revolution in military affairs (Thiesen 2003). So also, command and control relationships on the ground were worked out ad hoc to deal with the special contextual details (Rhyne 2004).

As mentioned above the initial manoeuver phase of the Iraq war went extremely well in 2003, demonstrating the power of the information-age changes. However, the U.S. military was utterly unprepared for the ensuing insurgency, which political leaders were slow in acknowledging. Matters turned into what has been called a fiasco (Ricks 2006).

Given the nature of conflict (insurgency rather than large-scale manoeuvre wafare), change was again necessary. Much of the impetus for change came from Generals James Petraeus (Army) and James Mattis (Marine Corps). One result was a new counter-insurgency field manual (Nagl et al. 2007). Perhaps most famously, the manual identifies the public of the conflict area to be a "center of gravity" and focuses not on kinetic warfare but rather on diverse activities to gain that public's support: by providing security and in other ways. A directive by General Petraeus in 2009 illustrates how different the new focus was to be (U.S. Central Command 2010):

> ...the center of gravity in this struggle is the Afghan people; it is they who will ultimately determine the future of Afghanistan ... Prior to the use of fires, the commander approving the strike must determine that no civilians are present. If unable to assess the risk of civilian presence, fires are prohibited, except under one of the following two conditions (specific conditions deleted due to operational security; however, they have to do with the risk to ISAF and Afghan forces).

Necessity was the mother of change in this case, but the changes drew on an older Marine Corps Small Wars manual (U.S. Marine Corps 1940) and the advice of social scientists. That said, the remarkable prowess developed in using special operations forces, air forces, and networked information was due to operational commanders and their staffs, who mastered application of new networking technology (McChrystal 2011).

Once again, what this transformation did *not* depend on was mainstream defence planning or its analysis. Moreover, senior civilian officials laboured mightily to provide what was needed in the war zone because the normal processes were so cumbersome. They had to create separate fast-track procedures.[7] Even then, the personal intervention of Secretary of Defence Robert Gates was necessary to force deployment of the Mine Resistant Ambush Protection vehicle (MRAP) (Gates 2014). Prior efforts to move it forward had been repeatedly stalled by the planning process because the MRAP was expensive and unlikely to be useful in what planners saw as normal military operations. Gates was more concerned about the lives of soldiers in the field than the niceties of long-term cost-effectiveness analysis.

The changes championed by General Petraeus and others were profound and the case fits well into this paper's theme. This said, the changes in technical capabilities, operational concepts, and organization were not enough to compensate for failures of strategy or the shortcomings of partner governments. Many papers exist on the failures of U.S. efforts in Afghanistan and Iraq over the last 17 years, including papers that decry the naïve enthusiasm that some had for counterinsurgency strategy a decade ago (Eikenberry 2013). That said – even if one agrees with the criticisms – the criticisms have to do with national and military strategy, not with defence planning.

The current era

The paper's last case is ongoing. Era B is a name given twenty years in reference to the period in which we now live. It follows an Era A (Figure 1) during which the United States enjoyed "overmatch" – the result of precision navigation, precision weapons, stealth, network centric operations, and other developments of the information age. As foreseen in 1998, Era A proved to be quite favourable to the U.S. and its allies militarily when fighting large battles, but – as foreseen in 1998 (Davis *et al.* 1998) – Era B is proving to be unpleasant due to the diffusion of technology and adaptation by adversaries, developments such an anti-access and area denial, North Korean nuclear weapons, and hybrid warfare. Further, impending discontinuities can be seen as a perfect storm (Figure 2) (Davis and Wilson 2011). Probably to the chagrin of the paper's authors, the paper has proven to have been too *optimistic*: it did not anticipate Russia's re-emergence as threat nor the rise of ISIS. Table 1, from that study, depicted the problems in terms of U.S. capabilities then and now (Era A and Era B). The problems are better recognized today, but are no less serious.

A troublesome feature of the new-era difficulties is that it requires being prepared to deal with different kinds of war and what some see as different revolutions in military affairs. As emphasized by Peter Wilson, these are not sequential but rather intertwined with complex action-reaction cycles as indicated in Figure 3. This includes revolutionary tactics (as in insurgencies) and gray-war tactics, rather as anticipated years ago (Van Creveld 1991), as well as advances in high-end warfare as the information-driven changes continue.

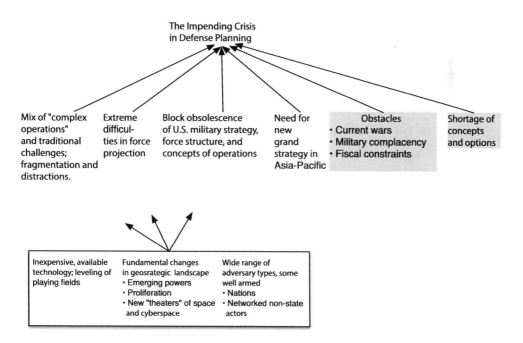

Figure 2. The impending crisis.

Table 1. U.S. capabilities then and now

Component	Previously	Now, and Increasingly in Near Future
Limited forward presence	Nonproblem	Restrained but not especially risky
Large-scale deployments to regional waters and bases	Nonproblem	Risky due to vulnerable bases and regional waters; risks stem from AIP submarines and precision antiship weapons (including land-based missiles); large standoff ranges will likely be needed.
Broad naval supremacy	Nonproblem	Challenges exist but are much less when not in close-in regional waters.
Achieving air supremacy	Nonproblem	Nonproblem in most domains, but not, e.g., close to Chinese mainland
Suppressing air defenses	Destruction is difficult because of cover and deception but suppression is quite feasible.	Risky for above reasons and advanced mobile and man-portable surface-to-air missiles
Offensive air operations	Strategic strikes are possible early with stealthy aircraft; large-scale operations are a nonproblem after suppression of air defenses against fixed and known high-value targets.	Risky and difficult because of modern air defenses, the need for long-range operations, and the difficulty of finding mobile and hidden high-value targets
Entry of traditional ground forces and infrastructure	Nonproblem after gaining air supremacy	Risky because of vulnerabilities of forces during entry and of bases and other logistics. Area weapons pose special concerns.
Later ground-maneuver operations with close air support and battlefield shaping	Supreme skill of U.S. forces Moderately risky, with air support constrained due to residual SAMs, and with vulnerabilities to residual precision weapons	Moderately risky, with air support constrained due to residual surface-to-air missiles, and with vulnerabilities to residual precison weapons
Large follow-up operations (e.g., stabilization in large countries)	Feasible on a small scale, or on the Iraq scale with mobilization; forces at risk due to improvised explosive devices and other asymmetric tactics; large manpower requirements	Feasible on a small scale, or on the Iraq scale with mobilization; operations are risky for adversaries having precision or area weapons and some defenses against drones. Special needs for mine-resistant vehicles, persistent surveillance and substantial manpower.

Scale from very dark: feasibility is in question to white: feasible with acceptable risk.

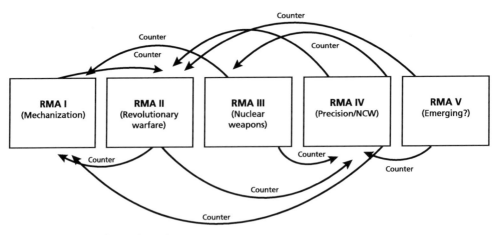

NOTE: NCW = network-centric warfare.

Figure 3. An era of intertwined revolutions in military affairs.

These challenges of Era B have hardly been lost on the Department of Defence. Secretary Hagel announced a "third-offset" strategy that, under successive Secretaries, has been attempting to exploit technology to maintain U.S. advantages (Hagel 2014, Work 2015). The jury remains out on what will emerge and how effective the changes will be. The Department has created a special office (the Strategic Capabilities Office (SCO)) and leaned on the Defence Advanced Research Projects Agency (DARPA) for innovations. The Defence Innovation Initiative is reaching out to Silicon Valley and other special sources of innovation. The tack being taken is very much different from that of normal processes. A recent paper refers to it as a case of "metagovernance" (Christiansson 2018).

The third-offset strategy has again included DoD officials going outside normal analysis channels. Actually, senior DoD officials have found themselves dissatisfied with mainstream analysis for some years. In the middle 2000s, they expressed dismay at receiving plentiful analysis on the kinds of problems that the community knew how to analyze (kinetic wars with major powers) but little or no analytic help on either the problems of the day (counterterrorism and counterinsurgency) or possibly catastrophic developments. They dramatized this by distinguishing among irregular, traditional, catastrophic, and disruptive threats and noting that the analysis they were receiving focused heavily on the "traditional" category. Thus, they firmly admonished the analytic community into broadening its horizons (Henry 2005). Given the forceful nudging, DoD's analytic community responded, especially with in-depth studies of the social science that should underlie counterterrorism and intervention,[8] as well as studies on the implications for high-end warfare of the continuing but maturing revolution in military affairs (Watts 2011). As of 2018, mainstream research and analysis is focusing on the high-end threats, including those in the realm of cyberspace.

It is not possible as yet to know how well the United States will respond to today's challenges, nor to know how its allies will do in this regard (Fiott 2016).

Observations from across the cases

Each of the cases above was different in kind as were mechanisms for addressing the challenges. Some generic features, however, cut across the set. Some of these are well described in the academic literature (e.g., addressing vested interests and incentive structures; having good leadership; recognizing that strategic planning and developing strategy are different). Many of these items are covered, for example, in Mintzberg's classic critique of strategic planning (Mintzberg 1994, Mintzberg et al. 2005). This paper elaborates somewhat on obstacles involving two related matters: failures of imagination and failure to confront deep uncertainty in analysis.

Failures of imagination

The term "failures of imagination" became famous after the Congressional report on the 9–11 catastrophe (National Commission on Terrorist Attacks 2004). As Chairman Thomas Kean noted:

> We were unprepared. We did not grasp the magnitude of a threat that had been gathering over a considerable period of time. As we detail in our report, this was a failure of policy, management, capability, and, above all, a failure of imagination.

Keane goes on to say that the 9/11 attacks were a shock, but should not have come as a surprise. The report's Chapter 8 is entitled "The System Was Blinking Red." But, as noted, "no one looked at the bigger picture; no analytic work foresaw the lighting that could connect the thundercloud with the ground" (p. 277). In one of the pithier passages of the report, the authors note "Imagination is not a gift usually associated with bureaucracies." (p. 344).

What can be done to avoid such failures? A good deal of literature exists on related matters, including a literature on thinking the unthinkable and using alternative scenarios (e.g., (Schwartz 1995, Wilkinson and Kupers 2003)). Some authors emphasize the need to maintain tensions (Pascale 1991, 1999). Another strand discusses analytic methods for planning under uncertainty generally, but with national-security issues in mind (Davis, 2003). One book specifically discusses avoiding strategic surprise in national security matters (Bracken et al. 2008). There is no shortage of methods for overcoming the problem of failures of imagination – if merely leadership wants to do so.

Implications about analysis for defence planning

Although shortcomings of analysis are only some among many obstacles to making important changes, they should be of particular interest to readers of *Defence Studies*. They relate to improving the imaginativeness of analysis (not just strategic thinkers) by foreseeing possibilities *and* using analysis to assist decisionmakers in planning accordingly.

A theme of related work has been the need for strategic planning to address *deep uncertainty*, something notably absent in mainstream defence analysis. This refers to materially important uncertainties that cannot be adequately treated as simple random processes and that cannot realistically be resolved at the time they come into play.[9] Raising the issue of deep uncertainty often conjures up images of paralysis by analysis, but that no longer needs to be a problem. As discussed in a recent study (National Research Council 2014, 36),

- Considerable technical progress has been possible due to the confluence of theoretical work, computational advances, empirical psychology, and other efforts. Addressing deep uncertainties need not mean paralysis; instead, it means pragmatically recognizing and bounding them, assessing the relative significance of the many such uncertainties, and identifying hedges and adaptations.

To exploit the advances it will be important for analytic organizations and analysts within them to revise their conception of their responsibilities. A suggested approach has been called "the FARness Principle" (Davis 2014).

- Analysis should help leaders find strategies that are flexible, adaptive, and robust: *Flexible* to accommodate changes of mission, objectives, and constraints; *Adaptive* to circumstances; *Robust* to events such as positive or negative shocks
- Leaders should demand analysis that does so.

A number of authors have made similar recommendations in various fields, although using different words or different connotations of words to mean the same thing, as in planning for adaptiveness (Davis *et al.* 1996, Pascale 1999), robust adaptive strategy (Beinhocker 1999), agility (Alberts, 2011), or robust decisionmaking (Lempert *et al.* 2003). The semantic confusion should not obscure the considerable consensus.

The FARness principle suggests a new responsibility for analysts. Analysts already have an ethic of making their assumptions known. This is excellent but not sufficient. The FARness principle suggests the following additional professional obligations:

- Routinely show how results vary with the major assumptions on which there is or should be disagreement; *it is not sufficient to show sensitivities to only one or a few issues while ignoring others that are also important.*
- Routinely identify and assess options for FARness, showing the value of affordable hedges to policymakers even in periods of austerity when hedges may seem like luxuries.

This contrasts starkly with the usual practice of mainstream defence analysis, e.g., the emphasis on standard scenarios, models, data bases, and measures of effectiveness, and on "optimization" based on them.

What would such planning and analysis look like? It might be akin to "capabilities-based planning" *as it was originally conceived* by senior DoD leaders. This approach emphasizes developing capabilities adequate (or as adequate as feasible given a budget) to deal with the range of possible conflicts *and* the range of ways that they can unfold, rather than fine-tuning for some best-estimate scenario. This requires hedging in various ways about what may be needed. Doing so has paid off historically, as illustrated in the cases above (e.g., when Saddam Hussein invaded Kuwait, despite that being regarded as quite unlikely, when U.S. forces were able to engage the Taliban deep in Afghanistan despite that not having been contemplated, or when – quite frequently over the years – U.S. Marines and naval battle groups have responded to diverse crises). Capabilities-based planning was a major thrust of the changes to defence planning introduced by Donald Rumsfeld in 2001 (Henry 2005). Unfortunately, implementation has sometimes distorted intent and buried uncertainty in ways that may be organizationally convenient but that are strategically destructive, as described in a Congressionally mandated study (Davis 2016). The term capabilities based planning now has very different connotations (both positive and negative), as reviewed elsewhere.[10]

It may be well to end this paper by noting that the long-term sustainability of the move toward addressing uncertainty by planning for FARness will be enhanced as the ideas are taken up, with one or another terminology, by academic scholars in more domains. It is already evident in work in some university groups, especially those doing interdisciplinary work to inform social policy decisions (Lempert *et al.* 2003, Haasnoot *et al.*, 2013), in the business literature on strategic planning (Quinn 1980, Mintzberg and Lampel 1999, Pascale 1999, March 2008), and in some of the organizational performance literature (Light 2004). On the one hand, such planning for FARness seems like nothing more than common sense. In reality, however, it is not natural for large complex organizations. Further, the analytic methods for doing are nontrivial and not yet broadly familiar.

Notes

1. (See Grimes 2008, 8). Other agencies have sought to emulate DoD's PPBE. For related discussion (see Tama 2018a, 2018b) and the larger special issue in which the paper appears. Official description of the PPBE can be found on the website of the Defense Acquisition University, http://acqnotes.com/acqnote/acquisitions/ppbe-overview.
2. A recent official history (Keefer 2017, 323–349) provides support for much of this case.
3. The "Wolfowitz report," *Capabilities for Limited Contingencies in the Persian Gulf*, was a study by the DoD's Office of Program Analysis and Evaluation. Reportedly declassified in 2013 (Gunzinger 2011), it does not seem to be publicly available on the Internet.
4. Major players included Robert Komer, the Under Secretary of Defence for Policy; Russell Murray, the Assistant Secretary for Program Analysis and Evaluation; and David Jones, the Chairman of the Joint Chiefs of Staff David Jones. The NSC Staff was also much involved.
5. The recapitalization focus is evident in U.S. General Accounting Office (1995). The preference for continuity (but with adequate funding) was evident in reactions of most senior DoD leaders who were briefed in a 1996 meeting on strategic options (Davis et al. 1997). A few of the leaders, however, exhibited much more interest in change.
6. Proponents for change included Andrew Marshall's Office of Net Assessment (Krepinevich 2002), the Defense Science Board (Defense Science Board 1998, Defense Science, 1996), the National Research Council (National Research Council 2000, National Research Council 1997), and such leaders in the Joint Staff as Admiral William Owens (Vice Chairman) (Owens and Offley 2000) and Vice Admiral Arthur Cebrowski (Cebrowski and Garstka 1998). Non-government studies also contributed (Frostic *et al.* 1993, Davis 1994, Davis *et al.*, 1998, Arquilla and Ronfeldt 1996, Davis *et al.* 1996, Ochmanek *et al.*, 1998, Hundley 1999).
7. Private communications with Under Secretaries of Defense and other officials in the mid- to-late 1990s. It seemed to them that everything worthwhile was being accomplished outside the mainstream processes (the PPBE, acquisition process, and that of the Joint Requirements Oversight Council).
8. This included large studies reviewing implications of the social-science literature for thinking about counterterrorism (Davis and Cragin 2009) and intervention operations (Davis 2011, Wong *et al.*, 2017).
9. A more formal definition is that deep uncertainty is "the condition in which analysts do not know or the parties to a decision cannot agree upon (1) the appropriate models to describe interactions among a system's variables, (2) the probability distributions to represent uncertainty about key parameters in the models, and/or how to value the desirability of alternative outcomes" (Lempert *et al.* 2003). The ideas have been developed for more than two decades at this point (Davis 1994, Lempert *et al.* 2003, Walker *et al.*, 2013, Haasnoot *et al.*, 2013). For links to many publications, see the website on robust decisionmaking http://www.rand.org/topics/robust-decision-making.html.
10. A history of capabilities-based planning, including criticisms and counters, appears in an appendix of a larger report (Davis 2014).

Disclosure statement

No potential conflict of interest was reported by the author.

ORCID

Paul K. Davis http://orcid.org/0000-0002-2913-2168

References

Alberts, D.S., 2011. *The agility advantage: A survival guide for complex enterprises and endeavors.* Washington, D.C: DoD Command and Control Research Program.
Arquilla, J. and Ronfeldt, D.F., 1996. *The advent of netwar.* Santa Monica, CA: RAND Corporation.
Aspin, L., 1993. *Report of the bottom up review.* Washington, D.C.: Department of Defense.
Beinhocker, E.D., 1999. Robust adaptive strategies. *MIT sloan management review.* March: 95–107.
Bexfield, J.N., 2001. . *Deep attack weapons mix study (DAWMS) case study.* Alexandria, Va.: Institute for Defense Analyses.
Bliddal, H., 2011. *Reforming military command arrangements: the case of the rapid deployment joint task force.* Carlisle Barracks, Penns: Strategic Studies Institute, U.S. Army War College.
Board, D.S., 1996. *Tactics and technologies for 21-st century military superiority (in three volumes).* Washington, D.C: Office of the Under Secretary of Defense for Acquisition, Technology, and Logistics.
Board, D.S., 1998. *Joint operations superiority in the 21-st century: integrating capabilities underwriting joint vision 2010 and beyond.* Washington, D.C.: Office of the Under Secretary of Defense for Acquisition and Technology.
Bracken, P., Bremer, I., and Gordon, D., 2008. *Managing strategic surprise.* New York: Cambridge Univ. Press.
Cebrowski, A.K. and Garstka, J., 1998. Network-centric warfare: its origins and future. *Naval Institute Proceedings*, 123 (1), 28–35.
Central Command, U.S., 2010. Gen. Petraeus updates guidance on use of force. Accessed at http://www.centcom.mil/MEDIA/NEWS-ARTICLES/News-Article-View/Article/884119/gen-petraeus-updates-guidance-on-use-of-force/.
Christiansson, M., 2018. Defense planning beyond rationalism: the third offset strategy as a case of metagovernance. *Defence studies*, 18 (3), 262–278.
Chu, D. and Bernstein, N., 1983. Decisionmaking for defense. *In*: S. Johnson, M. Libicki, and G. Treverton, eds. *New challenges, new tools for defense decisionmaking.* Santa Monica, CA: RAND Corporation.
Cohen, W., 1997. Report of the quadrennial defense review. Washington, D.C.: Department of Defense.
Council, N.R., 1997. *Technology for the united states navy and marine corps: 2000–2035.* Washington, D.C: National Academy Press.
Council, N.R., 2014. *U.S. Air force strategic deterrence analytic capabilities: an assessment of methods, tools, and approaches for the 21st century security environment.* Washington, D.C: National Academies Press.

Davis, P., 2016. *Capabilities for joint analysis in the department of defense: rethinking support for strategic analysis*. Santa Monica, CA: RAND Corporation.

Davis, P.K., 1982. . *Observations on the rapid deployment joint task force: origins, direction, and mission*. Santa Monica: RAND.

Davis, P.K., ed., 1994. *New challenges in defense planning: rethinking how much is enough*. Santa Monica, CA: RAND Corporation.

Davis, P.K., et al., 1998. *Transforming U.S. Forces: suggestions for DoD strategy*. Santa Monica, CA: RAND Corporation.

Davis, P.K., ed., 2011. *Dilemmas of intervention: social science for stabilization and reconstruction*. Santa Monica, CA: RAND Corporation.

Davis, P.K., 2014. *Analysis to inform defense planning despite austerity*. Santa Monica, CA: RAND Corporation.

Davis, P.K., 2013. Uncertainty sensitive planning. *In*: S. Johnson, M. Libicki, and G. Treverton, eds. *New challenges, new tools for defense decisionmaking*. Santa Monica, CA: RAND Corporation, 131–155.

Davis, P.K. and Cragin, K., eds., 2009. *Social science for counterterrorism: putting the pieces together*. Santa Monica, CA: RAND Corporation.

Davis, P.K., Gompert, D.C., and Kugler, R., 1996. *Adaptiveness in national defense: the basis of a new framework*. Santa Monica, Calif.: RAND Corporation.

Davis, P.K., Kugler, R., and Hillestad, R., 1997. *Issues and options for the quadrennial defense review*. Santa Monica, Calif.: RAND Corporation.

Davis, P.K. and Wilson, P.A., 2011. The looming crisis in U.S. Defense planning. *Joint Forces Quarterly*, 63, 13–20.

Department of Defense, 1992. *Final report to congress on conduct of the Persian Gulf war*. Washington, D.C.: Office of the Under Secretary of Defense for Policy.

Eikenberry, K.W., 2013. The limits of counterinsurgency doctrine in afghanistan: the other side of the coin. *Foreign affairs*, 92 (5), 59-62, 64-74.

Enthoven, A. and Smith, K.W., (foreword by Kenneth Krieg and David C. Chu), 2005. *How much is enough: shaping the defense program, 1961–1969*. Santa Monica, Calif: RAND Corporation

Fiott, D., 2016. Europe and the pentagon's third offset strategy. *The RUSI journal*, 161, 26–31. doi:10.1080/03071847.2016.1152118

Frostic, F., Lewis, K., and Bowie, C.J., 1993. *The new calculus: analyzing airpower's changing role in joint theater campaigns*. Santa Monica, CA: RAND Corporation.

Gates, R.M., 2014. *Duty: memoirs of a secretary at war*. New York, NY: Knopf.

Grimes, S.R., 2008. *Ppbs to ppbe: A process or principles*. Carlisle Barracks, Penns.: U.S.: Army War College.

Gunzinger, M.A.C.D., 2011. *Outside-in: operating from range to defeat iran's anti-access and area-denial threats*. Washington, D.C.: Center for Strategic and Budgetary Assessments.

Haasnoot, M., et al., 2013. Dynamic adaptive policy pathways: A method for crafting robust decisions for a deeply uncertain world. *Global Environmental Change*, 23, 485–498. doi:10.1016/j.gloenvcha.2012.12.006

Hagel, C., 2014. *Quadrennial defense review 2014*. Washington, D.C.: Department of Defense.

Henry, R., 2005. Defense transformation and the 2005 quadrennial defense review. *Parameters*, 35 (4), 5–15.

Hines, J.E., 1999. History of the Persian gulf war, and subsequent actions of the U.S. central command. Accessed at http://www.daveross.com/centcom.html.

Hundley, R.O., 1999. *Past revolutions, future transformations: what can the history of revolutions in military affairs tell US about transforming the U.S. Military?*. Santa Monica, CA: RAND Corporation.

Jensen, B., 2018. The role of ideas in defense planning: revisiting the revolution in military affairs. *Defence studies*, 18 (3), 302–317.

Keefer, E.C., 2017. *Harold brown: offsetting the soviet military challenge: 1977–1981*. Washington, D.C.: Office of the Historian, Office of the Secretary of Defense.

Krepinevich, A.F., 2002. *The military-technical revolution: A preliminary assessment.* Washingon, D.C.: Center for Strategic and Budgetary Assessments.

Lambeth, B., 1992. *Desert storm and its meaning: the view from moscow. R-3164.* Santa Monica, CA: RAND.

Lempert, R.J., Popper, S.W., and Bankes, S.C., 2003. *Shaping the next one hundred years: new methods for quantitative long-term policy analysis.* Santa Monica, Calif: RAND Corporation.

Light, P.C., 2004. *The four pillars of high performance.* New York, NY: McGraw Hill.

March, J.G., 1996. Continuity and change in theories of organizational action. *Administrative Science Quarterly*, 41, 278. doi:10.2307/2393720

March, J.G., 2008. *Explorations in organizations.* Palo Alto, CA: Stanford University Press.

McChrystal, S.A., 2011. It takes a network: the new front line of modern warfare. *Foreign policy*, March/April.

Mintzberg, H., 1994. *Rise and fall of strategic planning.* New York, NY: Free Press.

Mintzberg, H. and Lampel, J., 1999. Reflecting on the strategy process. *Sloan management review*, Spring, 21–30.

Mintzberg, H., Lampel, J., and Ahlstrand, B., 2005. *Strategy safari: A guided tour through the wilds of strategic management.* New York, NY: Free Press.

Nagl, J.A., et al., 2007. *U.S. Army/marine corps counterinsurgency field manual.* Chicago, Ill: University of Chicago Press.

National Commission on Terrorist Attacks, 2004. *The 9/11 commission report: Final report of the national commission on terrorist attacks upon the united states.* W.W. Norton & Company, New York.

National Defense Panel, 1997. *Transforming defense: national security in the 21st century.* Washington: Department of Defense.

National Research Council, 2000. *Network centric naval forces.* Washington, D.C: Naval Studies Board, National Academy Press.

Ochmanek, D.A., et al., 1998. *To find, and not to yield: how advances in information and firepower can transform theater warfare.* Santa Monica, CA: RAND Corporation.

Owens, W.A. and Offley, E., 2000. *Lifting the fog of war.* New York: Farrar Straus Giroux.

Pascale, R.T., 1991. *Managing on the edge: how successful companies use conflict to stay ahead.* New York, NY: Simon & Schuster.

Pascale, R.T., 1999. Surfing the edge of chaos. *MIT sloan management review* (Spring), 40 (3).

Quinn, J.B., 1978. Strategic change: logical incrementalism. *Sloan management review*, 20(1), 7–19.

Quinn, J.B., 1980. Managing strategic change. *MIT sloan management review*, 21, 3–20.

Rhyne, R.D., 2004. *Special forces command and control in afghanistan.* Fort Leavenworth, Kan: U. S. Army Command and Staff College.

Ricks, T.E.M., 2006. *Fiasco: the american military adventure in iraq.* New York, NY: Penguin Press.

Rosen, S.P., 1984. Systems analysis and the quest for rational defense. *The public interest*, 76, 3–17.

Schwartz, P., 1995. *The art of the long view: planning for the future in an uncertain world.* New York, NY: Doubleday.

Tama, J., 2015. Does strategic planning matter? The outcomes of US national security reviews. *Political science quarterly*, 130, 735–765. doi:10.1002/polq.12395

Tama, J., 2018a. How an agency's responsibilities and political context shape government strategic planning: evidence from US federal agency quadrennial reviews. *Public management review*, 20, 377–396. doi:10.1080/14719037.2017.1285114

Tama, J., 2018b. Tradeoffs in defense strategic planning: lessons from the U.S. quadrennial defense review. *Defence studies*, 18 (3), 279–301.

Thiesen, E.E., 2003. *Ground-aided precision strike: heavy bomber activity in operation enduring freedom.* Maxwell AFB: Alabama: Air University Press.

Tulkoff, M.L., et al., 2010. *Planning, programming, and budgeting system (ppbs)/multi-year programming reading guide.* Alexandria, Virginia: Institute for Defense Analyses.

U.S. General Accounting Office, 1995. *Future years defense program: 1996 program is considerably different from the 1995 program.* Washington, D.C.: U.S. General Accounting Office.

U.S. Marine Corps, 1940. *Small wars manual.* New York, NY: Skyhorse Publishing.

Van Creveld, M., 1991. *The transformation of war: the most radical reinterpretation of armed conflict since clausewitz.* New York, NY: Free Press.

Walker, W.E., Lempert, R.J., and Kwakkel, H.H., 2003. Deep uncertainty. *In*: S. Gass and M. Fu, eds. *Encyclopedia of Operations Research and Management Science, 3d ed.* NY: Springer, unspecified.

Watts, B.D., 2011. *The maturing revolution in military affairs.* Washington, D.C.: Center for Strategic and Budgetary Assessments.

Wilkinson, A. and Kupers, R., 2003. Living in the futures. *Harvard business review,* May, unpaged.

Wong, Y.H., *et al.*, 2017. The use of multiple methods in the joint irregular warfare analytic baseline (jiwab) study. *Journal of defense modeling and simulation,* 14 (1), 45-55.

Work, B., 2015. *The third U.S. Offset strategy and its implications for partners and allies (speech at willard hotel)..* Washington, D.C.: Department of Defense.

CONCLUSION

Coda: exploring defence planning in future research

Henrik Breitenbauch and André Ken Jakobsson

ABSTRACT
Through the contributions of this special issue, defence planning emerges as a strategic fact with a significance of its own. Defence planning does not merely serve as a conduit for external forces, but instead appears as an independent or intermediate variable as well as a discrete arena for national security processing. In this conclusion, we return to the overall issue of defence planning as an object of study as proposed in the introduction. We identify three analytical dimensions inspired by the contributions which offer avenues for future research on defence planning. These are process versus change, the issue of national versus comparative or international dynamics, and finally hybrid or interface dynamics. It is, in other words, important to account for the roles defence planning may play with regard to affecting change in strategic affairs, to deepen our understanding of the dynamics of defence planning in central national cases such as the US as well as the international and comparative aspects of such dynamics, and finally it is important to analyse the characteristics and effects of defence planning in its wider political, administrative and strategic contexts.

At the end of this special issue we are left with summing up the overarching proposal of the issue and with looking out in the future – tentatively planning as it were – possible future research contributions following from the path laid out in the preceding pages.

As the special issue began, we first proposed that the constitutive elements of defence and strategic studies could be considered "strategic facts" following Émile Durkheim's suggestion that social science should deal with and be founded on "social facts" (Durkheim 1982; Breitenbauch and Jakobsson 2018). Second, we argued, such foundational "strategic facts" ought to include not just the well-established questions regarding the use of force (what we drawing on Stephan de Spiegeleire termed "the downstream" issues), but also those everyday-important processes and activities that we find further "upstream" in the defence universe, namely those related to defence planning broadly speaking (cf. Spiegeleire 2012). We furthermore drew attention to how such studies of these phenomena would likely be concerned with subjects of a hybrid nature, often looking inside the black box of the state and its central administration, civilian as well as military. Because of this, we proposed the likelihood that a defence or strategic studies approach – normally considered to reside under the umbrella of the International Relations discipline – to defence planning would also open up for new engagements with issues that typically pertain to organizational studies or public administration (cf. Farrell 1996). While these opening proposals have come to fruition in the contributions of the issue, we would like additionally to emphasise three particular dimensions that appear across the articles and together help suggest opportunities for future research. These three dimensions are process versus change, the issue of national versus comparative or international dynamics, and finally hybrid or interface dynamics.

Three promising dimensions

For all of the articles, perhaps not surprisingly, defence planning manifested itself in various ways as a productive locus for interrogating different subjects of relevance for defence and strategic studies. Had the opposite been the case, defence planning would merely have served as a conduit for external forces, as a neutral relay mechanism, for example between the outside world and high-level political decision-making. Instead, defence planning emerged as a topic of importance, as an independent or intermediate variable as well as a discrete arena for national security processing – a true and significant strategic fact. In particular, contributors drew attention to how defence planning matters with regard to such a fundamental concern as *process versus change*. As Davis points out with regard to the central case of United States' formalised processes of defence planning, the processes and the analytical paradigms and concomitant assumptions underlying them, cannot remain static in a world of rapid change, but must instead seek to address these conditions. For Davis, this means embracing a principle of identifying flexible, adaptive and robust capabilities when organizing for defence planning (Davis 2018). In that vein, Mattelaer emphasises the requirement for NATO defence planning to change with the return of geopolitical tension at the borders of NATO itself (Mattelaer 2018). In the cases of Jensen and Tama, change appears to happen in spite or in circumvention of normal process or optimally as a trade-off between different options inside that normal process, while for Young change as an aspiration of control remained elusive in the absence of proper process (Jensen 2018, Tama 2018, Young 2018). Angstrom and Christiansson both conceive of defence planning in a macro-perspective, as a subset of a much larger context where the changing character of defence planning is either subjected to more general mechanisms of public management, or are part of such a wider mechanism of reproduction of bias in the state's strategic instruments (Angstrom 2018, Christiansson 2018). The examination of issues of process – orderly, or disorderly, organised and organisational processes – as well as their relationship to change in policy and larger reforms is thus one way of further engaging with the problems of defence planning. Examining practices within the world of strategy through their relationship to modern organizational concepts of strategy and planning (such as "emergent strategies" e.g.) could fall under this heading too (Minzberg and Waters 1985, Minzberg 1994). A recent example of such engagement (even if perhaps more from the strategy than the planning perspective strictly speaking) is Ionut Popescu's *Emergent Strategy and Grand Strategy* (Popescu 2017).

A second dimension that is already present in the contributions of the issue but which holds promise for additional investigations is the tension between the *national versus* comparative and international dynamics. For good reason, the case of the United States is central to both this special issue as well as to defence planning, in the West as well as globally, in the real world. Inside NATO, for example, the US not only plays an important role as security provider but also as a standard setter in developing new ways of "doing defence" both in terms of capabilities, doctrine and what we might term "first order" military practice, but also with regard to the "second order" military practices related to the organisation of defence planning. While Davis, Jensen, Tama, Angstrom and Christiansson all keep their main focus on the United States, Young and Mattelaer explicitly examine such international NATO contexts where more or less formalised standards of governance are part of the international defence policy landscape that smaller NATO member states must navigate and participate in. One obvious question that follows is the classical comparativist concern with how states adopt, emulate and transform internationally widespread forms of governance that they are exposed to (cf. Börzel and Risse 2011). In the case of defence planning, a burning issue then is how universal the concerns and experiences of the United States in defence planning are, and how easily they have been and are translated into smaller and/or non-Western national settings with very different political and administrative traditions?

A third and final dimension that can be identified in the contributions as a lead-in to fruitful future research has to do with the very existence of defence planning as strategic fact. Defence planning matters, has dynamics of its own and offers more than an automatic chemical reaction. Because of this, the *interfaces* between formal defence planning processes and other contextual elements that defence planning connects to come to the fore as places to examine for stories of conflict, exchange, and transformation. In particular we might draw attention to the link between defence planning and the security environment, to the interface between administrative and budgeting systems on the one hand and policy and strategy process on the other, and hence also to the distinction between ostensibly neutral planning processes and analyses and political level policy and strategy making, and therefore also to the difference between public administration and politics (see e.g. Allison and Halperin 1972, Allison and Zelikow 1999). Another interface logic that was also emphasized in the introduction as well as in several of the contributions has to do with the issue of practitioners and their experiences in the world of practice. Here, the literature and projects to support a bridging of the gap between academia and policy come in as an obvious counterpart to further analysing aspects of defence planning (Goldgeier and Gentleson 2015). From a more theoretical perspective, this might also mean engaging with practice theory (Bueger and Gadinger 2018). In this way, the big tent approach to studying defence planning as a strategic fact becomes also an encouragement to engage with a little-studied staple of the world of defence practitioners in ways that also theoretically open up to both the most recent IR scholarship as well as other disciplinary traditions such as public administration or organisation studies. While it may be difficult to predict – and plan – especially for the future, there are many opportunities for further pursuing the study of defence planning.

Disclosure statement

No potential conflict of interest was reported by the authors.

Funding

This work was supported by the Carlsbergfondet; Gerda Henkel Foundation.

References

Allison, G. and Halperin, M., 1972. Bureaucratic politics: a paradigm and some policy implications. *World politics*, 24 (1), 40–79. doi:10.2307/2010559

Allison, G. and Zelikow, P., 1999. *Essence of decision: explaining the cuban missile crisis*. 2nd revised edition Reading, MA: Pearson.

Angstrom, J., 2018. The US perspective on future war: why the US relies upon ares rather than athena. *Defence studies*, 18 (3), 318–338.

Börzel,T.A. and Risse, T., 2011. From europeanisation to diffusion: introduction. *West European politics*, 35, 1–19. doi:10.1080/01402382.2012.631310

Breitenbauch, H., and Jakobsson, A. K., 2018. Defence planning as strategic fact: introduction. *Defence studies*, 18 (3), 253–261.

Bueger, C. and Gadinger, F., 2018. *International practice theory*. 2nd. London: Palgrave-Macmillan.

Christiansson, M., 2018. Defense planning beyond rationalism: the third offset strategy as a case of metagovernance. *Defence studies*, 18 (3), 262–278.

Davis, P.K., 2018. Defense planning when major changes are needed. *Defence studies*, 18 (3), 374–390.

Durkheim, É., 1982. *The rules of sociological method*. New York: The Free Press.

Farrell, T., 1996. Figuring out fighting organisations: the new organisational analysis in strategic studies. *Journal of strategic studies*, 19 (1), 122–135. doi: 10.1080/01402399608437629.

Goldgeier, J. and Gentleson, B., 2015. How to bridge the gap between policy and scholarship, *War on the Rocks*, June 29, https://warontherocks.com/2015/06/how-to-bridge-the-gap-between-policy-and-scholarship/.

Jensen, B., 2018. The role of ideas in defense planning: revisiting the revolution in military affairs. *Defence studies*, 18 (3), 302–317.

Mattelaer, A., 2018. Rediscovering geography in NATO defence planning. *Defence studies*, 18 (3), 339–356.

Minzberg, H., 1994. *The rise and fall of strategic planning*. New York: Simon and Schuster. 1994.

Minzberg, H. and Waters, J.A., 1985. Of Strategies, deliberate and emergent. *Strategic management journal*, 6 (3), July-September, 257–272.

Popescu, I., 2017. *Emergent strategy and grand strategy: how american presidents succeed in foreign policy*. Washington, DC: Johns Hopkins University Press.

Spiegeleire, S., 2012. *Taking the battle upstream: towards a benchmarking role for NATO*, Report, Center for Technology and National security Policy, Institute for National Strategic Studies, National Defense University, Washington, DC, September, http://www.dtic.mil/dtic/tr/fulltext/u2/a582370.pdf

Tama, J., 2018. Tradeoffs in defense strategic planning: lessons from the U.S. quadrennial defense review. *Defence studies*, 18 (3), 279–301.

Young, T.-D., 2018. Questioning the "sanctity" of long-term defense planning as practiced in Central and Eastern Europe. *Defence studies*, 18 (3), 357–373.

Index

Note: **Bold** page numbers refer to tables; *italic* page numbers refer to figures and page numbers followed by "n" denote endnotes.

Abizaid, John 37
Adamsky, D. 62n3
Advanced Capability and Deterrent Panel (ACDP) 17, 20
advanced computing 11, 16
advanced weapons technology 3
Air Force 51, 56, 57, 76, 115, 126–8
AirLand Battle 91
AirSea Battle 51
Allied Command Transformation (ACT) 94
al-Qaeda's attack 127
Angstrom, J. 6, 8, 140, 141
anti-air system S-400 16
the Army 61, 76
Army Crusader 59
'Army 2006' modernization plan 115
Assault Breaker 56, 59
assumption-based planning 4, 109, 112, 116
assurance 95, 96, 114, 117
Auerswald, D.P. 78

balance of terror 56, 57
Ball, N. 113
Base Force 57
benchmarking 13
Berlin Wall, fall of 91
Better Buying Power 19–20
Bezos, Jeff 18
Brennan, M. 68
Brimley, S. 40
Brodie, B. 83n1
Brooks, R. 68
Brown, Harold 125
Budget Control Act 115
budget cycle 17, 20, 109
"building partnership capacity", notion of 35
Buley, B. 67
bureaucracy, Weberian centralized hierarchy 12
bureaucratic politics 12, 43, 59, 74

Bush, George W. 16, 41, 58, 67, 69, 73, 76, 127; war on terrorism 36
business models, private sector-style management with 13

capability-based planning 4, 133, 134n10; Berlin Wall, fall of 91; Iron Curtain, removal of 91; "out-of-area" missions 92
Carter, A. 16, 17, 18, 19, 22
Carter, Jimmy 125, 126
Cebrowski, A.K. 59, 134n6
Central and Eastern European (CEE) 6; defense institutions 112
Cheney (Vice President) 58
Christiansson, M. 6, 8, 140, 141
civil-military relations 4, 68; Huntingtonian 7; issues of 82; US context 23, 74, 79
Civil War 12, 68
Clinton, Hillary 20, 38, 59
coastal defense missile system SSC-5 16
Cohen, E.A. 57
Cohen, R.S. 45n1
Cold War 57, 87, 116
collective defense: and crisis management 93, 95, 97; force generation process 93; NATO 90
Combined Joint Task Force concept 92
command-and-control methods 14
command, control computer systems, and intelligence processing (C4I) 58
"congress-free zone" 59
congressional officials 39, 41
Cordesman, A.H. 22, 28
cost-benefit analysis 12
cost-informed plans 115
counterfactual analysis 61, 63n10
counterterrorism 37, 124, 127–8, 131, 134n8
Croatian defense plans (2006 & 2013) 119n4
cruise missiles 50, 56, 57, 59
cyber capabilities 16

Cyber Operations Centre 97
cyber-security 99

Daalder, I. 92
Daesh targets, in Syria 74
Dahl, B.R. 114
Davis, P.K. 4, 5, 7, 8, 12, 45n1, 140, 141
decision makers 3, 12, 22, 28, 30, 43, 68, 82, 106, 108
decision-making 18, 43, 111; cycle 58; formal/informal 73; political 3, 21, 140; procedures 70–3
deep uncertainty 2, 8, 131, 132; definition of 134n9
defense acquisition: advantages 19; planning process of 17
Defense Advanced Research Projects Agency (DARPA) 16, 56, 131
defense budget(ing) 13, 20, 28, 39, 78, 107–8, 111–13, 115, 116, 118
Defense Innovation Board (DIB) 17, 18, 20
Defense Innovation Initiative (DII) 15, 16–17; Advanced Capability and Deterrent Panel 17, 20; Defense Innovation Board 17, 18, 20; Defense Innovation Unit-Experimental 17, 18, 20; funding projects 20; goal-seeking learning process 17–18; Long-Range Research and Development Plan 17, 18, 20; signal awareness 22
Defense Innovation Unit-Experimental (DIU-x) 17, 18, 20
defense management and organization 39, **39**
Defense Nuclear Agency (DNA) 56
defense planning: analysis 123, 132–4; cases 124; characteristics 124; core elements 123–4; counterterrorism and counterinsurgency 127–8; current era 129–30; deep uncertainty condition 8; definition 4–5, 30; era of intertwined revolutions in military affairs 129, *130*; evolution of 8; failures of imagination 131–2; Huntingtonian civil-military relations 7; ideas & revolutions 50–1; long-term, historical relationship 5; military and civilian organization 6, 8; national security aspects 8; NATO, international defense planning 7–8; normal processes 126; periods of change 124, **124**; political decision-making 5; practitioners 3; principle, 1949 98; problems 124–31; programmatic actors 6, 8, 52–61; rapid deployment forces 125–6; revisiting RMA 55–61; and state planning 6; tenets 132; trade-offs 6; transformational or revolutionary 122; transformation efforts of late 1990s and early 2000s 126–7; U.S. capabilities 129, **130**; US defense policy and planning systems 7
Defense Planning Guidance (1992) 51
defense policy 13, 28, 29, 32, 38, 39, 43, 44, 54–6, 114, 117

defense programming 13, 31, 33, 52, 73, 76, 78, 108
defense reviews 13
Defense Science Board 134n6
defense spending 16, 36, 75, 78
Defense Strategic Guidance (DSG) 36
defense transformation 33, 37, 51; in Europe 10
Defense Transformation Act 16
Department of Defense (DoD) 15, 27, 122; characteristics 34; military services 36; National Defense Strategy 30; officials 131; ONA and DARPA 16; test ranges 19
discourse trap 80
discriminate deterrence project 56, 60
"downstream" issues 1, 4, 12, 43, 139
"dumb bombs" 127
Durkheim, É. 2, 139
Duyvesteyn, I. 83n1

Echevarria, A. 74, 80
effects-based planning 4
Egnell, R. 68
Eisenhower, Dwight D. 41, 91
electronic warfare systems 16
England, Gordon 40
Enlightenment 6, 72, 81
Enthoven, A.C. 107, 111, 116, 123
Era A 129, *129*
Era B 129

"the FARness Principle" 132–4
"fast tracking" key weapon systems 57
First World War 77
five-year military budgets *(Quinquennat)* 21
fixed-price contract structures 20
Flournoy, M. 27–8, 36
force employment 4, 6
force provisioning 4
Fortuna (Machiavelli) 2
Freedman, L. 66, 69, 71, 72
Frühling, S. 3, 4
future war: analytical tool **73**; civilian-military gap 68; civil-military relations 74; decision-making process 73; defense planning (2001–16) 67; dichotomy of Ares and Athena 67–70; long-term defense planning procedures 68, 69, 70, 71, 73, 81; military acquisition processes 74; military capabilities 71; open-source documents 74; planning procedures and decision-making procedures 70–2; prospective causality 74; representation of future war 70, 71, 72, 73; research design and analytical tool 72–4; separation of the power 70, 72–3; strategic illiterates 72; technological development 72; US defense planning (2001–16) 74–81, 82; waging war 70–1; *see also* defense planning
Future Year Defense Program (FYDP) 105, 108, 119n1

INDEX

Gates, R.M. 19, 34, 109, 119n6, 128
Genieys, W. 51
Giddens, A. 23
Global Trends 73
Global Trends 2015 80–1
Global Trends 2025 81
Global Trends 2030 81
goal-oriented service–delivery mechanism 23
Goldgeier, J. 92
Goldwater-Nichols Act 13, 20, 76
governmental decision making processes 43
GPS technology 16
Gray, C.S. 3, 21, 30, 69
GS14 or presidential appointee 55
Gulf War (1991) 126
Gunzinger, M. 35

"Hack the Pentagon" 18
Hagel, C. 15, 16, 17, 19, 20, 22, 131
Håkenstad, M. 30
Hanley, B. 71, 79
Herrschraft 52
Hicks, K.H. 28, 34
hierarchical relations, Weberian 10, 12
higher order governance 11, 14
Hindu Kush 88
Hintze, O. 3
Hitch, C.J. 13, 107, 108, 109, 119n2
Hoffman, Reid 18
Holman, R. 74
"horse cavalry syndrome" 57
Hungarian Ministry of Defense 118
Huntington, S.P. 33
Hussein, Saddam 126
hybrid conflict, Ukraine 89
hybrid warfare 129

imported programming methodology 115
incentive structures 12, 14, 15, 19, 23, 35, 39, 74, 78, 99, 125, 131
institutionalism 51
institutional self-evaluations 119
intelligence, surveillance, and reconnaissance (ISR) 58
International Monetary Fund 115
International Relations discipline 140
Internet technology 16
Iranian revolution 125
Iraq, invasion of 127
Iron Curtain, removal of 91
Iskander, cruise-missile 16
Islamic State 95
Islamist terrorism 3
ISSS-ISAC Annual Conference (2017) 2
ISTAR 99

JCS organization 57, 59, 60, 107
J8, QDR process 59

Jensen, B. 7, 8, 45n2, 69, 140, 141
Joint Force Command 97
Joint Staff's annual Joint Strategic Objectives Plan (JSOP) 119n2
Joint Support and Enabling Command in Ulm 97
Joint Vision 73, 79, 80
JSTARs 57

Kamp, K.-H. 93
Kean, Thomas 131–2
Kelley, Paul X. 126
Kelly, J. 68
Kendall, F. 17, 18, 19, 20
Kennedy, John F. 107, 108
Khalilzad, Z. 51
Knus-Larsen, K. 30
Komer, R. 134n4
Krepenvich, A. 50
Kroenig, M. 41
Kuwait, invasion of 126, 133

learning process 15, 18, 19, 23
legacy concepts 113
Leonhard, R.R. 87
Le Roux, L. 113
Lifting the Fog of War (Owens) 58
Littoral Combat Ship (LCS) 59
Lock-Pullan, R. 91
long-range accuracy 50
Long-Range Research and Development Plan (LRRDP) 17, 18, 20, 56
long-term defense planning (LTDP) 6, 67, 68, 78–9, 106, 113; case of Central and Eastern Europe 114–17; concept of 109; conflated concepts and nomenclature and muddled thinking 110–14; modern, origins of 107–10; sanctity of 107–17; *see also* defense planning
long term planning (LTP) 105; definition 30; documents preparation, formal structures 31; *see also* defense planning

Machiavelli's *Fortuna* 2
McKeon, Buck 38
Mackinder, H.J. 88, 90
McKitterick, J. 57
McNamara, Robert 13, 107, 108, 110, 123
Mahnken, T.G. 34
Mahoney, James 62n8
Mapping the Global Futures 2020 81
Marine Corps 76, 77, 126
Marshall, Andrew 50, 55, 56, 57, 62n1, 134n6
Mattelaer, A. 7, 8, 140, 141
Mattis, James 128
mechanisms, definition of 54, 62n8
Membership Action Plan, Bucharest Summit 92
Merkel, Angela 100
metagovernance 6, 131; military change and public administration 10–11; rational planning

and 11–15; and reflexive modernity 21–3; third offset strategy 15–21
micro-chip technology 16
military acquisition 70, 71, 73, 74, 78, 82
"military doctrine", legacy 112
military-industrial complex 14, 16
military technical revolution 57
Mine Resistant Ambush Protection vehicle (MRAP) 109, 114, 128
miniaturization 11, 16
Mintzberg, H. 119n5, 131
mission-oriented programs 111
modern communications technology 79
money, concept of 115
M-16 57
munitions, laser-guided 50
Murray, W. 21

National Defense Panel (NDP) 37
National Defense Strategy 27, 31, 34
National Intelligence Council (NIC) 73, 80
National Military Strategy 76
National Research Council 134n6
National Security Act (1947) 76, 107
National Security Council (NSC) 76, 125
National Security Strategy (NSS) 13, 76
NATO defense planning 3, 7, 44; capability-based planning 93; development of Allied doctrine 91; division of labour – or nodal defense 99, 100; European NATO allies 99, 100; functional approaches to defense planning 88–9; geographical factors 88–91; global NATO, notion of 92–3; methodological consequences 93; operational "level of ambition" 93; organisational evolution 92; post 1991: capability planning 91–4; post-Cold War environment 88; rediscovering of geography 100–1; regional division of labour 89, 98–101; road from Wales to Warsaw 89, 94–8; Soviet threat 99; Strategic Concept 88, 89, 90, 91, 92; strategic guidance 90; ten-year planning cycle 114; 2016 Warsaw Summit 89; *see also* defense planning
the Navy 76
"near zero miss" weapons 55–60
new business model 19
new NATO allies and PfP Partners, context of 114
"new product pipeline" 16
New Public Management (NPM) 7, 10, 12
new weapon systems 57
Nixon, Richard 50
non-nuclear weapons 56
Norheim-Martinsen, P.M. 7, 10, 23
North Atlantic Treaty 90
North Korean nuclear weapons 129
nuclear strategy 91, 92
nuclear weapons 56

Obama, Barack 17, 35–7, 41, 42, 67, 69, 73, 76
obligational contracts 15
Ochmanek, D. 35
Office of Net Assessment (ONA) 16, 50, 57, 60, 62n1, 134n6
Office of the Secretary of Defense (OSD) 32, 108, 110
official planning documents 112
offsetting 11, 57
Ogarkov, N.V. 56
"one size fits all" approach 30
one-year budgeting 111
OODA loop 58
operational war planning 77
Operations and Overseas Contingency funding 116
operations research 13
organizational theory 51
O'Sullivan, S. 22
"out-of-area" missions 92
"output/outcome control" 13
Owens, W.A. 57, 58, 59, 134n6

Partnership Goal General (PG) 0022 116
Pavel, Barry 34
Perle, Richard 50
Perry, William 37, 57, 58, 59, 60
Petraeus, James 128
Plan Black 77
planning, definition 4
Planning, Programming, and Budgeting System (PPBS) 13, 21, 108, 119n2; adoption of 111, 119n5
Planning, Programming, Budgeting, and Execution (PPBE) 106, 110, 116, 123; mainstream processes 123–4
Plan Orange 77
policy: role of 118; Western concept of 111
policy-makers 15; and civil servants 13
policy making process 43
political decision-making 3, 21, 140
Popescu, I. 140
PPBE *see* Planning, Programming, Budgeting, and Execution (PPBE)
PPBS *see* Planning, Programming, and Budgeting System (PPBS)
precision strike 11, 15, 57, 58
Presidential Directive (PD 18) 125
Presidential Review Memorandum (PRM) 125
problem-solving interaction 15
process reengineering 13
process *vs.* change 140
program budgeting 13, 20
programmatic actors: articulation 55; category formation 55; causal mechanisms 54; cause-effect relationships 52; encounter and activation/deactivation 54; European healthcare policy 53; framing 55; *Herrschaft*

INDEX

52–3; mobilization 54–5; organizations, capacity and resonance 53; policy formation process 53, 54; policy process literature 52; revisiting RMA 55–61; role of ideas in defense planning 52–5
programming creators 110
"programming" for Fiscal Year (1963) 108
programming method 107, 110
"proto-theory", defense planning 3
public agencies 10, 11, 14, 15
public relations, DoD's 39
public sector strategic planning 44
public strategy documents 110

Quadrennial Defense Review (QDR) 27, 77; assessments of **39**; defense strategy or innovation 27–8; DoD leaders, strategic thinking 28; fixed schedule 29, 41–2, 43; formal structures 27–8; inclusiveness 29, 33–8, 42; National Defense Strategy 31; new legislation 31; primary and secondary sources 32–3; research, statements 28; scholars and scholar-practitioners 32; transparency 29, 38–40, 42–3
Quadrennial Defense Review Independent Panel 37

RAND Corporation 5, 7, 13, 22
Rapid Deployment Joint Task Force (RDJTF) 126
rationalization 12, 20
rational planning: and metagovernance 11–15; origins of 6–7
Readiness Action Plan 95
Reagan, Ronald 20
reflexive modernity 21–3
relational sociology 51, 54
research and development (R&D) 16
Revolution in Military Affairs (RMA) 50, 55–61, 62n3; "automated reconnaissance-and-strike complex" 56; coercive response options 56; collective actors 51; conflicting articulation practices 61; discriminate deterrence 56, 60; Dominant Maneuver Working Group 57; group of like-minded actors 60; military technical revolution 57; new weapon systems 57; offsetting 57; organizational heterogeneity 59–60; precision in warfare, role of 56; series of Russian doctrinal publications 56; socialization forums 61; "system of systems" concept 58; transformation 58
Rivero, H. 91
roadmaps, creation of 40
robotics 11, 16
Roche, James G. 56–7
rogue states 92
Root, Elihu 77
Rosen, S.P. 57, 62n5
Rumsfeld, Donald 33, 50, 57, 58, 127

SAIC 57, 59, 60
"St. Andrew's Prep" 60
Schmidt, Eric 18
"science projects" 117
SECDEF 108
security threats 2, 40, 98
Selva, P. 19, 23
September 2001 attack 93
sequestration mechanism 36, 115
Serbian Defense White Paper (2010) 115
service–delivery mechanism 12
Shalikashvili (Chairman) 57
short-term budgets 13
short-term strategic planning 77–8
"should-cost model" 20
Simpson, E. 67
Smith, K.W. 107, 111, 116
Smyrl, M. 51
social facts 2, 139
Soviet threat 99, 125, 126
Spiegeleire, S. de 1, 139
state planning 6
Stojkovic, D. 113, 114
Stone, J. 67
Strategic Analysis Center (SAC) 57
strategic bombing 90
strategic budgeting 110, 111
Strategic Capabilities Office (SCO) 131
Strategic Concept (2010) 95
strategic decisions, DoD leaders 39
strategic illiterates 72, 83n1
strategic planning: classic critique of 131; definition 30
Sullivan, General 57
supersonic fighter jet F-22 Raptor 74
Supreme Allied Command Atlantic (SACLANT) 94
Supreme Allied Commander Europe (SACEUR) 91
systems analysis 13

Tama, J. 7, 8, 23, 73, 140, 141
technique of war 67
technological innovation 17, 106
ten-year technical modernization program 115
"third-offset" strategy 11, 51, 131
Thomas, Jim 28, 34, 35
threat-based planning 4
3D printing 11, 16
Tilly, C. 6, 82
tradeoffs: advantages and disadvantages 43, **43**; external actors, transparent review 29; multiple principal-agent relationships 44; national security and defense strategies 30–1; public sector organizations, benefits for 31; scheduling strategic planning 29; strategic review 29; U.S. Quadrennial Defense Review 31–42; *see also* defense planning

INDEX

transformation process 5, 20, 33, 34, 37, 51, 57–9, 61, 92, 126–7
turf wars 12
Two Major Theater War planning strategy 51, 57

Ukrainian strategic bulletins 112
uncertainty 3, 22, 69, 77, 88, 91–4, 107, 115, 117, 126, 132, 133
"upstream" activities 2, 4, 8, 12, 43, 139
US Army Field Manual 100–5 Operations 91
U.S. Central Command (USCENTCOM) 126
U.S. civil–military relations 23, 74, 79
U.S. defense bureaucracy 51
U.S. Defense Innovation Initiative *see* Defense Innovation Initiative (DII)
US defense planning (2001–16): deterministic and without agency, future representation 80–1, 82; future war as military undertaking 79–80, 82; separation of planning processes 76–9, 82; separation of power to wage war 75–6, 82; *see also* defense planning
U.S. Defense Planning: A Critique (Collins) 3
U.S. Department of Defense *see* Department of Defense (DoD)
U.S. Navy's Thirty-year Ship Building Plan 106
U.S. planning procedures 1

Vallance, A. 94
Vedby-Rasmussen, M. 21
Very High Readiness Joint Task Force (VJTF) 95, 96

Vietnam War 77, 116
Vine, D. 67

Wales Summit, 2014 94
Wales Summit Declaration (2014) 95; alliance's neighbourhood 95; Readiness Action Plan 95
war on bureaucracy 58
War Powers Act (1974) 75
Warsaw Pact, NATO and 87
Warsaw Summit, 2016 89, 94, 96
Washington Treaty 92
Watts, B. 33–4
weapon systems 11, 57, 111
Weighley, R. 68, 80
Welby, S.P. 17, 18
Western alliance 98, 111, 116
Western modernity, advent of 6
"Westphalian Europe", re-emergence of 100
White House, Reagan 56
Wilson, P.A. 45n1, 129
Wohlstetter, A. 50, 55, 56, 57, 59, 60
Wolfowitz, Paul 50, 126
Wolfowitz Report 125, 134n3
Work, R.O. 17, 18, 19
World War II 12, 126

Yarger, H.R. 71
yearly budget-cycles, context of 109
Young, T.-D. 5, 6, 7, 8

Zakheim, Dov 57